CLASSIC WALKS IN
Southern England
by Kev Reynolds

The Oxford Illustrated Press

This book is dedicated to my parents—with thanks and love.

© Kev Reynolds

ISBN 0 946609 85 3

Published by:
The Oxford Illustrated Press Limited, Haynes Publishing
Group, Sparkford, Nr Yeovil, Somerset BA22 7JJ, England.
Haynes Publications Inc., 861 Lawrence Drive, Newbury
Park, California 91320, USA.

Printed in England by:
J.H. Haynes & Co Limited, Sparkford, Nr Yeovil, Somerset.

British Library Cataloguing in Publication Data
Reynolds, Kev
   Classic walks in Southern England
   1.   Southern England – Visitors' guides
   I.   Title   II. Series
   914.22'04858

   ISBN 0-946609-85-3

Library of Congress Catalog Card Number
89-85544

CONTENTS

ACKNOWLEDGEMENTS

I would like to thank all those who offered suggestions, practical information and advice, and who walked some of the routes with me.

Special thanks for their company on some of the best days of all: Nigel Fry, Alan Payne, Ilsa and Linda Reynolds and Derek Roberts.

For first-rate West Country hospitality: Mary and Ralph Hurne, Avril and Alan Payne, Gina and Alan Sanders.

For the use of a splendid backpacking tent: Ken Rawlinson of Phoenix Mountaineering Ltd.

Southern England has a wonderful network of footpaths and green lanes to entice the walker into an exploration of the countryside. Here the path of the North Downs Way leads above the great expanse of the Weald.

INTRODUCTION

Southern England. What pictures do those two words conjure up in your mind? Could it be an overcrowded landscape of concrete and brick, with one town jostling against another? Or perhaps a spaghetti twist of motorway choked with traffic? Or do you immediately think of green-thatched downland rolling as far as the eye can see; the calm warbling of a dawn chorus bringing alive a beech wood on a hill; the thunder and crash of waves pounding a stark granite cliff-face; a vast tract of moorland with wind-sculpted tors and bilberries at your feet; or bluebells creating a haze of smoky light along a raised bank in springtime?

Much will depend, I suppose, on your mode of travel. For as Richard Jefferies so rightly said a hundred years ago: 'They only know a country who are acquainted with its footpaths. By the roads, indeed, the outside may be seen; but the footpaths go through the heart of the land.'

If you follow the footpaths through the heart of this land you'll be delighted with what you find. If your eyes and ears are alert you'll discover the trade-routes of fox and badger, of rabbit, vole or hare—highways of another kind. You'll find the hedgerows are a-bustle with life, with colour and fragrance and sound. You'll notice the difference in texture of various trees and grasses, and learn to recognise habitats favoured by the creatures with whom you share that land.

Walking the footpaths of southern England is a joy and an education. It goes far beyond the physical pleasure of simple exercise in a glorious setting. You are a witness to history, for this countryside is a tapestry of the past and everywhere you go there are signs and symbols of all the ages of man: long barrows, stone rows, earth banks that tell of hillforts, Roman villas and Roman roads, Saxon churches, strip lynchets, castles built by invaders from Normandy, medieval manor houses, Elizabethan cottages, sunken tracks carved by heavily-laden wagons, furnace ponds and watermills and parks laid out by Victorian gentry with exotic plants that have escaped to invade the surrounding countryside. And being a witness to history you will begin to

realise how vulnerable this land really is. How the environment is under increasing pressure from politician, developer and farmer alike. And, hopefully, you will grow determined to help protect it for future generations.

This land is ours—but it is merely on loan from the future and the only true way to an understanding of it, and thence to properly value it, is to walk through it, absorbing its essential qualities through the soles of your feet, breathing the fragrance of its rich vegetation, listening to the creatures that live in it, sniffing the breeze.

There are footpaths everywhere. Some, official long-distance paths or trails like the South Downs Way, that lead you on a walk in the sky with orchids and cowslips at your feet, skylarks trilling fit to burst overhead. Others, like the Medway Riverside Walk, that avoid hills altogether, yet explore the heartland of a county in a manner that is bound to display qualities unguessed by those who merely stick to the roadway. Footpaths wander along the fretted edge of an escarpment, or up and down, helter-skelter like around our magnificent coastline where generations of coastguards tramped in the course of their duties. Coast paths are in a class of their own. Often hard walking, they are sometimes like wandering a tightrope between the land and the sea, where you savour some of the best of both.

Classic Walks in Southern England is designed to open the eyes of all who think of the south as one great urban sprawl, for what is on display is a glorious variety of landscapes—some breathtakingly dramatic, some gentle and quietly lovely. The walks chosen to represent this variety of scenery range from a single day's outing along a river bank in Kent, to the epic South-West Peninsula Coast Path that will require around six weeks to complete. And there are walks of varying lengths and degrees of commitment in between. They cover most of the counties of southern England, and most of the different types of landform too, from wild moor to fertile farmland, and from chalk downland to Mendip limestone and Wealden clay, from the Thames towpath to

a weekend along a disused railway.

What makes a walk classic? That was a question I had to face from the outset, so I asked a number of friends and fellow wanderers to give me their opinions. And we all agreed that there are no set criteria. A walk can be a classic because of its scenic quality, or because of its place in history. A walk might be accorded the status of a classic from the natural history angle—the birds or plants that will be met along the way—or by its very concept.

Suggestions were made and arguments raged! But I listened to them all, then made my own choice. No doubt others would have made a different list. That is the way it should be. What I do know is that the year or so spent putting this book together gave me some of the happiest days and weeks of walking I've ever enjoyed, and in so doing confirmed my deep love of this land; the countryside in which I was born and raised.

Apart from a short period spent working in the Alps, I have always lived in southern England. First in Essex, then later in Kent. I had the happiest childhood imaginable because fields and streams, woods and hedgerows were all easily accessible, and I was given the freedom to roam. Only a fence separated the bottom of my garden from them. They were my playgrounds. I made camps in the hedges and hid my treasures in a hollow oak, and paced every horizon with a sense of wonder. That wonder has never left me.

A teacher at Junior School inspired me with a passion for the world of nature. He would take us on rambles that were explorations every bit as exciting as any I have since taken part in among some of the world's most dramatic mountains. With him we never went beyond the county boundary. Yet what we saw filled us with amazement, for he had the marvellous ability to draw out the extraordinary nature of the countryside about us. Stepping through winter-bare woods that dripped and spun webs of fantasy, was to become aware of the world of squirrel and jay and badger. We strode across summer fields head high in crackling wheat, eye to eye with poppy and dormouse, and chewed on leaves and fruit from the hedgerows. I shall never forget the gifts that man bestowed upon us, nor the way he opened my eyes to the fascinating world about me.

All our early family holidays were spent somewhere in the south of England and I grew steadily more familiar with folding hill and curving bay, beginning to understand that every county had its own particular flavour worth testing and tasting.

Then, as a Youth Hostel Warden for almost twenty years, it was my pleasure to direct others into the natural world on my doorstep. Many came by default from the far corners of Britain—and elsewhere throughout the world—to spend the night in transit to somewhere better known for its landscape drama. And then it would please me no end to hear their admission that they'd had no idea the south could be so lovely! Over the years we found scores of converts who would return time and again to explore the green hills and chequerboard valleys of southern England; praising the views and the variety, the colour and the history—all discovered from the winding pathways that lead out of our village.

I never tire of wandering these paths. Nowadays my work takes me into some of the world's most spectacular scenery. Yet I'm always happy to come home to the greenest land I know, to a countryside that throbs with life. And practically every day spent at home I'll find time to go walking along the ridge of hills above the village, through the woods and down into secretive coombes. Sometimes by night, stepping quietly through the pitch dark alleyways of those woods, listening to the sounds of nocturnal creatures; sometimes going up to a favourite viewpoint to capture the magic of daybreak; sometimes to watch the sunset; sometimes alone, sometimes with my wife or daughters or friends, or leading a group of adults eager to share some of the mysteries of this secret land. We've even bivouacked above the village on a hilltop overlooking three counties, just to experience the world spinning beneath the same stars that gleam on mountains far away.

The countryside of southern England is a part of me, and when I was asked to write and illustrate this book of classic walks through it, I jumped at the opportunity. It was not only an opportunity to explore areas I'd not yet properly seen, but it also gave me the excuse to return to parts of the country that had brought me pleasures in the past.

There was not a dull day's walking anywhere. Sometimes the rain lashed down. On occasions I slopped through ankle-deep water or shivered in a raw wind. But often I strode hour after hour on sunlit hills serenaded by birdsong, and became almost intoxicated by the fragrance of wild flowers, or the blossom in tree and hedgerow, or by the rich scent of newly mown hay.

This book, then, suggests where to walk and how far, which maps and guides to study, what the essential qualities of each area are, and then attempts to unravel the splendours of some of the finest walks to be found in all of lowland Britain. Some of these walks will be well-known to most southern ramblers, but I trust there will be fresh discoveries to be made too. There are walks included—the North Downs Way, for example—that have been popular challenges for some time, and could not be left out. Then you'll also find within these pages a traverse of Dartmoor National Park that follows very few tracks at all, and is included as an illustration of how in some areas it is still possible to go off and create an original outing of your own. There are several Ways officially approved by the Countryside Commission and plenty of others dreamed up by assorted groups of ramblers, local authorities or even individuals with an enthusiasm for a particular corner of the country. All have one thing in common: they lead to visions of glory.

As well as the fifteen walks described in the main body of the book, I have included a selection of ten additional routes, treated to potted outlines only, to show the tremendous scope that exists for southern walkers. Yet these are merely a handful of possibilities and are long-distance routes only. I have specifically avoided the temptation to include any short day walks since it would be almost impossible to give a proper geographical coverage to such a large area of country. Be it sufficient to say that every long route described can be happily broken into isolated day walks. Bearing this in mind, *Classic Walks in Southern England* represents somewhere in the region of 150 days of activity!

Each of the main walks in this book is treated to an essay designed to tempt others to pull on their boots and follow the route for themselves. Each chapter begins with a few introductory paragraphs outlining the character of the route or the countryside it passes through, and in some cases a brief history of how the walk was devised. Then

the route itself is described, with suggestions, in some instances, of places where accommodation is available. The Fact Sheet accompanying each walk is a précis of useful information, giving such details as the distance, the time required to tackle it (this is, of course, only a guideline and will need to be modified to suit each individual walker), the type of walk it is (with any specific difficulty noted), the start and finishing point, and which maps and guidebooks to use.

Gearing Up

A certain mystique has been created around the subject of outdoor clothing, and anyone setting out to equip themselves for a walking holiday for the very first time could be forgiven for becoming totally confused. Walk into any specialist supplier's shop and you'll be confronted by a bewildering array of equipment. Happily most of these shops are staffed by enthusiasts who not only sell the gear but use it themselves on their days off. They will provide all the advice required; don't be afraid to ask. All the customer requires is an understanding bank manager.

In good weather most of these lowland walks could be tackled in trainers. (The rough terrain of Dartmoor, however, will require good lightweight boots to protect your ankles.) In wet conditions you'll need something rather more substantial than trainers and in any case, on almost any walk there will be stretches of mud to negotiate. Personal preference means that I invariably wear lightweight walking boots to give maximum ankle support, with a good Vibram or similar sole to give grip, which is as important on a damp slope of downland as in the mountains. Made of a soft leather these modern boots need practically no 'breaking in' and at the end of a long day's walking you may find, like me, that your feet hardly ache at all. Most 'experts' proclaim the need to wear two pairs of socks, but I only ever use one pair. Of course you must make your decision on this when you choose the boots and go with the right combination of socks when you try the new boots on in the shop. (I once trekked with a very keen walker who had made the mistake of trying on a new pair of boots without his usual walking socks, and who was in rather too much of a hurry. As a result he suffered with terrible blisters the first time out, and only after days of experiment did he find that the right combination to suit his new boots was

Backpacking gives the ultimate freedom on a long walk. The Phoenix Phalcon is an ideal tent for use in all weathers, and is seen here on the Dorset Coast Path.

no less than three pairs of woollen socks and two pairs of cotton inners!) Boots should fit comfortably with room to wiggle your toes.

Shorts are fine on bright summer days, although you may find the occasional bramble or thicket of nettles to negotiate; then you'll wish for better leg protection. Jeans are not a good idea. Once wet (either from rain or from long dew-wet grass) they can feel extremely uncomfortable. They take ages to dry out and soon make you very cold. If you can afford them, lightweight travel slacks (Rohan or Mountain Equipment make them) are becoming very popular among walkers, and are probably seen more often now than walking breeches. A pair of gaiters can be handy in winter to keep mud off your legs and the worst of the water out.

No-one should set out on a long walk in

Britain, in Devon as in Scotland, without carrying waterproofs; cagoule and overtrousers, preferably made of one of the 'breathable' fabrics such as Gore-Tex or Sympatex. Unless you are backpacking (and I'll discuss accommodation below) a medium sized rucksack should be ample to carry spare clothing, food for the day, water bottle, small first aid kit, guidebook, map and compass. Most of the walks in this book are well waymarked and signposted, yet a map and compass should be taken in any case—although you should first learn how to use them. Do not set out on a Dartmoor crossing without that knowledge.

Accommodation

If you plan to tackle multi-day walks then one of your main considerations will be accommodation. I suppose, having been a YHA member for something like thirty years, as well as a Warden, I'm biased in favour of Youth Hostels. This may also be excused by the fact that YHA has the largest network of lodgings anywhere in the country

and that most long-distance paths or trails have one or more hostels situated along them. Add to this the fact that you're likely to meet other outdoor enthusiasts in them, that rucksacks attract no adverse comment or second glance, and that in most hostels you can either have meals provided for you or, if you arrive at an inconvenient time, there'll be a simple kitchen where you can knock together a meal for youself.

There are disadvantages, of course. Not everyone approves of the idea of dormitory accommodation, nor will you necessarily appreciate arriving worn out after a long day in the countryside only to find a rather boisterous school party in attendance. Having experienced both sides of the counter, I'd say: be patient and remember when you were young!

The annual *YHA Guide* gives all the information needed with regard to the location of hostels in England and Wales. YHA is, of course, a membership organisation, and the address of its National Office is given at the end of the book.

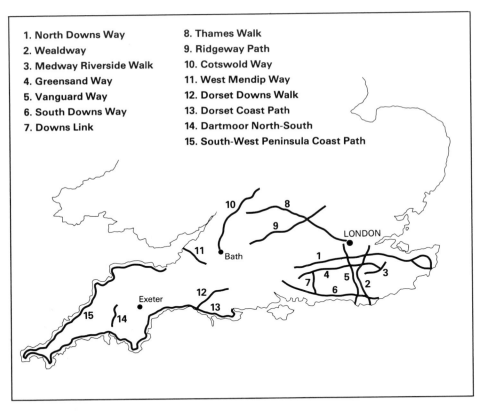

1. North Downs Way
2. Wealdway
3. Medway Riverside Walk
4. Greensand Way
5. Vanguard Way
6. South Downs Way
7. Downs Link
8. Thames Walk
9. Ridgeway Path
10. Cotswold Way
11. West Mendip Way
12. Dorset Downs Walk
13. Dorset Coast Path
14. Dartmoor North-South
15. South-West Peninsula Coast Path

Recommended bed and breakfast establishments are listed in the annual *Ramblers' Association Yearbook* (available to members only). Almost everywhere I have enjoyed my stay in a private b&b when there were no hostels. Alone, especially, one can relax in a homely room and prepare for the next day's walking without disturbance, and I must admit to being happier with b&b than hotel accommodation when on a long trek. Standards of comfort and food provided can vary considerably, of course, but most proprietors have an affection for walkers that makes a welcome almost guaranteed. But do take the precaution of telephoning first to make sure there will be room when you arrive.

Finally, backpacking; the ultimate freedom. This, to me, is the finest way to travel. Put your home on your back and set out for a week or two firm in the knowledge that you have all the requirements of accommodation and food in the rucksack, and your mind can range untroubled over hill and dale. Unfortunately, in lowland country this is not always practicable, for it is not always possible to find a farmer willing to allow you to pitch your little tent in the corner of a field, and whilst you may personally have few misgivings about an isolated spot away from habitation, you won't always be able to locate sufficient water for safe drinking and the preparation of food.

Where there are approved camp sites of course, these problems do not occur, and certain Youth Hostels also allow members to pitch a tent in their grounds. (Study the *YHA Guide* for details of these.) But there are few wild pitches to be had in the area covered by this book. Long stretches of the South-West Peninsula Coast Path can certainly be backpacked. So can Dartmoor, and my lightweight Phoenix Phalcon tent has been used in a number of idyllic situations in the south-west, where memorable nights have been spent as enjoyably as many others among wild mountain sites.

Transport

Public transport is a subject of great significance for walkers, whether you have your own vehicle or not. Trains and buses offer a useful means of access to the countryside and if you plan to tackle a long-distance linear route, rather than a circular one, you are almost certainly going to be in need of some form of public transport—either to reach the start, or to return home upon completion of the walk.

British Rail still has a very fine network serving southern England, with main lines radiating in all directions from London, and with other regional centres giving access to various parts of the country. However, most minor branch lines offer a reduced service on Sundays and some stations may even be closed one day a week. Check specific details before you travel.

The fare structure on BR is bewilderingly complex. There are various discount schemes, including the Young Person's Railcard for those under 24 years of age and in full-time education, and a Senior Citizen's Railcard for those of retirement age. For long trips certain 'Saver' fares are available, except for use on Fridays and Saturdays in the main holiday season. It often pays, therefore, to travel midweek if you can.

There are numerous bus and coach operators in existence that offer a competitive service and it is worth making enquiries to see what is available to get you to or from the end of your chosen walk. Tourist information offices and public libraries generally have addresses. But there is an invaluable publication that lists bus services, timetables and prices. *Doe's Directory of Bus Timetables* may be ordered from Barry Doe, Travadvice, 25 Newmorton Road, Moordown, Bournemouth, Dorset BH9 3NU.

Finally, walking these routes and putting the book together has brought me untold hours of pleasure. May you too be inspired to make some journeys of discovery through southern England, and in so doing gain as much happiness as I have. While you walk, please remember the Country Code. It reiterates principles set by one of the founders of the National Trust, Octavia Hill, who wrote at the turn of the century:

> Let the grass growing for hay be respected, let the primrose roots be left in their loveliness in the hedges, the birds unmolested and the gates shut. If those who frequented country places would consider those who live there, they would better deserve, and more often retain, the rights and privileges they enjoy.

Like its predecessors in the Classic Walks series this book is an appreciation, in words and photographs, of some truly delightful countryside. It is a rich and vibrant countryside, a countryside that only those who take to the footpaths can properly know.

Let this, then, be your waymark to journeys of discovery along some of the *Classic Walks in Southern England*.

WALK 1: *The North Downs Way*

The sandy track on St Martha's Hill that is used by the North Downs Way.

Distance: 141 miles (227km).
Time Required: About 10 days.
Type of Walk: A long but fairly easy walk. Mostly along the edge of the North Downs escarpment. Often among trees, sometimes on quiet country lanes. The paths and tracks are for the most part clearly defined.
Start: Farnham, Surrey.
Finish: Dover, Kent.
Maps: O.S. Landranger series 186, 187, 189, 178, 179.
Guidebooks: *A Guide to the North Downs Way and Pilgrims' Way* by Christopher John Wright (Constable). *The North Downs Way* by Denis Herbstein (HMSO). *North Downs Way* by H D Westacott and Mark Richards (Penguin). *Discovering the North Downs Way* by D J Allen and P R Imrie (Shire).

From Farnham in Surrey to the White Cliffs of Dover

The wall of the North Downs acts as the one sure deterrent to London's complete domination of the south-east. The city and its suburbs have greedily pushed out towards its northern rim, but the southern escarpment is too severe for development and it remains for the most part distinctly rural in aspect, with far-reaching vistas from the crest. Some of the most breathtaking panoramas in all of southern England are to be gained from it.

But the North Downs wall is much more than a natural suburban barrier. It is a major geological feature, one of several ridges of high land radiating from the hub of Salisbury Plain; a rib of chalk remaining

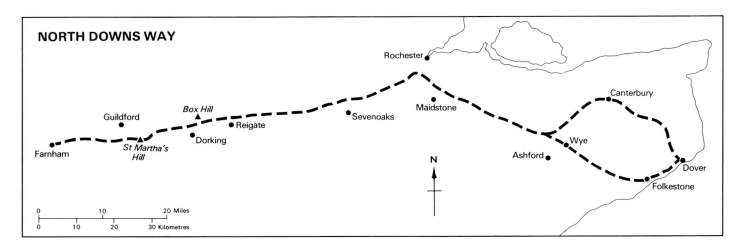

NORTH DOWNS WAY

from the great dome that once covered much of the land that is now Kent and Sussex, and of which the South Downs ridge forms an obvious counterpart.

'From the Straits of Dover to Farnham,' said Hilaire Belloc, 'Nature herself laid down the platform of a perfectly defined ridge, from which a man going west could hardly deviate, even if there were no path to guide him.'

Along this ridge there have probably been trackways of one sort or another for many thousands of years. No doubt some of the first nomadic tribes to inhabit southern Britain used the arc of downland as an important route of communication on journeys from what we now know as mainland Europe, for the Weald of our Mesolithic forefathers was largely an almost impenetrable forest doomed with swamps, while the chalk scarp would have been a much drier, more accessible feature, and one that offered kinder conditions for hunting forays and journeys to and fro.

If its accessibility was one of the major features of the Downs in prehistoric times, it is no less important today. But it is not swamp and forest that the journeyman of the twentieth century seeks to avoid by wandering along the North Downs, but rather the dual intrusions of motorway and housing estate that threaten the lower lands. The south-east of England is under threat as never before from both private and government backed development, and much of the North Downs, being contained within the Surrey Hills and Kent Downs Areas of Outstanding Natural Beauty, stands aloof from landscapes that could so easily become both political and environmental battlegrounds in the near future.

Above: **The North Downs curve in soft mouldings above Hollingbourne.**

Left: **The Way crosses the River Mole outside Dorking by a series of stepping stones before climbing Box Hill.**

There are two routes for walkers along these Downs; one that sticks mainly to the crest, the other which seeks a lower course and exploits the no-man's land between the scarp edge and the great bed of clay that is the Weald. The first is the North Downs Way. The second, and lower, route is that of the Pilgrim's Way. The first stretches from Farnham to Dover via Canterbury; the second from Winchester to Canterbury. In places the two combine, but elsewhere they run parallel with one another. While the North Downs Way (which perhaps ought to be called the North Downs Ridgeway) is mostly footpath and trackway, long sections of the Pilgrims' route follow metalled lanes.

The North Downs Way, with which this chapter is concerned, was opened by the Archbishop of Canterbury in 1978 as Britain's eighth national long-distance footpath. Promoted and financed by the Countryside Commission, it is waymarked with the standard acorn symbol of such routes. In Surrey these are carved on oak signposts, while through Kent low stone plinths are

provided. It's a popular route, not only with long-distance walkers from our own shores, but also with ramblers from Europe—especially with visitors from Belgium and the Netherlands.

If the original tracks along the Downs were most likely to have been made by migrations heading west, the modern North Downs Way is better served in the opposite direction, going from west to east, as though on a pilgrimage. Even without following any true or imagined pilgrims' route, one really needs a distinctive finishing point; something on which to set your sights, a concrete goal that will lift the heart. Either Canterbury's glorious cathedral, or the splendour of the White Cliffs of Dover, will supply that goal, and make the ending as memorable in its way as the journey itself.

It is 141 miles (227km) from Farnham to Dover, and the walk will take anything between a week and ten days to complete. There are several Youth Hostels on or near the route, and numerous inns, hotels and bed and breakfast establishments along the

11

way to ease the problem of where to stay overnight. And of all the long routes in this book, there are probably more opportunities to find public transport links than on any other, thereby making it a convenient walk to tackle in broken stages of a weekend or so at a time.

Days 1–3: Farnham to Westerham

Curiously, the walk does not start on the ridge of the Downs as such, but south of it to capture a flavour of greensand country with its big broad Wealden panoramas, and the route is quite 14 miles (23km) old before it gains the North Downs proper at Newlands Corner to the east of Guildford. But those initial 14 miles are well worth having; especially on the hilltop perch of St Martha's above the village of Albury, before you bear north to join the Downs. They are varied miles that go through country known to the much-travelled William Cobbett, who wrote of it: ' . . . the soil is good; the houses are neat; the people are neat; the hills, the woods, the meadows all are beautiful.'

Cobbett was born in Farnham itself, and although he walked nowhere unless it was absolutely impossible to ride, he knew with an unchallenged intimacy the Downs and the Greensand Ridge, the Weald of Kent and so much of the countryside through which our route travels today. It is, of course, a very different series of landscapes that the modern long-distance walker strides through compared to that of Cobbett's nineteenth century scene, but it's grand country nonetheless.

Farnham too, has changed from the prosperous town known far and wide for its large corn market in the late eighteenth and early nineteenth centuries, to become a cosy Georgian place on the edge of the stockbroker belt, with a blend of heath and woodland, so typical of this western edge of Surrey, on its very doorstep. There is an ancient history here, for in 893 the Danes were defeated in battle by Edward, son of the Great King Alfred, and on the site of this battle there now stands the twelfth century

Farnham Castle, which was used as a residence for successive bishops of Winchester right up to 1927. The Castle stands on the edge of Farnham Park to the north of the River Wey, but the route of the North Downs Way ignores this by leaving the station and heading out of town between the river and the railway line.

The river curls southward, off towards the ruins of Waverley Abbey, before veering to the east and making for Guildford. However, you cross this and skirt a golf course below the rise of Crooksbury Hill and come to the village of Seale. Above the village to the north runs the narrow ridge of the Hog's Back between Farnham and Guildford. Steep on both sides, the ridge here is busy with traffic throughout the year,

The hilltop church of St Martha's on the outskirts of Guildford enjoys a magnificent panorama.

while on a summer weekend it can be a scene of unbearable madness. Happily for the walker the North Downs Way keeps well to the south of it, and south of Seale too, across fields and through pine woods to the neat little village of Puttenham, while the Pilgrims' Way takes the course of a narrow road a little farther to the north. The two routes combine on the outskirts of the village.

The churches of Seale and Puttenham would both have been visited by pilgrims on the road to Thomas à Becket's shrine at Canterbury as, no doubt, would the church at Compton. Seale's is an attractive building, still with the original timber porch some six hundred years old, and that of Puttenham, dedicated to St John the Baptist, is also worth visiting today—as is the curious terracotta Watts Mortuary Chapel on the way to Compton. Facing Puttenham's church is a pub that could well be found around lunch time on the first day out from Farnham, and it's a little over halfway on the walk to Guildford.

The North Downs Way does not stray into Guildford itself, but it would be a shame to miss this town, for it has much to commend it, and for those who prefer a gentle, undemanding start to a long-distance walk, the 10 miles (16km) or so from Farnham might be sufficient for a first day out. The route proper skirts Guildford to the south, crosses the River Wey and climbs through Chantries Wood on a steep sandy track to reach the lonely church of St Martha's, perched high above the villages of Chilworth to the south and Albury to the east.

A lovely place, is St Martha's Hill (573ft/175m), and one that I've visited on a number of occasions to enjoy the glorious views and the sense of peace that one gains there. (It also begins the path of the Downs Link, described elsewhere in these pages.) On a clear day, so they say, you can see six counties. That may be so; I've never counted. But there is no disputing that the views are extensive, for they stretch along the greensand hills and out to the wooded expanse of the Weald; over Guildford and into Hampshire beyond it.

The church, which is the parish church of Chilworth, stands on what is thought to have been a Bronze Age site. The first Christian chapel was built here in the eleventh century but by the early 1800s it was virtually in ruins—although services were still held in the chancel. St Martha's—

the only church in England so-named—was virtually rebuilt in 1850 and despite its isolation, is still in use to this day.

The North Downs Way passes along the south side of the church and follows a well-trodden sandy track among bracken, pine and birches. In places the track is being re-seeded and brief diversion paths are used until the effects of erosion have been successfully addressed. A short distance to the east of the church you pass a wartime pill-box, but just before reaching it you'll see the marker indicating the start of the Downs Link path, which goes for 33 miles (53km) to Botolphs below the South Downs. As you descend St Martha's, splendid views of the Greensand Ridge are a constant companion. Then you bear northward and, at the bottom of the hill, emerge through a stand of pine and birch to a tranquil valley, on the far side of which stretch the North Downs.

The Downs here are known as Albury Downs, and the path leads up onto them at Newlands Corner, a well-known and invariably busy viewpoint beside the A25 road. If the views from St Martha's are extensive, those from Newlands Corner are even more so, being a little more elevated. All things being favourable, Chanctonbury Ring can be seen way off in the distance on the South Downs, but after the tranquillity of St Martha's there is rather too much humanity here; too many cars and bustle, and one tends to hanker after a resumption of peace and the company of birds and butterflies once more.

Having crossed the A25 the route now heads eastward along the crest of Albury Downs and Netley Heath high above the valley of the Tillingbourne stream. The Pilgrims' Way remains lower, but later it climbs the hillside towards the North Downs Way again at Ranmore Common where YHA members will be tempted to spend the night in the delightfully eccentric Tanners Hatch Youth Hostel. Much of the charm of Tanners lies in its isolation, hidden as it is on the edge of the deer-and-badger-busy beech woods just south of the National Trust's Polesden Lacey. Tanners is a throw-back to another age; it has no electricity supply, no road running to it. Yet it is one of the most popular of all YHA hostels—especially with youngsters weened on all the benefits of our technological age. Tanners is an experience.

East of Ranmore Common the Downs have been sliced by the River Mole, one of only a handful of river-cut breaches along the walk. (The others are forced by the Wey,

Darent, Medway and Stour.) Below in its gap stands the old market town of Dorking, while across to the east rises Box Hill. The path avoids Dorking altogether, drops from Ranmore, ducks beneath the A24 and heads down a tree-lined track to the river for the classic crossing by way of a series of stepping stones. (Downstream by half a mile is the Burford Bridge Hotel, formerly known as the Fox and Hounds where Nelson and Lady Hamilton said farewell before Nelson set out for Trafalgar. If the river is high and the stepping stones submerged, there is a footbridge nearby, or a more dry but uninteresting way across the Mole by the hotel, where a path may be taken from its north side onto Box Hill.)

The path onto Box Hill from the stepping stones is a steep one. It climbs up to one of the most famous of all picnic spots in southern England: open grassy meadows dotted with box trees and crowned with some extremely handsome beeches. Dorking's rooftops cluster far below, and beyond them rises the famous tower on Leith Hill which just reaches 1000 feet (305m) above sea level. Between Box Hill and the Weald runs the parallel line of the Greensand Ridge, heavily wooded and masking some of the glory of its views. It is from this ridge that Leith Hill Tower rises above the trees.

From Box Hill towards Reigate the Way continues along the edge of the escarpment and across lovely open downland hills: Buckland Hill, Juniper Hill, Colley Hill. On Colley Hill the North Downs Way is joined again by the Pilgrims' Way, and a little north of this the deep trench of the M25, London's notorious orbital motorway, is filled with a constant roar of traffic.

A footbridge takes the path from Reigate Hill over a deep cutting through which runs the A217, and on the eastern side you now turn off the Downs to go through Gatton Park, a one-time rotten borough that up until 1832 returned two full Members of Parliament, whilst having no more than twenty-three houses in the village. The Park is part of an extensive estate whose house was destroyed by fire in 1934. On the site there now stands the Royal Alexandra and Albert School, next to the fifteenth-century church of St Andrew and a tiny town hall built in 1765.

Merstham is reached about a mile (1.6km) from the Park with a frenetic amalgam of motorway interchange and two railway lines enclosing the village in a nightmare grasp. Poor Merstham, it was

once famous for the quarries that provided sandstone for parts of Westminster Abbey and Windsor Castle, for St Paul's and London Bridge. It would have been a place of back-breaking labour then, but after the last war it was chosen as the site for a London overspill estate and the village now has the air of suburbia, with just Quality Street's lovely tile-hung or half-timbered houses putting on a brave face against so much nearby opposition. Yet surprisingly, once the motorways have been crossed and the Downs regained, the walk resumes its country ways with huge views over the Weald.

The long crest continues from White Hill to Gravelly Hill south of Caterham, and across the A22 with Kentish hills ahead drawing you on. On Oxted Down the path drops to the foot of a steep meadow and enters the woods bordering Titsey Park where the Romans had a villa. Then up again to Botley Hill, highest point on the North Downs at 876ft (276m), marked by a tall communications aerial. Here the Downs

show their breadth. To the south the scarp plunges steeply among trees but northwards they level out before sloping into coombes that drain towards Croydon and the grey spillage of London.

The North Downs Way remains high; the Pilgrims' Way edges the lower slopes on a metalled road and, parallel with one another, they leave Surrey and enter Kent at Betsom's Hill. Down below, in the Holmesdale Valley not far from where the Darent rises, lies the little former market town of Westerham. On the green stands General James Wolfe, sword held aloft in triumph. A few paces away Sir Winston Churchill sits slumped in bronze. Both were Westerham heroes in different centuries and in different ways. Both are revered and their former homes now each belong to the National Trust.

Days 4–6: Westerham to Hollingbourne

Between Westerham and Hollingbourne the Downs are broken by the Darent and the

Across a shoulder of Box Hill the clean outline of the Greensand Ridge blocks views of the Weald.

Medway. Whilst it is not difficult to appreciate the power and strength of the Medway in past aeons to break through the great chalk dome, the Darent is less easy to come to grips with, for in reality it's little more than a meagre stream whose banks rarely give way to a sudden recollection of former times when it sliced north through the downland wall to find the Thames.

The Darent rises among greensand hills, flows north-eastward through the Holmesdale Valley and then heads north at Otford. The North Downs Way is ignorant of this fact until it drops from the escarpment to pass along the edge of Chevening Park, and out beside its lovely flint-studded church, before tackling the crossing of the M25. Here the motorway heads north towards the Dartford Tunnel under the Thames but the walker breaks across the Darent Gap to Otford with its promise of a welcome return to soft turf under foot and the breezy open sweep of the Downs once more.

In the heart of Otford there's a duck pond overhung with willows and with a line of pleasant cottages forming a background. Nearby stand the ruins of one-time Otford Palace that housed Becket for a while during his time as Archbishop of Canterbury. In times gone by it was a huge place, more than 400 feet (122m) long and 200 feet or more wide, but all that remains today is an empty tower and sections of walling.

It is difficult to comprehend Otford's historic importance as you wander through, yet its position at the mouth of the Darent Valley was obviously of considerable strategic significance. For the Romans were here (they were everywhere in the Darent Valley) some two thousand years ago; and in 774 Offa, King of Mercia, fought a momentous battle against the men of Kent in the Darent Gap. Again, in 1016, Offa's battlefield was the scene of more bloodshed when the Danes were routed by Ironside and chased eastward to the Medway. Once more Otford came into focus five hundred years later (more peacefully this time) when Henry VIII, and his retinue of some five thousand, came through on his way to France and the Field of the Cloth of Gold. But for all that, Otford is quite unspectacular today and not a place in which to linger, and the need to return to open spaces spurs the walker on.

Beyond Otford Station the Pilgrims' Way continues to Kemsing as a narrow metalled road, but the North Downs Way climbs onto the Downs, among dark yew trees and scrub with the tentacles of old man's beard (Travellers' Joy, or wild clematis) clambering everywhere. Edward Thomas's words capture the scene admirably:

The smoke of traveller's joy is puffed
Over hawthorn berry and hazel tuft . . .

On Green Hill above Kemsing there are more splendid views. Down in the southwest the flooded gravel pits of Chipstead Lakes, now a wildfowl reserve, are clearly seen. So is Sevenoaks with the darkly wooded Greensand Ridge stretching either side of the town. The path then draws back away from the scarp edge for a while, dodging in and out of tree-lined avenues before rejoining the Pilgrims' Way near Wrotham.

Wrotham village (pronounced Rootum) is an oasis of calm and worth 'spending a

little time in before continuing to Wrotham Hill. The sturdy-looking church is particularly fine, with a gallery of exquisite brasses and echoes of centuries long past. Yet more motorways hurtle nearby but the village somehow manages to remain undeterred by it all and this air of calm will remain with you on the walk to Trosley Country Park.

The stage from here to the Medway Gap is a grand walk. The scarp edge is wooded, but sudden huge vistas burst through and when these occur you can see far across the Medway Gap to the south-eastern curve of

Having left St Martha's the path then cuts across a gentle valley before climbing onto the North Downs proper.

the Downs, a blue wall blending to a distant sky. In the valley below Trosley Country Park slumbers the village of Trottiscliffe (pronounced Trosley), with its little church standing apart across the fields, huddled in a dip with Court Lodge Farm next to it. A little farther to the east, and reached by a

15

track from the village and another from the North Downs and Pilgrims' Ways, are the remains of a Neolithic long barrow, the Coldrum Stones. (See details in the chapter on The Wealdway walk.)

The path goes over Holly Hill where the North Downs scarp has been blunted by the Medway, and you walk northward, largely shielded from industrial sights, before being led across the river on a footway alongside the M2 motorway. Rochester Cathedral and Castle are seen on the eastern bank downriver, dominating the scene.

Breaking away from major roads now, the path takes you south to the noted local viewpoint of Bluebell Hill where you gaze south and west over the deep trench of the Medway and out to the vast expanse of the Weald. It is an immense panorama, but one that I love best of all on a winter's afternoon when much of the Medway is pulsating under a skein of mist, and the sinking light adds a touch of magic to what is no more then than a hint of distance.

A short stretch alongside the A229 road follows, then you cut away to follow a tall hedge-lined track leading down to a second Neolithic site, known here as Kits Coty House. This is the best-known of the Medway group of Neolithic monuments and, apart from the dreadful iron railings that cage it, the most impressive too. Like the Coldrum Stones near Trottiscliffe, and the Countless Stones below near Aylesford, Kits Coty House represents a burial chamber whose earth covering has long since eroded away. What we see are three bulky upright stones, taller than a man, and topped by a ten-ton capstone; though how this was raised to its present position without sophisticated lifting gear, remains one of the mysteries of prehistory.

The site is wonderful. Far across the Medway the Downs, retrospectively, continue their westerly line. Across the Gap, unseen now and camouflaged with distance, stand the Coldrum Stones. Were these great burial chambers once used as waymarks, to direct our forefathers across the river? We may only speculate. And dream.

Above the county town of Maidstone the North Downs Way and the Pilgrims' Way continue their parallel lines with little but steep slopes between them. Yet again the Pilgrims' route is along peaceful lanes that bypass Boxley and go through Detling, while our path crosses open pasture and edges woodland, with the 'inner' Downs spreading wide and even, and with an occasional

distant sighting of the north Kent coast announced by a glint of sunlight on water. Much of this section hugs the very lip of the Downs and views are across the depths of the Weald. But on the escarpment, away from roads, this is a lonely landscape with some interesting names: Civiley Wood, Coldblow, Cold Harbour. A little to the south of these, and on the route, is the great Norman earthwork of Thurnham Castle on the very scarp edge, enjoying tremendous views. The Pilgrims' Way continues below.

Hollingbourne is tucked against the ankles of the Downs, on the spring line between chalk and clay. Coming to it, the long-distance walker shares a moment with Cobbett, who wrote in 1823:

> When I got to the edge of the hill and before I got off my horse to lead him down this more than a mile of hill, I sat and surveyed the prospect before me, and to the right and to the left. This is what the people of Kent call the Garden of Eden.

Hollingbourne is another of those charming little villages that gather peace around them. It has the Downs as a safe and sturdy backdrop, the tranquillity of low meadowlands before it. There's a fifteenth-century manor house with a lovely garden of herbs and flowers; another with tall Tudor chimneys; while black and white timber-framed buildings add further to the sense of graceful age. A stream rises near the church and flows south-westwards to join the River Len on the edge of the great park, laid out by Capability Brown, that surrounds Leeds Castle. Should you have time to spare, I would urge you to stray from the route in order to visit this glorious place, considered by Lord Conway to be 'the loveliest castle in the world'.

Day 7: Hollingbourne to Boughton Lees

Between Hollingbourne and Boughton Lees where the Way divides, the North Downs Way and the Pilgrims' Way share a common route, easy-going and extremely pleasant walking, with practically no need to consult the map. Sometimes you wander along hedge-lined tracks, sometimes on tarmac lanes, often on the soft downland turf. Lenham is off the route. So is Charing—but only just. If you need accommodation for the night, you might find it by wandering half a mile south of the Way. In any case, Charing is worth a visit for the harmony of its typically Kentish weatherboarded and

timbered houses, its Georgian frontages, its grey ragstone church tower and former archbishop's palace—another of those palaces, like Otford's, where Henry VIII stayed on his way to meet the Emperor Charles V at the Field of the Cloth of Gold.

East of Charing, the route takes you past a limeworks and chalk pit at Burnt House Farm, then along the edge of a lengthy stretch of woodland to the pleasant little hamlet of Dunn Street, whose name Belloc took as significant evidence of the existence of an ancient road. (Belloc annexed numerous justifications for his assertion of a true Pilgrims' Way existing between Winchester and Canterbury. Village names merely added to his catalogue of 'proof'.) A short distance to the south of Dunn Street, and not on our route, Westwell commands a minor crossroads. This too, is worth a short diversion to see. It has a pub (excuse enough at lunch time), a fine, ancient church, and a disused watermill now converted to a private dwelling and set beside the road. Around the village the wild flowers in spring are a joy to behold.

Back on the North Downs Way and just before reaching Boughton Lees, you come to the sad but romantic remains of Eastwell church standing above the forty acres of a green lake in Eastwell Park. The Park is a considerable estate through which you wander for nearly half an hour before coming upon Boughton Lees in the valley of the Great Stour. Here the Downs have curved away, but they resume again on the far side of the valley above Wye. But the route of the North Downs Way now divides, with one branch heading north in company with the Pilgrims' Way still, making for Canterbury and then on to Dover. The other, more straightforward, route continues across to Wye and follows the scarp south-eastwards to Folkestone and Dover.

Northern Spur via Canterbury Days 8–10: Boughton Lees to Dover

It's a little over 13 miles (21km) to Canterbury, and in those 13 miles there are several places of interest to cause a slackening of pace and to delay your arrival in the city. The first is Boughton Aluph, a tiny hamlet with a church whose size and capacity far exceeds even the most optimistic dreams of the diocese. The next is Chilham, a wonderful village invariably cluttered with camera-snapping tourists. But between the two the Way crosses Soakham Downs and

King's Wood (otherwise known as Challock Forest) above Godmersham, in whose park Jane Austen frequently stayed in her brother's house. 'Kent,' she wrote, 'is the only place for happiness.'

All streets that climb into Chilham have a way of making you feel that you've just discovered something rather special. As indeed you have. The village is a treasury of half-timbered, brick and stone, projecting-gabled cottages of various periods, all of which harmonise surprisingly well. There's a superb church with a flint and stone tower, and a 'castle' which is, in fact, a Jacobean mansion hidden behind high walls. Jousting matches are held in the grounds on a number of Sundays through the summer and in the woods there is England's oldest heronry.

The North Downs are seen as a great natural wall behind Hollingbourne.

Chilham has often been called Kent's prettiest village and it is certainly a victim of its own loveliness. Throughout the year when the sun shines (and often when it doesn't), the streets are crowded with visitors and the square between castle gates and church, packed with cars. I've been there only once to find the place almost deserted, and that was on a wet Tuesday in December!

This is orchard country and much of the way to Canterbury leads among acres of fruit. You wander through Old Wives Lees and past Nickle Farm on footpaths to Chartham Hatch, and then via the twenty-five acre site of Bigbury Iron Age hill fort to Harbledown. Here you pass a spring known as the 'Well of St Thomas', or perhaps more famously as 'Black Prince's Well'.

Once a village with its own identity on the outskirts of Canterbury, the city has virtually swallowed Harbledown now, and you are faced with a succession of streets leading inevitably across the Great Stour and up to

one of England's best-loved buildings: Canterbury Cathedral. As you emerge through Christ Church gate with its ornate heraldry and enter the cathedral precincts, there surely will come bursting upon you (as upon every pilgrim down the ages) a wonderful sense of home-coming. The cathedral rises before you, as does Bath Abbey at the end of the Cotswold Way and Winchester Cathedral at the finish of the South Downs Way, as the ultimate goal of all pilgrims in southern England.

By contrast the continuing walk to Dover must almost inevitably be something of an anti-climax, and in stopping here the Pilgrims' Way walker scores a point over we who are still bound upon the North Downs Way. Canterbury has broken the rhythm of the walk, but this may be resumed to the east of the city along the old Roman road that linked Durovernum (Canterbury) with Rutupiae (Richborough)—now prosaically known simply as the A257. But then you head through orchard country to Patrix-

bourne, cross the Nail Bourne stream and climb onto Barham Down to draw away from the busy Dover road.

By way of Womenswold and Woolage you wander roughly south-eastwards. From Shepherdswell (otherwise known as Sibertswold) there is an obvious direct country road route to Dover but the North Downs Way ignores this to make a long curve eastwards before sniffing the sea and heading south along another Roman road towards the Channel and journey's end.

*Left: **The Neolithic burial chamber of Kits Coty House stands exposed today on an open hillside, but sadly it has been caged as though to contain a wild animal.***

*Below: **A short diversion away from the North Downs Way will give the opportunity to explore Leeds Castle, often called the loveliest castle in the world.***

Direct Route via Folkestone
Days 8–9: Boughton Lees to Dover

In many respects the direct route from Boughton Lees provides better walking and more extensive views. What is lost by not visiting Canterbury, is more than compensated for by the landscape.

Between Boughton Lees and Wye winds the Great Stour, a charming river in places, and one that is navigable to Canterbury. You cross this by Wye railway station and walk towards the church where the footpath route takes you through the churchyard and on a track heading between experimental fields laid out by students at Wye Agricultural College. The wall of the Downs rises directly ahead, and on it can be seen a large crown cut out of the chalk by students to mark the coronation of Edward VII in 1902. The path climbs steeply among trees well to the left of this crown, then wanders along the scarp edge of Wye Downs and Broad Downs with enormous views that encompass the flatlands of Romney Marsh spreading at your feet. It was along here that the ceremony took place to open officially the North Downs Way in 1978, on a magnificent chalk grassland that is also National Nature Reserve. In spring and early summer the turf is bright with flowers, and throughout the summer it is a splendid place for butterflies.

The path, faint in places but waymarked at important junctions, takes you along the edge of the Downs, among sheep and always with superb views. There are few villages and one gains an impression of space and the lonely vigil of isolated farms. South of Stowting you cross Cobb's Hill, then round by Farthing Common and on to Etchinghill.

Drawing ever nearer to the Channel, outside Folkestone there is at present all the reshaping of the landscape due to the demands of the Channel Tunnel. On Castle Hill clear days give views to France. But steeply below lies the Cheriton rail terminal for the Tunnel, and on the final stretch of the walk to Dover across Shakespeare Cliff, one is aware that this small patch of Heritage Coast has been betrayed by politicians and private enterprise alike. Not even a rare patch of Heritage Coast is sacrosanct when it comes to a political grand gesture.

And at the final stage of this long walk, perhaps more than on any other, the walker is certain of one thing: our landscapes are vulnerable and all who care about them must remain vigilant at all times to the threats that come from every direction. Lest they be lost forever.

If nothing else, the North Downs Way teaches all who walk it that single valuable lesson.

Canterbury Cathedral stands as a natural destination for all pilgrims in southern England. The North Downs Way walker is drawn by its lovely mellow stone.

WALK 2: *The Wealdway*

Hales Court Farm, half-hidden in a lush countryside, is the first building in Sussex met on the path of the Wealdway.

Distance: 82 miles (132km).
Time Required: 5–6 days.
Type of Walk: An ever-varied walk across the grain of the land; over chalk Downs, greensand hills, heath, woodland and heavy clay.
Start: Gravesend, Kent.
Finish: Beachy Head, East Sussex.
Maps: O.S. Landranger series 177, 188, 198, 199.
Guidebooks: *The Wealdway and the Vanguard Way* by Kev Reynolds (Cicerone Press). *Wealdway Long-Distance Footpath* by The Wealdway Steering Group. *A Guide to the Wealdway* by John H N Mason (Constable).

A Walk to link the River Thames with the English Channel

From Thames-side to clifftop, from the river to the sea. In its 82-mile (132km) journey across the grain of the land the Wealdway explores some of the richest and most varied landscapes in the south-east.

It begins on the river bank at Gravesend and finishes with a view over the English Channel from the airy clifftop perch of Beachy Head outside Eastbourne. But between the two there is a fascinating, multi-dimensional countryside contained by the outstretched arms of the North and South Downs. These Downs are arranged in a rough horseshoe shape and within their embrace lies the great clay basin of the Weald of Kent and Sussex, one of the most important geographical features in this corner of the country. In it will be found the orchards and hop gardens of the Garden of England. Through it flows the Medway, that major waterway of Kent whose birth is in the black bog of a Sussex hillside. Across it runs the lovely Greensand Ridge, like an inner lining to the North Downs, while the breezy upland heath of Ashdown Forest marks one of the true high-spots, not only of the Weald, but also of the Wealdway.

In ancient times *Anderida*, as the Weald was known by the Romans, was densely forested for a distance of about 120 miles (193km). This forest was mostly of oak, with areas of swamp which added considerably to the problems of communication. That great woodland cover has now, of course, mostly gone. It was cleared over many centuries to gain land for grazing or for crops, for house-building purposes, to fire the furnaces that smelted iron and to make the ships of Britain's fleet. But today's south-bound wanderer still plunges into numerous oak-and-beech woods along the route of the Wealdway, and from the belvedere outposts of the Downs and the greensand hills it is to a patchwork of woodlands that the eye is inevitably drawn.

The concept of a long-distance walking route linking the Thames with the Channel was raised in the early 1970s by members of the Ramblers' Association. With the backing of the Countryside Commission, the County Councils of Kent and East Sussex, a number of amenity groups, District Councils and the South-East England Tourist Board, a route was devised to link existing rights of way.

It is a surprisingly scenic route; an ever-varied route, full of charm and history, full of colour, fragrance and birdsong. It leads through an unfolding series of landscapes that have been tended and cared-for through all the ages of man's occupation of these isles. The walk traverses meadows and woodlands, soft downland pastures, orchards, hop gardens and beech-clad hilltops. There is the life of the hedgerows, spinneys and shaws to brighten the day. There are sunken lanes that tell of centuries of travel by ox-drawn wagons cutting through the notorious Wealden clay. There are rivers and streams to follow. There are abandoned mills, oasts, crooked barns, medieval timbered manor houses, romantic cottages, fine churches that beckon from afar. On the

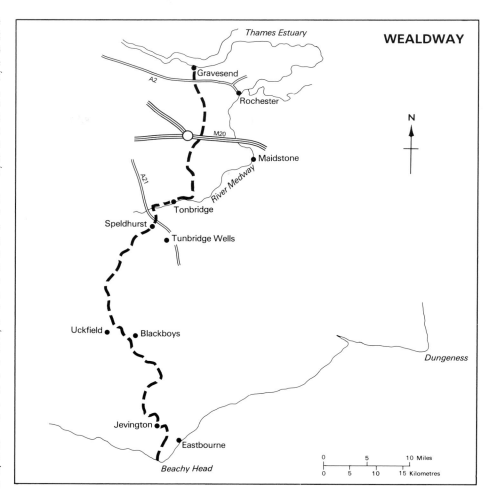

borders of chalk and clay below the North Downs scarp we find the remaining upright stones of a Neolithic burial chamber. On Coombe Hill in Sussex the Wealdway crosses a 'causewayed camp' used by settlers of the New Stone Age—about 2500 BC—and passes at the feet of the Long Man of Wilmington, England's largest chalk figure whose pedigree is still unknown. Along the route of the Wealdway the wanderer passes through several delightful villages and 'lost world' hamlets that seem to owe little to the twentieth century.

And this, in the 'overcrowded south-east'. Who but the walker would believe it possible to travel through Kent and Sussex for many hours at a stretch before finding a village large enough to boast a single shop? Who, in this crowded corner of Britain, would appreciate that it is natural to walk for dozens of miles through the countryside without coming into contact with anyone other than the occasional farm worker?

When I wandered this route one glorious June, I was only 8 miles (13km) from my journey's end before I met another walker—although there are thousands of ramblers living within easy reach, and many hundreds of miles of footpath open and easily accessible.

The map shows a conglomeration of towns, villages, roadways, industrial estates and railways strangling this south-eastern corner of England. That picture is all too true but there is another reality which only the wanderer of footpaths can possibly know. That reality produces a landscape washed with distant hills; a landscape painted with bluebells and orchids. It is peopled by deer, by rabbits, hares and foxes. There are badgers' trails to read. There are news reports announced by jay and magpie. There are adders and lizards dozing in the sun-warmed heaths, and stonechats nervously flitting from one gorse bush to another as you stroll past.

21

The walker's reality is a fragile one, yet it is only by taking to the footpaths that we are able to see the whole—and to know just what we stand to lose without vigilance. Walking the Wealdway will open many an eye to the vitality, gentility and desperate vulnerability of England's green and pleasant land.

Days 1–2: Gravesend to Tonbridge

At first glance Gravesend has little appeal, although for the long-distance walker it has the distinction of starting two multi-day routes: the Wealdway and the Saxon Shore Way. A grey town on a grey river it may be, but it does have an indefinable atmosphere all its own, and it's a haunting place when all but deserted. The town owes its existence and prosperity to the Thames, for long ago it proved to be the first convenient landing for ships having entered the estuary bound for London. Pepys knew it well from his work with the Navy Board, coming here often on business and commenting on the life of the town in his Diary.

Today Gravesend depends less on the river than in the past, though in June it turns to the Thames for the spectacle of sailing barges mustering, their rust-coloured sails and tar-black timbers making a romantic sight with the wind behind them. And plying a daily trade back and forth across the water, the Tilbury Ferry dodges other river traffic on its short link with Essex, and where the ferry discharges its passengers, there the Wealdway begins. (In truth, the official start to the walk is on the outskirts of town, beside the ancient Roman road of Watling Street. It also officially finishes short of Beachy Head at East Dean Road, just outside Eastbourne. But there is considerably more purpose in beginning the route on the Thames river bank and ending on one of the finest clifftops of the South Coast.)

Wandering through the town, first along the pedestrian precinct of the 700 year-old High Street, the long-distance walker feels a little conspicuous with his rucksack among the shoppers but 2 miles (3km) later, Watling Street is crossed near the Tollgate Moat House; the first WW sign met as countryside takes the place of town and pavement is exchanged for footpath. Ahead stretch broad flat fields, a row of willows and the promise of good things to come.

Heading south and passing beside orchards, the path leads to the quiet little hamlet of Nash Street, no more than a handful of cottages with tangled hedges and fields all around. A tunnel of trees takes the route into a meadow or two, across a couple of country lanes and through a wood to emerge in the village of Sole Street which is on the London–Chatham railway line. On the southern outskirts the Wealdway follows the boundary of Camer Country Park before crossing the line of the London Countryway and tackling a chessboard of fields and woodlands in the very heart of the North Downs—although that fact seems hard to believe. It is only later that the Downs properly announce themselves but by then you will already have chalked your boots and trodden the first thousand or so flints.

With a woodland path behind you the Downs fold neatly into little valleys, and views stretch out to encompass a rich landscape of far-off hills, beech-clad knolls and marching hedgerows. Steeply below, in a bowl of light and tree-shadow, rests the hamlet of Luddesdown. It is a scene of tranquillity in which only the distant sentry-like pylons with their cats' cradles of power lines intrude. Lovers of the countryside may well seethe at this brazen intrusion but how much worse it all might have been a few years ago had the Ministry of Defence been allowed its way? Much of this land, these fine rolling acres, almost became lost as a tank training ground. Imagine, tanks rumbling where primroses bloom, where rabbits play and rooks break the silence with their mournful cry! A battle with the MoD naturally commenced. It was, happily, a battle on behalf of the countryside that the countryside won. But still the pylons intrude.

The Wealdway passes through Luddesdown, a tiny, ancient place with a long history. There was a settlement here in Stone Age times, and in the Iron Age too. The Romans were here next, for pieces of their pottery have been found on the slopes above the hamlet and there are Roman tiles set in the lower walls of the church. Next to the church stands Luddesdown Court. One of the oldest inhabited houses in Britain, it has been continuously occupied for some nine hundred years—ever since William the Conqueror's Bishop Odo lived in it. The hamlet can hardly have grown at all in those nine centuries, for today it merely consists of a clutch of houses, a pub, farm, the church and the manor. All around the downland slopes rise to bird-thrashing woods. Footpaths lead away like the legs of a spider into this peaceful, hidden land. Yet not half a dozen miles (10km) away there are traffic-congested streets and unsightly industries—lost to view and sound, fortunately.

After the first hillside has been traversed out of Luddesdown, the path leads along a delightful sweep of valley known as The Bowling Alley, and this in turn takes the walker to a narrow twisting lane in the hamlet of Great Buckland, a place of tidy farms and isolated houses set among trees in a back-of-beyond country. Nearby stands the sorry little church of Dode, a tiny building barricaded against the world by a high fence. The community it once served was wiped out in 1349 by the Black Death.

Another field or two, then through Whitehorse Wood the Wealdway leads on to the lip of the North Downs escarpment which rewards with a vast panorama overlooking a rich green landscape. This is a sudden revelation, for while there have been occasional distant views thus far, they have mostly been narrowed by the rise and fall of intervening hills. Often views were constricted by woods—grand in themselves in their concentration of individual aspects, but limiting in extent. Now, though, the eye scans a broad and extensive patch of country: the Weald of Kent, a green wash of meadow, field and woodland running blue towards the southern horizon. Off to the left the Downs curve south-eastward across the Medway Gap. Below the neat criss-cross pattern of hedges contain fields of barley, wheat or rape. There are meadows grazed by cattle or sheep, solitary farm buildings, a cluster of houses marking a village, a dark jigsaw of woods and spinneys. To the right you see the Downs reaching on towards the west, off to Surrey along the line of the North Downs Way.

There is a steep descent of the scarp slope banked by hedges wrapped around with wild clematis, the chalk underfoot a mite

Right above: **Dreaming by Highlands Pond I was surprised to find a number of deer wandering blatantly through a neighbouring field.**

Right below: **Near Withyham the path heads alongside a modest stream which is, in fact, the infant Medway.**

slippery after rain and requiring some caution. Near the foot of it you come onto the Pilgrims' Way. A few paces along this the path heads south and the Wealdway deserts the chalk of the Downs in favour of the clay and sand of the Weald. Moments later you come to the Coldrum Stones, or Coldrum Long Barrow; a meeting with an ancient past.

On this site, some five thousand years ago, Neolithic man buried his dead in a chamber tomb. Two dozen weighty stone pillars were raised in a circle measuring 160ft in circumference, capped with stone and covered with earth. Four of the original pillars remain upright, the rest lying in a rough circle in the grass. In 1910 when the site was excavated the bones of twenty-two people were discovered. This chamber, along with others at Addington and Kits Coty on the Downs above Aylesford, form part of what has become known as the 'Medway Culture'. They share similarities with tombs discovered in the north of Germany and in Scandinavia, and it is thought they may have been erected by a northern race who worked their way along the Medway Valley. In 1926 the National Trust accepted responsibility for the Coldrum Long Barrow in memory of Benjamin Harrison, the amateur archaeologist and grocer from nearby Ightham.

The Wealdway continues to head south through Ryarsh Wood, across low-lying fields and beneath the M20 motorway. Happily the wanderer soon loses the drone of traffic and exchanges it instead for birdsong on the final mile or so to Wrotham Heath.

Rhododendron-lively woods bring you to the edge of the village of Platt where quiet lanes with pretty cottages beside them lead to the first of the day's orchards, and into Mereworth Woods, one of the largest remaining woodland areas in Kent where wild boar used to be hunted. Much of this woodland today is coppiced but with fine groves of beech and oak bringing a more stately aspect to it. For 2 miles (3km) the path—often muddy—wanders through the woods and comes to Gover Hill where the Weald is again seen falling away to the south.

Down an easy slope now, with lovely views and a big country spreading on either side of the path, it's not long before you enter orchards with oast houses in view, and far across the valley the curious Hadlow Tower standing out above the trees. Into the village

of West Peckham, one of the prettiest met on the Wealdway; a group of cottages, the weatherboarded Swan Inn and a Saxon-age church seen across the village green. It's an attractive vignette of a village mentioned in the Domesday Book.

From West Peckham a series of meadows and flat fields are typical of this corner of the Weald. Then a few hop gardens and orchards again, with oast houses painting the countryside with their white cowls. Some are still in use as drying kilns for hops; some are used for storage, while others have been converted into dwellings. There are long views ahead, huge skies and scattered farms, snaking lanes shoulder-high with cow parsley along their verge, old barns and wild flowers in the hedgerows.

At Barnes Street the Wealdway crosses by a handsome timbered house dating back to the fourteenth century but then heads through a farmyard, among orchards once more, and very soon comes to the banks of the River Medway. The route keeps company with it on both sides of Tonbridge for a delightful 6 miles (10km).

Following a river there is always something to see. There is wildlife in the water and along its banks. There are flowers by the towpath, birds in the trees and high reeds, and ever-changing vistas of the valley ahead.

At first you cross the Medway on a footbridge, then walk upstream a short distance before recrossing to the left bank at East Lock and continuing upstream for another 4 miles (6km). It's a lovely summer-indolent river in which you may see numerous birds, as well as various pleasure craft. Sometimes the path is fully open to the sun; at others it creeps through tree shade with dappled patterns thrown in the water and the joyful warbling of birdsong overhead. Tonbridge comes into view almost too soon.

Days 3–4: Tonbridge to Blackboys

Tonbridge has been around for a long time. One of the first major trackways through the great Wealden forest of *Anderida* came via *Dun Burgh*—the ancient name for the settlement that grew on the banks of the River Medway. In the Iron Age there was a hill fort here—*dun burgh* means 'hill fort'—and it is thought probable that the Saxons too had a fortification on this strategic river crossing. Certainly after the Norman Conquest a wooden castle was quickly built here but this was destroyed by fire soon after, in 1087. It

was rebuilt at once, this time using stone, and it is the remains of these massive walls and central keep overlooking the Medway that the Wealdway wanderer sees as he sets out on the stage to Fordcombe along the northern bank of the river.

Heading west the town is soon left behind. In its place there are fields and woodland shaws and lovely views across low-lying meadows to the rise of the Greensand Ridge. There is a long canal-like stretch of river known as the 'Straight Mile' where a century and more ago attempts were made to pursue the Medway's navigation as far as Penshurst. This attempt gave out near the modern Flood Relief Barrier at Haysden. Now the route crosses the river a hundred yards or so short of the massive grey gates of the Barrier, dodges beneath an arched brick-built railway bridge and shortly after reaches the hamlet of Haysden, whose pub, the Royal Oak, is usually found too soon in the day to be of much use to walkers.

A lane leads to a farmyard and this, in turn, gives access to a meadow with a tunnel leading beneath the busy Tonbridge by-pass. This is soon left behind with a long pull up the northern slope of one of the High Weald ridges—first alongside Beechy Toll Wood, then through the wood itself to reach the B2176 road at Bidborough, occupying one of the classic belvederes of this corner of Kent. Within a few paces of coming out of the wood, a magnificent view draws the eye to the north. The hillside plunges away among gardens extravagant with rhododendrons and azaleas; down, down to the Medway's valley, then across this to the line of the Greensand Ridge—a lovely wall whose glory is but a hint from this distance—and north-east to the blue haze of the North Downs, a day and a half's walk away. It is a view to slow one's pace; an excuse to rest awhile, leaning on a wall and dreaming into the spaciousness of this 'crowded south-east'.

Sir Thomas More—he who upset the conscience of Henry VIII and lost his head for it—once lived at Bidborough, and it is said that his friend, the noted Dutch scholar Erasmus, preached in the little ragstone church here. It is a glorious church dating from the twelfth century, crowded with the silence of eight hundred years broken only by the heavy swinging of the clock's pendulum. It stands high above cottage rooftops, with a fine view across the surrounding countryside. The Wealdway passes through the churchyard, where gravestones lean with age, coloured with lichen, and then heads out by way of well-worn steps of stone through the lych gate and onto a sloping lane that plunges once again into the tight fold of yet more hills.

Steep meadows, lazy meandering streams, shading trees and a little woodland all maintain interest on the walk from Bidborough to the charmingly-named Modest Corner. Not a village, and barely a hamlet, Modest Corner is little more than a row of cottages facing a common. In the midst of the cottages stands the white weatherboarded Beehive pub.

There follows a short stretch of quiet country road, then back to fields and meadows with the hills falling away and the church at Speldhurst beckoning above intervening trees. An old watermill, now no longer used as such, stands beside its swan-loving pond deep in a hollow formed by the circling hills. Soon after you come up a slope to the attractive hilltop village of Speldhurst where the George and Dragon inn is conveniently placed for lunch time refreshment. It's an interesting building in its own right; a very popular pub with fourteenth-century beams and dark corners. Opposite stands the Victorian Gothic church with stained glass windows by William Morris and Burne-Jones. The village, on the edge of the Wealden ironmaking region, was first mentioned in a document dated AD 768, although it is not in the Domesday Book.

The path exchanges Speldhurst's street for a sudden broad panorama. A crown of hill leads to a woodland, and down through this to Bullingstone Lane with a smattering of aged cottages, some of the fifteenth century, set in a tranquil backwater. The Wealdway passes between two of these romantic crooked-walled cottages and enters Avery's Wood; an enchanting place, a small mixed woodland with a stream flowing through. A place of birdsong, wild flowers and imagination, for there are numerous gnarled trunks ideally suited for transformation into Disney-esque characters. This is a wood straight out of Grimm's fairy tales!

Avery's Wood leads to more meadows, a couple of ponds, a country lane with an oast house beside it, and into the village of Fordcombe, which sits on a crossroads overlooking a splendid patch of countryside above an adolescent Medway.

From Gravesend to Fordcombe the walk has been a constantly-evolving introduction to the countryside of the south-east. There

have been a couple of towns and a few villages and hamlets along the route. Mostly, though, the footpaths that link them have exploited the varied nature of Kent's hidden places, making the most of its unsung heartland, prising its secrets from secluded hollows or revealing its splendour from one ridge after another. After Fordcombe, however, habitations grow more scarce. Sussex is entered and the wanderer of footpaths becomes accustomed to lengthy stretches of undulating landscape practically devoid of any real community, just the occasional isolated farm or cottage to give

the countryside the reassurance of population. It is still a worked land, though. The south-east has no wilderness, and the nearest you may approach to one will be found on the crossing of Ashdown Forest.

Half a mile or so of broad-visioned

Avery's Wood, near Bullingstone Lane, is a magical place where you almost expect the trees to take life and move in a Disneyesque dance!

hedgerow path separates Fordcombe from Stone Cross. Off to the right a valley lies hidden by the slope of fields. In it winds the Medway, and beyond it to the west rise more hills of the High Weald—lovely walking country for other days. Stone Cross has a collection of converted oast houses beside the path, then you plunge through a tunnel of trees and hedges and emerge into a blaze of light shining over Sussex. From a green meadow sloping to the south comes one of the finest of all the Wealdway's views. It gazes over the last of Kent and into the first of Sussex. There are chequerboard fields and meadows—barely a building in all this wide panorama—and woodlands crowning the hills ahead, with Ashdown Forest hinted in the blue rise and fall of the horizon. It is a stunning view, made even more attractive by the prospect of walking through it.

Going down the meadowland slope the route of the Sussex Border Path is crossed. Then under a railway bridge, over an insignificent stream and into the county of East Sussex. A farm track takes the Wealdway towards Hale Court Farm, whose single oast makes a pleasing picture above the track. Breaking away to the south now, a path leads alongside another innocent-looking stream: the Medway. A couple of miles (3km) later, having crossed the line of the former Forest Row to Groombridge railway which is now the Forest Way Country Park, you come to a lane climbing uphill with the fascinating church of Withyham standing off to the left, and a furnace pond below to the right. The church is well worth visiting; in it will be found a collection of monuments to the Sackville family (the Sackvilles of Knole, Sevenoaks), for some fifteen generations of them lie here in the awesome peace of rural Sussex.

For a little over a mile a quiet lane leads across an exposed brow of countryside, through rolling parkland with stately trees and huge views, and comes to Five Hundred Acre Wood. Those who have not yet forgotten their Winnie the Pooh stories will recognise this as *Hundred Acre Wood*; A. A. Milne, the creator of the Pooh series, lived at nearby Hartfield and translated this woodland and parts of Ashdown Forest beyond into his books. Five Hundred Acre Wood is a dense stand of oak and beech; originally part of Ashdown Forest, it was enclosed as long ago as 1693, and the trees of today are descendants of those earlier plantings. Some of the trackways through the wood are notoriously muddy, but as you

gain height on the southbound journey, so the tracks give way to footpaths, and these are considerably more pleasant to walk along.

Then the wood suddenly falls behind and you find yourself on the great open heath of Ashdown Forest; 6000 acres of it, a sweep of gorse, bracken and umbrella stands of pine. A stunning vista displays the vast extent of the Weald, for here you come onto the brow of the country, and look off to the south to see the line of the South Downs hovering far away, then spin in 180 degrees to gaze off to

the North Downs and the Greensand Ridge, and the confusing ridges of the High Weald marking the ribs of the land. Up here the breeze blows free.

On the southern side of Ashdown Forest the footpath, guided by special Forest markers bearing the WW symbol, dodges to and fro, sometimes in spinneys, often across open bracken-tangled country, and finally leaves the Forest near the grandiose gates of Oldlands Hall whose estate, 500 years ago, was heavily involved in the iron industry. Hard to believe though it may be for the

Above: **Handsome cottages, tile-hung as is typical of Sussex, line the churchyard in Hellingly.**

Left above: **High above Wilmington the path treads the frontiers of earth and sky, and grants wonderful views over the low-lying Weald.**

Left below: **England's largest chalk figure is the Long Man of Wilmington. The Wealdway goes right to his feet before breaking away to the left and climbing onto the South Downs.**

passing walker, this whole area was for centuries caught amid the clamour of iron. The Romans worked it, and in a nearby field great deposits of ash dating from Roman times have been found, indicating that they were smelting here. Remains of a Roman building, skeletons and numerous pieces of first century pottery have been unearthed in this peaceful, unsuspecting countryside. To the walker, though, all this is a confusion of history. Passing through it is the fragrance of bloom and blossom, the song of the birds, the flash of a deer, the far-off views that are absorbed. The clang and crash of hammers belong to another age.

Something over 3 miles (5km) of woods, meadows and country roads lead to Buxted Park, and meandering through the Weald-way enjoys the company of rhododendrons and stately trees, but then swings away to find the little River Uck which it follows to the converted mill house of Hempstead Mill. Uckfield stands about a mile or so off to the west while the route heads east, away from

the river and across undulating meadow-lands, past a farm and over a railway cutting, to a quiet lane near Highlands Pond. The pond makes a colourful corner. In it reeds attract dragonflies. Flowers and trees burst with life; there are fish lurking in the depths, and once when I was there I spotted several deer trespassing through a neighbouring field.

There follow more fields, more meadows, a short stretch of country lane, another stream to stroll beside, and then you arrive before Tickerage Mill; an attractive hidden corner with a bright mill pond and fine house on the outskirts of Blackboys, where there's a Youth Hostel at the end of a rather long, but enjoyable day's walking.

Days 5–6: Blackboys to Beachy Head

Almost immediately upon leaving Blackboys the Wealdway heads into a countryside of meadows and woods, and within the first hour it comes to New Place Farm, a splendid mansion on the site of an iron foundry. You

wander alongside a bright landscaped garden with intimate waterfalls tumbling from a lake amid trees and shrubs, then leave the grounds for a broad series of fields, one after another with the footpath sometimes difficult to locate when June's growth is lush and thigh-high.

East Hoathly, set on a dog's leg on the A22 Eastbourne road, is better seen by the walker than the motorist, for the path goes beside the church whose Tudor door is adorned by the Pelham Buckle—a sword buckle won by a member of the Pelham family at the Battle of Poitiers, and presented by King John II of France in 1356. The village has opportunities for refreshment, but the Wealdway continues through, heading east now, then south-east and running parallel with the route of the Vanguard Way which is less than a mile away to the north. Both routes cross again in the next village, Chiddingly.

There's not much to Chiddingly. It's just a handful of houses, the Six Bells pub, a Post Office Stores and a charming church whose lofty stone spire dominates the surrounding countryside. The spire makes a useful landmark, while the body of the church is a comforting place in which to sit for a few minutes to gain strength for the continuing journey.

Leaving Chiddingly the footpath takes you on a long south-easterly sweep of meadows, passing some handsome farm buildings, duckponds and streams, and then along a short stretch of lane into Hellingly. Walking through the tile-hung cottage-lined churchyard you tread history, and soon after, come before the fourteenth-century timbered Horselunges Manor, passing alongside its romantic moat. Horsebridge nearby is bland by comparison, but it is only a few short minutes before soft countryside takes over again with a sequence of fields that lead down briefly to the young Cuckmere, that river of character which rises in

Above: **The Norman keep of Tonbridge Castle stands above the River Medway.**

Right: **Blackboys Youth Hostel, built to house refugees from the Spanish Civil War, offers accommodation for walkers on both the Wealdway and Vanguard Way.**

the High Weald and flows in ox-bows through the South Downs and out to freedom beside the Seven Sisters.

Out of Upper Dicker the Downs suddenly appear to be closing ahead. More meadow paths lead again to the banks of the Cuckmere, but once more you desert its company in order to cut across country to visit the Saxon church at Arlington. Passing Arlington Reservoir a rough marshy area leads on towards a rising hill which overlooks the Downs, and there comes a sense of anticipation as the South Downs signal the final obstacle to tackle on the journey from the Thames.

Wilmington, with its delightful street, its ancient Priory ruins, its flint-walled church, its huge chalk figure and the great wall of the Downs behind it, is a fitting place to pause before tackling the last 9 miles (14km) to Beachy Head.

Probably the best of the Wealdway has been saved for the end. Nine miles make for an easy final day but there are the Downs to ascend, and so many magnificent views to enjoy that one is tempted to dawdle when the weather is set fair; to sprawl in the cropped grass with orchids or cowslips around you and larks warbling high overhead; with huge vistas over the Weald or the sea; with history in the very bones of the land, and a walk in the sky as a worthy conclusion.

Wilmington itself challenges the walker to stay on—just a little longer. It has much appeal for it is, surely, one of the most charming of the many charming villages of Sussex with its long romantic street, bright with roses in summer, leading to the haven of the Downs. It is in every respect a village of the Downs, for the smooth green slopes rise just behind it to the clean line of a ridge stretching far off.

If it is the challenge of the Downs that encourages the walker away from Wilmington, it is the Long Man who signals the way. England's largest chalk figure (another is the Cerne Abbas Giant on the Dorset Downs Walk), the Long Man stands 226 feet (69m) high, naked on the hillside with a stave held in each hand. No-one knows exactly how old he is, nor what he represents. Speculation abounds: could he be a product of the Bronze Age? or is he a Roman engineer—with sighting posts, rather than staves? or Saxon perhaps? Various theories are outlined on a plaque fixed below the figure. In 1873 the Long Man was etched in yellow brick, but in 1969 white blocks were placed upon him for greater impact, and to protect the exposed chalk of the original. He rests in the care of the Sussex Archaeological Trust which also looks after the remains of Wilmington Priory.

The Wealdway takes a fenced path to the Long Man's feet, then veers away to the left on a steady ascent of the hillside and with an enormous view of the low-lying Weald spread below. This is one of the finest footpath sections of the whole route, and it leads in a mile or so round the northern spur of the Downs, then drops among trees to the tiny hamlet of Folkington. There is very little of Folkington: a Victorian manor house, a farm and the flint and stone-walled thirteenth-century church with its weatherboarded bell tower, set among trees beside the path. This path soon becomes a sunken track between bushes and trees climbing towards converging hills; a sunken track that once was the road between Jevington and Folkington. Once over a saddle in the Downs the old trackway descends then to the secluded village of Jevington.

Jevington is a firm favourite with lovers of the South Downs, and it is easy to understand why. It's an ancient place nestling in a fold of the Downs. Unspoilt, historic, attractive, with the Downs crowding around to protect rather than threaten.

Above the village, and reached by a flight of steps opposite the Eight Bells pub, a climbing path takes you onto Coombe Hill, site of a 'causewayed camp' where, about 4500 years ago, immigrant farmers of the New Stone Age created enclosures of land in which they experimented with the growing of grain. Later, Bronze Age Man (about 1500 BC) came to Coombe Hill to bury his dead. It is so obviously an important site; one of the finest viewpoints of the Wealdway it presents a 360 degree panorama of peace and beauty. From it one gazes over the Weald, over Pevensey Levels, to the sea, into a green bowl of downland, off to Butts Brow and Willingdon Hill.

Beyond Willingdon Hill's high point you descend among bushes towards Eastbourne and on coming to a road beside Beachy Head Youth Hostel the Wealdway officially ends. It is an unsatisfactory conclusion; as unsatisfactory as beginning the long walk two miles from the Thames, so you head up the road a short distance, then break away onto a clifftop path that climbs among gorse bushes and low wind-bent trees, the sea dazzling off to the left. The faint indent of a path leads on, and suddenly there's the dramatic lunge of Beachy Head's great chalk bastion into a froth of surf, 532 feet (162m) below, with its famous lighthouse dwarfed by the cliffs and the green switch-back of the Seven Sisters rolling away ahead. There's the taste of salt in the breeze; gulls overhead, waves far below. And no further progress south.

WALK 3: *Medway Riverside Walk*

Standing above the river is East Farleigh. The church, standing on a crossroads, is typical of this corner of Kent. It overlooks the Medway Valley, and sits on the edge of a land of orchards and hop gardens.

Distance: 16 miles (25km).
Time Required: 1 day.
Type of Walk: A gentle towpath outing, virtually level all the way. It treads a peaceful countryside but passes close to several villages with a number of opportunities for refreshment. There are various places along the route where public transport is available to whisk you back to the start, or ahead to the finish.
Start: Tonbridge, Kent.
Finish: Maidstone, Kent.
Map: O.S. Landranger series 188.
Guidebook: *Walking in Kent* by Kev Reynolds (Cicerone Press).

A Gentle Stroll Beside Kent's Major River

Southern England has no great waterways to match the broad swirling rivers of Scotland. But then the landscape of Southern England is devoid of mountain systems that give rise to such features. However, the modest streams and rivers that do flow through these gentle lands have a considerable impact on the region's charm. Elsewhere in this book a chapter is devoted to following the course of the Thames, and few rivers of Britain have had a more profound effect on the nation's history than that. Kent, one should remember, shares some of the banks and the estuary of the Thames, but it also has the Great and Little

Sometimes hugging the shade of trees, sometimes across open meadows, the towpath is never dull.

the county, bestowing as it does a benevolent gesture of grace and calm.

From Tonbridge to Maidstone the Medway eases itself for about 16 comfortable miles (25km) through a peaceful landscape of fields, pastures, orchards and hop gardens. A gentle, untroubled river, it traces the heart of a gentle and seemingly untroubled countryside. Along its banks a towpath maintains a close companionship, sometimes tree-lined and shady, sometimes through open meadows, often beside locks, the occasional weir, or beneath a medieval bridge. There are views of the wood-crowned greensand hills. There are hillsides neat with fruit bushes, villages standing above the river, manicured lawns sneaking down to the water's edge, attractive churches nearby, boat yards and oast houses and lively riverside pubs. On the walk beside the Medway there will undoubtedly be river craft seen slowly chugging along, or negotiating the half-dozen or so locks that regulate the levels. There may well be anglers sharing the bank, canoeists quietly skimming through the dappled waters, oarsmen in training.

Mostly, though, there will only be the birds and animals and insects for company. Never is the river dull or uninteresting.

As Kent's major waterway the Medway cuts right across the county making an unequal division between west and east, and in times gone by this division gave rise to the oft-quoted distinction between Kentish Men and Men of Kent; Kentish Men being raised to the west of the Medway, Men of Kent to the east.

In common with all rivers the Medway has many sources, one being a black bog on Ashdown Forest in Sussex. On the journey to its estuary of oozing mud banks, marshes and little islands trapped between Sheppey and Grain to the north-east of Rochester, it draws other streams from the greensand hills, from the chalk of the North Downs and from the broad lesser slopes of the Weald, and in so doing becomes transfused by the vitality of the Garden of England.

Being born among Sussex hills, for a while the infant stream forms the county boundary, but by the time it has reached historic Penshurst it has grown somewhat and, like an adolescent, misbehaves now and then when heavy rains encourage it to flood the low-lying meadows below Penshurst Place, one of England's finest stately homes. In one such meadow, not far from the tree where England's last bear was reputedly

Stour, the Darent, Beult and Teise, and a number of lesser streams. None of these today match the Thames in volume or importance, of course, although in historical terms the Stour was once linked with a channel (the Wantsum) that made Thanet an island at the county's eastern extremity.

The Medway, on the other hand, still claims some importance and remains Kent's major river. It casts a gleam of light across shot, the Medway is given a boost by the inflowing River Eden and, thus encouraged, winds on to Tonbridge.

From Tonbridge to the sea the Medway is navigable, a factor which assured the town's prosperity in the eighteenth century. Access to London markets being gained along the river and into the Thames, Tonbridge could then transport locally grown hops, fruit and timber to the capital. This occurred from the 1740s onwards. But Tonbridge stood guard over the river for many centuries before that navigation came, and the remains of the Norman castle still overlook both town and waterway from the huge motte that was thrown up nearly a thousand years ago. Nearby, several other interesting and historic buildings give the town a character that modern Town Planners have failed to match, although the recent Medway Wharf development is pleasing enough for these architecturally soulless times.

Tonbridge to Maidstone

This is not a tough walk. There are no hills to tackle, no need for constant reference to map and compass, even though there are no Medway waymarks (you simply stay wth the river throughout). There are convenient refreshment halts at a number of places, sometimes on the route itself, sometimes by a short diversion from it. And since the towns at either end of the walk are linked by public transport (by Maidstone and District buses, and by British Rail via Paddock Wood), it is possible to arrange a return to Tonbridge at the end of the day. There are also several intermediate stages on the journey where either train or bus could be taken to shorten the walk by those who consider the distance rather too long for one day.

It begins not far from the castle in Tonbridge High Street, on the south side of the bridge that crosses the river. The Castle pub stands beside the bridge on the corner of Medway Wharf Road, and a short distance along this little back street it is possible to join the towpath on the right bank heading downstream. Within a few paces the first lock (Town Lock) is reached where a side

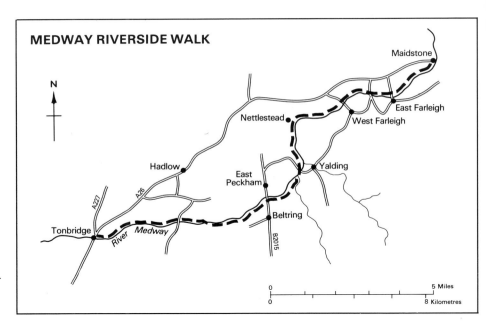

MEDWAY RIVERSIDE WALK

From Tonbridge to Maidstone the Medway is navigable. The riverside walk starts here, in the heart of Tonbridge, a few paces from the Norman castle.

stream flows in from the north. This is one of several tributaries draining out of the Wealden hills to bolster the Medway, and where the two streams converge used to be a busy, industrious place. It is now a fairly tranquil haven secreted away from the town's commercial heart.

Continuing to the east along the asphalt towpath you pass below the town's gasworks and come to a road which serves an expanding industrial estate. Crossing the road bridge the towpath is rejoined, although it's no longer surfaced and has taken to the left (north) bank of the river with the boathouses of Tonbridge School nearby. (You'll often see rowing crews in training along the initial section of the walk.) Almost immediately Tonbridge is left behind, and in its place there are meadows and trees and bushes, with the greensand hills rising in the distance off to the left and more open country spreading away to the south. For the next $3^{1}/_{2}$ miles (5.5 km) the route remains on the left bank to enjoy a deepening involvement with the river.

For some time your attention becomes focused on a peculiar, yet not unattractive, Gothic tower rising digit-like across the fields. Because of the river's meanderings this lofty tower is occasionally seen ahead, sometimes off to the left, but ever watchful of your progress. This is Hadlow Tower, or May's Folly, the solitary remains of one-time Hadlow Castle, a considerable mansion built in the last year of the eighteenth century. The tower was added as an afterthought by a wealthy and eccentric industrialist, Walter Barton May who, it is said, wanted to keep an eye on his wife after they had parted. (Another suggestion is that he wished to be able to see the coast way off in the east—but the feasibility of this strikes me as being most unlikely.) It stands 170 feet (52m) high and is a fanciful concoction of crenellations and spires, and it makes a striking landmark, considerably dwarfing the church that stands next door.

Two more locks are passed while the river broadens among low, open meadows. Then you come to the rather bland Hartlake Bridge which carries a minor road through orchard country from Tudeley to Golden Green and Hadlow. This bridge replaces an earlier, rather frail timber structure that was the scene of a tragedy in the autumn of 1853. A party of thirty-five hop-pickers (or 'hoppers' as they were known) were returning by wagon to their camp after the day's harvesting when one of the lead horses stumbled against a rail and broke it. The crowded wagon, and a second close behind, toppled through into the river, and all thirty-five hop-pickers—men, women and children—drowned. Hadlow church has a memorial to them.

Rivers provide a rich and diverse habitat for numerous creatures and in common with others this walk enables the quiet and observant rambler to witness not only the wildlife of bank and river but also a profusion of plants along the way. When these are in flower colour dazzles the eye, often with the indolent drift of butterflies tacking from one flower-head to another around you. In springtime almost every step of the way will be gladdened by birdsong; chiffchaff, willow warbler, blackcap and so on. There are dragonflies and damselflies too, winging in uncertain to-ings and fro-ings where reeds offer a site for their eggs. There are mallard, moorhen and coot maintaining their mid-stream business and it's quite possible that you will catch sight of a heron or two standing alert on a mudbank for an unsuspecting meal passing by. And there are mysterious trails of various bankside creatures to unravel, too. The life of the river, the towpath and the surrounding countryside keeps you ever-attentive as you wander along.

About $3^{1}/_{2}$ miles (5.5 km) downstream of Tonbridge you come to East Lock. A footpath here breaks away to the north towards Golden Green among hop gardens and by the side of oast house clusters. But unless you are drawn to a diversion that gives the opportunity to visit Hadlow just beyond Golden Green, you should ignore this and cross to the right bank which is now followed as far as the medieval bridge, lock and weir at The Leas, outside Yalding.

For about 3 of these riverside miles (5 km) the Medway leads through a peaceful, almost deserted patch of countryside; the most remote section of the whole walk. There are woods and meadows in view, with orchards and hop gardens in the distance. Other footpaths plunge away through the fields to far-off anonymous villages, unseen from the river bank. There are occasional footbridges teasing across the Medway and more locks, presenting opportunities to gaze on boats patiently negotiating their way through. But it is the countryside that dominates. This, after all, is the heartland of Kent, the soul of the county and it is for some the very epitome of rural England; a mixture of worked and unworked land. A dynamic agriculture rubbing against a fallow, resting countryside. There are crops and fertile strips of grassland spiked with rough bush and woodland shaw—a haven for wildlife, the habitat of numerous plants. It is a land that needs protecting.

South of the straggly village of East Peckham the towpath brings you onto the B2015 road opposite a small industrial area. A little under a mile down this road stands the Whitbread Hop Farm at Beltring, a great cluster of oast houses with a museum on the hop industry open to the public. This industry, once so important to the county's rural economy, is in decline in Kent, and the amount of land devoted to hop growing is now less than a quarter of what it was at the turn of the century. However, there is still a good acreage of land along the Medway Valley put to hop cultivation today, but production is governed by a quota system organised by the Hop Marketing Board at nearby Paddock Wood.

The Medway walk continues along the right bank, heading through the brief interruption of the little industrial area and soon passing beneath a railway bridge. The river is shaded by trees for a while, then it becomes brighter and more attractive on the approach to Yalding. At The Leas there is almost a seaside holiday atmosphere. The river is joined by the Teise—a delightful stream when seen in its infancy far away on the county boundary west of Lamberhurst, where one branch flows by the ruins of Bayham Abbey and another by lovely Scotney Castle. On joining the Medway it sacrifices its individuality and almost immediately flows beneath the medieval splendour of Twyford Bridge. There is a weir and more lock gates, a busy pub, a cafe and a boat chandler's here. Always, it seems, there are people. People fishing, canoeing, gazing in the water, leaning over the bridge, throwing sticks for dogs in the adjoining meadows. Through the archways of the bridge you look to the north-east where the ridge of sun-loving hills above Yalding is rich with husbandry; row upon row of fruit fields and orchards. A busy, neat and productive land that Cobbett much admired.

In his *Rural Rides*, he wrote of the country between Maidstone and Tonbridge:

'I believe it to be the very finest, as to fertility and diminutive beauty, in the whole world . . . There are, on rising grounds . . . not only hop gardens and beautiful woods, but immense orchards of apples, pears, plums, cherries and filberts, and these, in many cases, with gooseberries and currants and raspberries beneath.'

The hillside backing the village of Yalding and spreading east to Linton and beyond towards Chart Sutton, could well be the country Cobbett was thinking about. Yet much of the hill slope rising from the right bank of the Medway between Yalding and Maidstone is similarly husbanded, for it is indeed a fertile valley with much 'diminutive beauty' on display. Yalding itself is worth a short diversion to visit. It's an attractive village with a fine main street and a lovely church, and from it footpaths lead on delightful journeys of exploration—through the valley of the River Beult, or along the ridge of fruit-cropped hills, or deep into the Weald.

In meadows beyond Twyford Bridge the Medway swings anti-clockwise and is joined by the River Beult coming from the southeast. A navigable canal cuts away to the north immediately before the bridge and flows beside the B2162 road for a short stretch of a few hundred yards. As there is no public right of way alongside the main sweep of the river for this section, it is necessary to cross the weir-side lock and follow the canal. It takes you beside a factory, then practically straight away rejoins the Medway proper and, now on the left bank, you wander northwards through a rough stretch of giant hogweed, scattered trees and bushes. It is, perhaps, the most untamed section of the walk, and it leads for almost 2 miles (3 kms) to Wateringbury. On the way the footpath passes below the musty, yet delightfully simple old church of Nettlestead. A short diversion to it by way of a weathered pathway along the boundary of medieval Nettlestead Place, is worth taking. The church of St Mary, an unpretentious cool place of whispers and solitude, had its stained glass damaged by a storm on 19th August 1763 when hailstones, said to be 10in (25cm) in diameter, smashed the windows and wrought havoc throughout the neighbourhood.

The riverside at Wateringbury is like a seaside resort in miniature, but it takes only a few moments to pass through, gaining once more the peace of an uncluttered countryside. More meadows then lead to Teston. Another weir, another lock, another splendid medieval stone bridge spanning the river with five arches and, on the far side, a

heavily overgrown wall of what appears to be a one-time mill. Beside the river here, at Teston Bridge Picnic Site, there is a small car park and public toilets. The village is but a short stroll away.

Between Teston and Maidstone the Medway passes through a bountiful region of orchards and hop gardens and beneath two more notable bridges; the first, below East Barming, is the only timber-built bridge on the river, the second being the connoisseur's bridge at East Farleigh. This, the third of the medieval bridges on the walk, is best of all. Some five hundred years old and measuring 100 yards (100m) long, it strides across the river by way of a number of ribbed arches. In 1648 Cromwell's men, under the command of Fairfax, marched across Farleigh Bridge before taking Maidstone in a battle that saw three hundred Royalists dead and another 1300 taken prisoner.

On the southern slope above the river, East Farleigh presents an attractive scene with its church, its oasts and black and white houses forming a neat group. That scourge of the slave traders, William Wilberforce, spent his old age here when his son occupied the seventeenth-century vicarage as incum-

Approaching Yalding a cluster of oasts appear on the left bank.

bent, and in the churchyard lies one of Kent's keenest advocates, Donald Maxwell, a man whose books conjure so well the atmosphere of many of the county's odd corners. He knew the Medway intimately, not only from living above it, but from explorations along its banks and through its waters by boat.

Between river and tree-hidden railway the Medway towpath then brings you to the best of Maidstone, county town of Kent. It delivers you out of countryside and onto a concrete walkway with a mellow collection of church, college and Archbishop's Palace rising almost from the water on the opposite bank. There's a mixture of historic association and twentieth-century development, a blasphemous torment of one-way streets choked with traffic—and hidden corners of charm to be discovered.

There are ducks up-tailing in the river yet, a few paces beyond, the full bustle of town. One steps from the sublime to the ridiculous.

WALK 4: *The Greensand Way*

From the ridge at the Devil's Punchbowl, a long view shows Leith Hill in the distance.

Distance: 75 miles (121km).
Time Required: 5–6 days.
Type of Walk: Basically an easy walk on well-defined paths and tracks. Waymarking is mostly good but a little obscure in places and the route cards should be studied with care. As there are many interesting National Trust properties along the way, it is tempting to stray from the route to visit some of them.
Start: Haslemere, Surrey.
Finish: Yalding Station, Kent.
Maps: O.S. Landranger series 186, 187, 188.
Guides: Two packs of route cards have been published: *The Greensand Way,* Surrey section published by Surrey Amenity Council, Jenner House, 2 Jenner Road, Guildford GU1 3PN. *The Greensand Way Long-Distance Footpath,* West Kent section published by The Ramblers Association (Kent Area), 11 Thirlmere Road, Barnehurst, Bexleyheath, DA17 6PU.

Beech Woods and Big Panoramas

The Greensand Ridge serves as an inner lining to the chalk wall of the North Downs. To my mind it's a finer ridge than that of the Downs, with broader views, uncluttered and crisply outlined with the Weald of Kent and Surrey holding the eye to the south; a patchwork of meadow, field and woodland, a tartan plain predominantly green.

Much of the Wealden plain is wood or farmland and it is the rich agricultural heritage of this wide vale that gives Kent its epithet of the Garden of England. There are small towns settled in it, of course, and numerous villages too. Yet from the ridge of hills that contain them, the vast majority remain undetected—until night falls, that is. Wander onto the crest after dark and you will be astonished at the glittering, twinkling

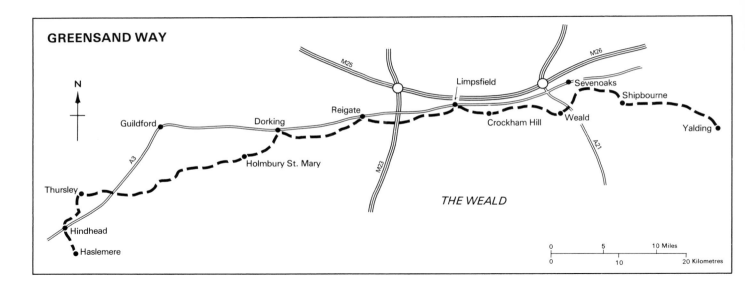

GREENSAND WAY

N

Guildford   Dorking   Reigate   Limpsfield   Sevenoaks   Shipbourne

Holmbury St. Mary   Crockham Hill   Weald   Yalding

Thursley

Hindhead

Haslemere

THE WEALD

M25   M26   M23   A3   A21

0   5   10 Miles

0   10   20 Kilometres

array of lights far below that reveal individual farms and clustered communities lost by day in a blanket of foliage.

It is this seemingly deserted landscape that gives the Greensand Way one of its most precious and memorable virtues.

The ridge, as its name suggests, is composed of greensand; a soft, golden-coloured stone that weathers to a tinge of mossy green. The Kentish ragstone that is quarried from this range of hills has been prized as a building material for centuries, and along the walk a good many cottages, as well as grand country houses and even churches, have used it in their construction.

This greensand is unlike the chalk of the neighbouring Downs. It has a different texture and encourages a brighter range of vegetation than does the downland chalk. Along the hills there are heaths, rampant with waist-high fronds of bracken, ablaze with rhododendrons in May and June while bilberries cluster in the shade of tree and shrub and offer their fruit to summer ramblers. There are stands of pine and extensive beech woods crowning the ridge. Silver birch grow in company with sweet chestnut, oak and hazel thickets, so there is colour throughout the year, whether or not there are leaves. On the southern edge of the escarpment projecting prows look out over immense panoramas that are generously displayed, with horseshoe-shaped coombes cutting back on either side. Underfoot in places the soil is distinctly sandy; there are no flints poking through, such as will be found on the Downs. There are springs bubbling from the turf covering, and cheery

streams flowing from them.

They're lovely hills; walkers' hills.

The Greensand Way has been developed in sections, and at the time of writing is not quite complete. [1] When it is finished the walk will traverse all of Surrey and most of Kent, starting at Haslemere in the south-western corner of Surrey near the boundaries of Hampshire and West Sussex, and cutting in a long arc round and across the Weald to link with the Saxon Shore Way near Hythe on the Kent coast. The walk described here travels some 75 miles (121km) from Haslemere to Yalding on the River Medway. Fifty-five miles (89km) in Surrey; twenty (32km) in Kent. The route, which is waymarked with small arrows bearing the letters GW, goes through, or near, Hindhead, Thursley, Shamley Green, Pitch Hill, Holmbury Hill, Leith Hill, Dorking, Reigate, Nutfield, Tandridge and Limpsfield. Continuing into Kent it crosses Crockham Hill, Toys Hill, Ide Hill, over meadows to Sevenoaks Weald and into Knole Park, then to Ightham Mote, Shipbourne, West and East Peckham and down to Yalding in the Medway plain.

It's a splendid walk dominated by big views. But there are plenty of individual places of interest along the way too; Nature Reserves, stately homes, deer parks. There are several Youth Hostels on or close to the route; at Hindhead, Holmbury St Mary, Tanners Hatch, Crockham Hill and Kemsing. Elsewhere country inns and private houses offer bed and breakfast at reasonable rates, while a range of hotels in small towns not far from the path have competing

facilities at widely varying prices.

For lengthy sections of the Greensand Way the escarpment is clothed with magnificent woodlands. Until the autumn of 1987 that woodland cover was even more extensive, beech woods that were part of the glory of the south.

Then, in the early hours of October 16th 1987, terrifying winds roared across the south-east of England and reshaped the landscape. Officially the force of those winds fell a little short of that required to make the storm a hurricane. But for those of us who lived through it, official designation is an irrelevance. The wind came sweeping across the low-lying acres of the Weald and smashed against the resisting wall of the Greensand Ridge with incredible force. Roofs were torn from village houses and whole woodlands were laid flat. At Toys Hill near Sevenoaks, 200 acres of beech wood were decimated. Knole Park received a battering; Seal Chart took on the appearance of a battleground. Elsewhere the story was much the same. Yet fortunately the reaping wind came in swathes, and whilst vast areas of glorious mature beech and oak and chestnut were felled and plucked from the ground, neighbouring spinneys and individual trees showed little or no sign of damage. Alas, the nature of this walk was inevitably altered, as was some of its routing.

But the story is not one of hopeless despair and already the greensand hills are showing signs of recovery. It cannot happen overnight, of course, for newly planted hardwoods take years to mature. But nature is getting to grips with the problem—as are landowners and councils—and year by year the landscape will bear fewer scars and gradually be restored to some of its former beauty. Meanwhile the Greensand Way remains a splendid walk. In places fresh views have been opened by the absence of tree cover. In others, the lush bowery of leaf and network of branch continue to sift the sunshine across the path in pillars of light. Wandering through, serenaded by birdsong, catching the fragrance of the warm earth or a thousand seasons of leafmould underfoot, with now and then a soft and distant view of Wealden meadows far below, the Greensand Way walker discovers one more aspect of the 'overcrowded south'.

[1]. The route was completed and officially opened by R.A. President, Fay Godwin, in the spring of 1989, and now measures some 105 miles.

Days 1–2: Haslemere to Holmbury St Mary

The old heart of Haslemere is lovely to look at, and it makes a fitting start to this long walk. Comfortable among the hills it's a prize for London-bound commuters but for all the housing pressure that must have come its way, development appears to have been contained within acceptable bounds and Haslemere retains a distinctly rural atmosphere; an old market town, with the Old Market House at its centre. In the mid-nineteenth century a number of well-known people came here, including Tennyson and George Eliot. Haslemere was home to Josiah Whymper, father of the first man to climb the Matterhorn, and its links with mountaineering also embrace the last years of John Tyndall, the Victorian scientist who studied glaciers and then became an enthusiastic and noted climber with a fine record of achievements in the Alps (he came very close to beating Whymper to the Matterhorn's summit). Tyndall built his home nearby among land that is now owned by the National Trust—one of whose founders, Sir Robert Hunter, also lived here for a while, as did Conan Doyle and George Bernard Shaw.

In the first hour of the walk you head up to Hindhead Common, more than a thousand acres of it in the care of the National Trust, and come onto the A3 by the Devil's Punchbowl Hotel at Hindhead. Hindhead and its huge views are known and loved far beyond Surrey's borders. Yet Cobbett denounced it as 'the most villainous spot God ever made'.

Skirting away from the road a little you edge the hillslope onto Surrey's second highest summit. At around 850 feet (259m), Gibbet Hill retains the gruesome memory of the murder of a sailor here in 1786, and of the three convicted felons who hung in chains from the gibbet for all to see. Dickens obviously knew the spot from his travels, for he worked the scene into *Nicholas Nickleby*:

They walked upon the rim of the Devil's Punch Bowl, and Smike listened with greedy

Ightham Mote, one of England's finest moated manor houses, is approached on the route of the Greensand Way.

interest as Nicholas read the inscription on the stone, which, reared upon that wild spot, tells of a foul and treacherous murder committed there by night. The grass on which they stood had been dyed with gore and the blood of the murdered man had run down drop by drop into the hollow which gives the place its name. 'The Devil's Punch Bowl', thought Nicholas, as he looked into the void, 'never had better liquor than that.'

The Greensand Way paces the rim of the Punch Bowl from where there are wonderful views; to the north-east Leith Hill can be seen quite 16 miles (26km) away across a corner of the Weald, all tree and bracken in shaded undulations. To the south low hills of Sussex show clearly, while you peer westward into the deep cut of the Punch Bowl itself onto a dense mattress of greenery that warbles with birdsong. The path runs clearly on a slope of heath, in and out of shade and down to a minor road, eventually coming into the churchyard at Thursley where the murdered sailor, remembered on Gibbet Hill, lies buried. On his tomb the inscription reads:

No dear relation, or still dearer friend,
Weeps my hard lot, or miserable end;
Yet o'er my sad remains, (my name unknown)
A generous Public have inscrib'd this Stone.

Most of the 'iron village' of Thursley, and there's not a lot of it, lies just to the north of the church, but our walk heads off to the east, crosses the A3 again and takes to green tracks and fields, crossing as it does one or two neat streams that flow northward out of the hills and on to collections of ponds and lakes. A footbridge takes you across the railway outside Witley Station, then on a sandy track up onto Hambledon Common where more lovely wide views have you gazing south over the Weald and into Sussex. This is one of those unknown corners of Surrey, a 'hinterland' visited only by those with business to be there. There are woods and little lanes, and open landscapes in which to catch the sun and smile. It's good to have the excuse to discover it.

Given time one could wander onto the summit of Hydon's Ball, half a mile off the route, and enjoy yet more wonderful views. The hill was given to the National Trust in 1915 in memory of one of its co-founders, Octavia Hill, who died three years earlier. This remarkable Victorian lady is remembered in many different places along the Greensand Ridge; particularly in Kent, where she lived for some of her last years (our path wanders close to her home on Crockham Hill Common) and she now lies at rest on the ridge's southern slopes.

East of Hydon's Ball you cross Holloways

Heath and enter the little village of Hascombe opposite its nineteenth-century church and the White Horse pub. The village is set among wooded hills, with Winkworth Arboretum along the lane to the north and Hascombe Hill rising to the south where Iron Age settlers smelted iron two thousand years and more ago. Now you break away heading north-eastwards, crossing first the A281 Guildford to Horsham road, then the dismantled railway line known today as the Greenway along which both the Downs Link and the Wey-South Paths go, then the former Wey and Arun Canal, and finally come to the edge of Shamley Green where, by a short diversion, you can find refreshment.

From Shamley Green the route is once more resumed along a more easterly course on a linking of lanes and footpaths that head among fields and woods. The scarp slope drops away from the route over Winterfold Heath and Reynard's Hill where extensive views south over the Weald hold your attention again. Easy tracks lead on to Pitch Hill (otherwise known as Coneyhurst Hill) at 843 feet (257m), passing along the way a windmill and another pub. Those Wealdon views never grow stale, no matter how often one wanders along the ridge. They reflect the seasons' changing tides, and hour by hour the angle of light creates new islands and green oases picked out as the sun beams among flotillas of cloud. It's a landscape known and trodden for thousands of years, yet every day is a fresh awakening and there's always something delightful to be discovered there.

Iron Age man was on Holmbury Hill as well as on Hascombe Hill. Up here, on this wonderful viewpoint that overlooks both North Downs and South Downs, an earthwork of about eight acres can still be made out. As the scarp edge cuts back to enclose an indented coombe, you could drop through the woods a short distance to find Holmbury St Mary Youth Hostel, an unimaginatively designed flat-roofed brick building, but in as secretive a setting as you could wish.

Days 3–4: Holmbury St Mary to Crockham Hill

The wooded ridge that runs between Pitch Hill and Leith Hill is often fondly called 'Little Switzerland,' and is one of Surrey's most popular walking areas. Much of it is common land. There's a lot in the care of the National Trust and footpaths explore every-

where; among pine trees and rhododendrons and waist high bracken. Leith Hill is best of all and is the crown of Surrey at 965 feet (294m). The nearest land to rival this height to south and west is 100 miles (160km) away in the Mendips. You walk up to it in less than an hour from Holmbury on a clear track and a bit of a lane, and then stand at the base of a 60-ft (18-m) tower that was raised more than two hundred years ago by Richard Hull, the eccentric squire of Leith Hill Place, who is said to be buried *upside down* beneath it.

From the topmost platform of the tower there's a vista of memorable proportions. The Channel may be seen through the Shoreham Gap in the South Downs, and in the opposite direction the Chilterns, 50 miles off, while the dome of St Paul's can be picked out far beyond the North Downs. It is recorded that in 1844 a group of surveyors managed to identify no less than 41 of London's church towers from this platform, while before them—and before even the tower was built—John Evelyn claimed in his diary that from Leith Hill 'may be discerned twelve or thirteen counties on a serene day'.

Soon after leaving Surrey's much-lauded summit the route breaks away to the north on a sandy track heading downhill, thereby losing for a while those extensive Wealden views and, having almost reached the bed of the Holmesdale Valley, with the wall of the North Downs rising on the far side, veers to the right and picks a way round the southern edge of Dorking. Now I like Dorking as a town, but not midway on a walk such as this. Give me the hills and the woods and long views of an empty countryside and I'm content. Happily the interruption of town is soon left behind as you head across farmland to Brockham Green, so-named for the great number of badgers that used to tunnel near the banks of the River Mole. Other memories tell of W.G. Grace who played cricket here on the green.

The way from Brockham leads across the Mole to nearby Betchworth, and beyond that to Reigate Heath with its lovely view of the Downs, and its curious windmill, owned by the local golf club but leased to the parish for occasional use as a church. From the outside it appears to be nothing more than a

This track was once an important pack horse route. Ahead can be seen the oasts of Ightham Mote Farm.

disused mill but inside there's a simple altar and seating for a handful of congregation. Apparently there was not only once a chapel on the site of the mill but also a gallows; which makes this windmill church seem even more incongruous.

Dorking's intrusion on the Greensand Way was a very low-key, innocent affair when compared to that of Reigate and Redhill, but even so the path's surveyors have done their work as discreetly as possible when faced with the southward urban spread of these twin towns, and despite the over-heavy printing of pink upon the map, countryside is soon restored again. Earlswood Common and its golf course act as a green lung. Then through the grounds of the Royal Earlswood Hospital and over fields to a lane which takes you past an eighteenth-century watermill and into South Nutfield on the northern side of the railway.

A track leads beneath the M23 London to Brighton motorway, through parkland and northward over Castle Hill. On the edge of Bletchingley there are few remains left of the great castle that changed hands many times during the reign of King John. But the village itself is one of the loveliest of all in the Holmesdale Valley, and deserves a brief visit. It has a wide main street, signifying that Bletchingley was once an important settlement, a fine Norman church and an attractive Tudor street leading to it. Anne of Cleves lived at Bletchingley Place, of which only an arch remains, and Catherine of Aragon met Cardinal Wolsey here. History has not always been kind to the village, but happily the present seems to be—especially since it has been relieved by the construction of the M25 of the monstrous traffic problems that used formerly to curse it.

The Greensand Way, however, remains a little south of Bletchingley and strikes off eastward to wooded Tilburstow Hill where you gaze across the Weald to the heights of Sussex far off. Tandridge is the next place to aim for. A small straggling community with a Norman church famed for its tower and for the ancient yew in its grounds, and with the nearby Court marking almost the top of the hill. It's virtually a one-street village, but the parish is all of 10 miles (16km) long and gives its name to a District Council that includes far more crowded places than this. Oxted and Limpsfield are two such, and they are next in line.

Footpaths take you up and onto the neat hills and over their brow with views north to the Downs, scarred ahead where the Oxted chalk pits have laid an open wound in their southern flanks. Through Broadham Green then and on to Limpsfield Common where stockbroker houses group themselves among splendid trees on the scarp edge. With the coming of the railway to nearby Oxted in the nineteenth century, the beauties of the Greensand Ridge were 'discovered' by the rich and influential who built their homes in a rash of late-Victorian development on some of the finest sites of all to be found between Limpsfield and the Surrey/Kent border. By the turn of the century many noted figures of the time would be seen on neighbourhood footpaths enjoying the huge vistas and fragrant woods as they visited their contemporaries, on business and for pleasure. They included H.G. Wells and Galsworthy, while it is said that Baden-Powell and 'Buffalo Bill' (William Cody) experimented on Limpsfield Common with kites capable of raising a man off the ground.

The Greensand Way veers from the scarp edge at Limpsfield Chart, exchanging Wealden panoramas for views across the Holmesdale Valley to the wall of the North Downs. There's a pub, the Carpenter's Arms, opposite the heather-trimmed green, and a golden burst of broom and gorse on the edge of the woods. A broad track leads through a dark plantation, followed by an enclosed footpath that whispers its way out of Surrey and into Kent between trim gardens, across a road that leads to Westerham, and onto Crockham Hill Common. There are shops, pubs and restaurants a mile or so down the northern slope in Westerham. Hotel accommodation is available there, too, while a downhill stroll to the south takes you into Crockham Hill village for a shop, a pub or a bed for the night in the Youth Hostel.

Days 5–6: Crockham Hill to Yalding

Some of the finest Wealden views of the whole route are experienced along this section, and during the first part of it a brief diversion from the main path will give an impressive canvas of depth and colour. At all times of the year it is a magnificent landscape; in places given scale by the appearance of an oast house or old tile-hung farm, the land sweeping away in a bounty of green, the hills crowned by a tiara of beech or oak or chestnut, the far horizon bathed in the blue undulations of Ashdown Forest, the Weald itself blotched with patterns of meadowland and spinney, speckled white with sheep where once hops clambered on forests of twine. In winter stark outlines of branch and twig on outpost hills make a web against the sky. In spring and early summer bluebells wash against the shadowed slopes like woodsmoke drifting; in summer the long broad vistas are patched with ripening wheatfields; in autumn the Weald often lies anonymous beneath a vast sea of mist, with just the tops of trees rising from it like an archipelago of land-locked islands. It is a landscape of which I never tire.

Within half a mile of joining Kent you come to a triangle of tracks with a framed view looking south-west. There are two or three houses on the slope gazing south, the first of which was built for Harriott Yorke and Octavia Hill shortly before the National Trust came into being. When Miss Hill died in 1912 she left a request that she be buried in the village churchyard below, planted on the sunny slopes of the ridge she had come to know and love so well.

The Way continues among trees and the storm-battered remnants of trees that fell in the 1987 hurricane, and across a clearing with shoulder-high bracken where a vast panorama opens to the right. Sadly, and unaccountably, the route misses what would have been one of the loveliest stretches (the crossing of Mariners Hill) by breaking 'inland' a little and heading straight for the north side of Churchill's Chartwell. The route it takes is pleasant enough, but it could have been spectacular. A study of the map will show the slight diversion necessary above Froghole to explore the prow of Mariners Hill, the last piece of land Octavia Hill saved for the National Trust, having received a cheque ensuring its future only the day before she died.

So much of the route from Crockham Hill to the Medway plain passes through or by National Trust property. After Mariners Hill the eastern portion of Crockham Hill Common leads the Greensand Way beside Chartwell, home for more than forty years of Sir Winston Churchill, and since his death one of the Trust's busiest houses. The western side of the house is, quite frankly, ugly. Yet its south and east faces are full of character, while the view from it through a shallow coombe to the glory of the Weald, is as lovely a view as any house might hope to capture for its own.

The path climbs up to a transverse ridge and comes to the lost hamlet of French Street, with one or two cottages straight out of Rip Van Winkle. A fine narrow valley sloping towards the Holmsedale Valley cuts

a swathe between French Street and Toys Hill, and the walk through the devastated woods of Toys Hill—once one of my favourite lowland walks anywhere—is now a sad reminder of the temporary nature even of the landscapes of southern England. Nothing is forever; and nature is in a perpetual state of evolution.

After Toys Hill you drop into a deep coombe, cross a stream and climb to Ide Hill, an over-popular village on a bright summer's day when the green is crammed with picnic parties and the narrow lanes are a-snarl of traffic. The walker has the best motive of all for dodging back to the footpaths that rim the scarp edge. A mile or so out of Ide Hill a waymark indicates the point where it becomes necessary to leave the ridge and descend over meadows as though attempting to climb into the Wealden canvas that has become so familiar with the miles.

The elegant nineteenth-century Wickhurst Manor, set among neat lawns, is passed on the way to the village of Sevenoaks Weald where W.H. Davies wrote his *Autobiography of a Super Tramp* in a cottage found for him by that restless poet, Edward Thomas, who also lived here for a while. The village is a suntrap, and with those vast panoramas and so much fine accessible countryside around it, offers a good number of rewarding day walks. The Greensand Way, however, barely touches the village itself, but rather passes a little above it, near the parish church, then across fields to duck beneath the Sevenoaks by-pass and up onto the ridge once more to make a crossing of Knole Park.

This is one of the greatest deer parks in all England, with one of the nation's finest houses set within it. The park occupies 1000 acres; the house has 365 rooms and a staircase for every week of the year. Knole was begun in 1456 by Thomas Bourchier, Archbishop of Canterbury, but Henry VIII took it over a century later and Elizabeth I gave it to the first Earl of Dorset, Thomas Sackville. It has remained in Sackville hands ever since, but the National Trust assumed responsibility for the running of the house in 1946 and throughout the summer it is a major attraction for visitors. But whilst Knole itself is open to the public only at set times, the park has permanent rights of way through it and the herds of fallow deer have grown, if not overly tame, at least a mite indifferent to walkers passing by.

The path taken by the Greensand Way remains well to the south of the house and soon makes an exit through the high deer-proof fencing that surrounds the park, crosses a minor road and heads through woods again, then out to yet more fine views over the Weald. Beyond One Tree Hill a track that was once a major pack-horse route leads below the scarp edge and along the hillslope, sometimes among trees but often with broad uninterrupted views. You come to a little eyeless cottage owned by the National Trust, but empty now, that used to be an ale house. There's a splendid footpath route from here across fields to Shipbourne, whose church can just be seen between some trees off to the south-east. However, our route continues ahead along the track and reaches Shipbourne later, after first having the opportunity to visit Ightham Mote, a magnificent medieval moated manor house—again National Trust owned.

The waymarked route veers southward near the entrance to Ightham Mote but as in Knole Park, a public right of way goes right past the house itself, alongside the moat with its ducks and geese and swans, and a second footpath breaks away soon after, to allow you to rejoin the proper route once more in Shipbourne churchyard.

Now you're down in the Weald, with the Greensand Ridge sweeping in a long and attractive line across the low northern meadows. Then, to the east of Plaxtol, that line of hills pushes south, wooded on the summit of Gover Hill, but with orchards and hop gardens on the slopes. The walk is clearly drawing closer to the Garden of England.

Over fields and streams, by the side of farms and small contained orchards of Kentish cobs (hazel nuts) you come to the hamlet of Dunk's Green with its pub, the Kentish Rifleman, on a junction of lanes. The stream that flows through the little valley below is the River Bourne; an insignificant-looking stream but one that was used in the past to power mills in the paper-making industry. One of these, Roughway Mill, can be seen just to the left of the lane as you wander down it. A few paces beyond the bridge you bear right and follow another path skirting the hills.

The footpath takes you above a large house called Oxen Hoath, in whose grounds (unseen from our route) is a landscaped lake with a bridge crossing it in a most pleasing situation. But although the Greensand Way misses this, it has plenty of other features to enjoy as it joins the route of the Wealdway among more orchards into West Peckham. Little more than an hour's walking remains, for it is not quite 4 miles (6km) from West Peckham to Yalding. The Wealdway and the Greensand Way part company east of the village green and you take an alternative field path that evokes the age of iron-making

in the Weald, as you pass a one-time furnace pond and come to Forge Farm on the A26 Tonbridge–Maidstone road. A minor road leads across this and passes the former church of East Peckham, deserted since the village it served moved 2 miles and more away, down by the Medway.

The Medway is to the south and to the east, making its sinuous route round the base of the hills. And as you leave Nettlestead Green and cut over the last few fields of the walk, the river adds a fresh sparkle and you follow it to Yalding Station, where for now the Greensand Way makes only a temporary halt.

Coming down towards Sevenoaks Weald, spring lambs block the pathway.

WALK 5: *The Vanguard Way*

South of Dry Hill the path winds past a farm pond with expansive views ahead of Sussex hills and meadows.

Distance: 62 miles (100km).
Time Required: 4-5 days (recommended, but could be achieved in less).
Type of Walk: A medium-grade lowland walk that enjoys a variety of landscapes in its journey across the grain of three counties. As with the Wealdway it crosses the North and South Downs, Greensand Ridge, the low Weald, High Weald ridges and Ashdown Forest.
Start: London Borough of Croydon.
Finish: Seaford Head, East Sussex.
Maps: O.S. Landranger series 177, 187, 188, 199.
Guidebooks: *The Wealdway and the Vanguard Way* by Kev Reynolds (Cicerone Press). *The Vanguard Way* written and published by the Vanguards Rambling Club.

From London's Suburbs to the Channel Coast

During the mid-Sixties a group of keen ramblers from South London would often escape the bustle of the city to wander footpaths in various distant locations, returning by rail on a Sunday evening uplifted by their weekend adventures. One Sunday their train back from Devon was so busy that they had to occupy the Guard's Van—an experience made marginally more comfortable by the help of a bottle of Drambuie. Out of that experience the group decided to gather themselves into an informal rambling club: the Vanguards.

Several members of this club were also active in both the Youth Hostels Association and the Ramblers' Association and over the years they became involved in footpath clearance, in marathon walks, orienteering and walking rallies. In 1980, to celebrate the fifteenth anniversary of the founding of the Vanguards Rambling Club—which also coincided with the Golden Jubilee of YHA and the Ramblers' Association's own *Footpath Heritage '80*—they devised a long-distance walking route of their own; 'from the suburbs to the sea'.

Thus was the Vanguard Way born. It was a fitting manner by which to mark any one of these celebrations and a worthy tribute to the dedication of a relatively small but enthusiastic band of walkers.

The Vanguard Way travels 62 miles (100km) from East Croydon to Seaford Head; from the frenzy of commuter-land to the trim green baize of the Downs; from soul-less tower blocks to the salt-laden breeze off the sea; from a concrete wilderness to the welcome sight of the Seven Sisters rolling away beyond Cuckmere Haven. The contrasts are bewildering to conceive but delightful to experience.

As with the neighbouring Wealdway, this route soon escapes the tedium of London's ever-encroaching tentacles to wander across the broad shoulders of the North Downs—open, elevated and breezy. Then it's the turn of the Greensand Ridge on the very borders of Surrey and Kent, with huge views overlooking the Weald from high, tree-clad hills. Down then into the low valley of pastures and woodland shaws, heading south towards the first of the High Weald ridges where Iron Age Man made a camp around 500 BC. There are orchards clothing these hills, a riot of blossom and bees in spring, but south again, the Vanguard Way heads into an undulating countryside of woods and rhododendron banks leading to Ashdown Forest. This, of course, is Sussex.

Being quite unlike anything else along the route this Forest heath, broken here and there by gorse bushes, stands of pine and birch thickets, marks a convenient half-way point. Behind, in the far distance, runs the blue line of the North Downs hiding London's sprawl. Ahead, beckoning from afar, the South Downs block the sea. It's a surprisingly vast panorama that one gains from the elevations of Ashdown Forest and beyond it the route southward to the Downs takes you through another rolling land of great charm as far as Blackboys, a village which also shares the Wealdway.

For a while beyond Blackboys the Weald-way and Vanguard Way run parallel with each other but several fields apart so that one experiences different scenes, different visions of the Sussex landscape. The Downs draw the walker on. Suddenly low fields are exchanged for rising hills and the Downs roll

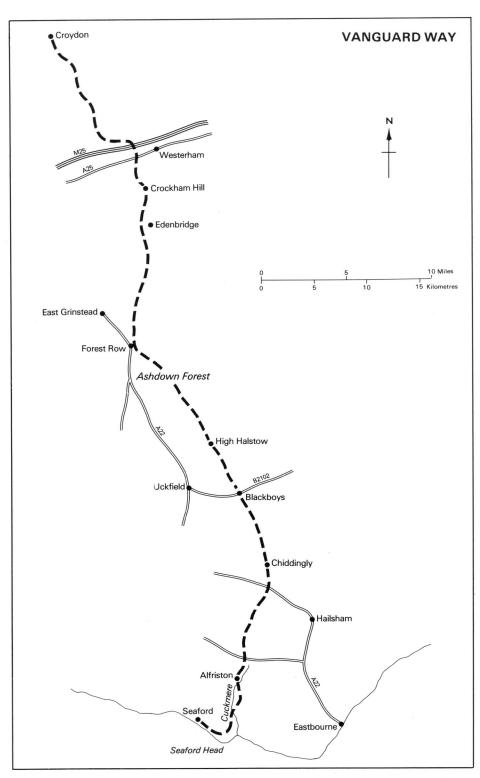

VANGUARD WAY

out their welcome; old, old hills they are, bowed down with the weight of centuries, with round shoulders along which footpaths and ancient trackways lead in the sun. In their shadow lies Alfriston, that much-loved village on the banks of the Cuckmere. From it there goes the final easy stage along green hills overlooking the river's lazy windings, through Friston Forest and down to the riverside for a short stroll south towards Cuckmere Haven. Off to the left rise the cliffs of the Seven Sisters. To the right slopes Seaford Head—journey's end with the sea beyond.

The Vanguard Way consists of footpaths, historic tracks and a few stretches of country lane. Unlike 'officially approved' long-distance walking routes there is no waymark symbol to guide you. However, the latest Ordnance Survey Landranger maps are being printed to show the line of the route, and all but a few short footpath sections deep in Sussex are clearly defined.

But most walkers will discover that a detailed guidebook to the Vanguard Way is indispensible for following the precise route. It will require about four or five days to complete with comfort, so it is well-suited for a bank holiday period, or even to be nibbled at over two or three weekends.

There are three Youth Hostels along the route, and several hotels, guest houses and private bed and breakfast establishments offering accommodation.

Day 1: East Croydon to Crockham Hill

The Greater London Borough of Croydon long ago lost any semblance of the flowering vale from which it derived its name in Saxon times. (It was first recorded in AD 809 as *Crogedene*, which means 'saffron valley'.) Today its multi-storey office blocks of concrete, glass and steel dazzle the sun on a maze of bland shopping precincts where pop music roars and crowds jostle for the latest bargain. On flyovers and under-passes the traffic races in a constant frenzy of free-for-all madness, while those drivers misguided enough to attempt to steer a route through the town, soon find themselves wedged between red London buses in a nose-to-tail procession.

The long-distance walker is fortunate indeed to be heading for the sea!

The Vanguard Way begins its journey towards the rich variety and hospitality of the southern countryside outside commuter-busy East Croydon railway station. Within a

surprisingly short space of time the crowded pavements and tower blocks are left behind, and in their place generous green parks ablaze with rhododendrons and azaleas in early summer. Coombe Woods, alive with birds and squirrels, stand on the edge of the one-time hamlet of Broadcombe, and as you wander alongside it you catch one of the last views of the Croydon tower blocks beyond a screen of trees.

A few residential streets lie between Coombe Woods and Littleheath Woods, but once you are following the footpath through the latter there is a belief that real country is here at last. In spring Littleheath Woods are bright with bluebells. There are badger setts and foxes earths, a symphony of birdsong, rabbits breaking away in a panic. Then you come to another estate of houses and busy Selsdon Park Road, yet this is really the last outpost, the final pronouncement of suburbia, for once the fenced area of Selsdon Woods Nature Reserve is entered you can relax with the certain knowledge that between this point and the South Coast footpaths will lead into the very heart of the countryside, visiting only a clutch of small towns, villages and hamlets along the way.

The 200 acres of Selsdon Woods were acquired by the National Trust in 1935. The path climbs through among wood anemones, primroses and bluebells in their season, and then, leaving the fenced area and following another path, comes to yet more woods. A sunken track, overhung by trees and bushes and sometimes muddied by horses, takes the Vanguard Way from this last woodland to open fields, past a farm and on to the little hamlet of Farleigh, whose church dates from 1083. Standing here in the morning peace it is difficult to believe that London's boundary is but a few paces away, for the collection of farms, cottages and the Norman church belong to a rural landscape as much today as they have done since Farleigh (or Fearnlege as it was named in AD 880) originated in Saxon times. Yet the Greater London boundary creeps towards its field limits with an unnerving stealth.

To the south the path leads briefly to Chelsham Common and soon beyond this a short woodland section is exchanged for the broad open expanse of the North Downs—not a downland of sheep-cropped grass as you might imagine it to be but a high and wide acreage of farmland, hungry beneath huge skies where cloudscapes are often as interesting as those of the land itself. Gazing

north for a moment you bid farewell to London's immense sprawl, seen grey and forbidding in a distant hollow. Down then into a coombe on the edge of Woldingham before climbing once more on a bridle path towards a wooded hill from whose upper rim a lovely rolling parkland folds off to the west. Minutes later you come to the very lip of the Downs. A green slope drops away to a valley carved by London's orbital motorway, the M25. That is a crude intrusion on an otherwise delightful sweep of the North Downs drawn in an arc towards the west, with jutting spurs green with beeches, and far off a faint wash of blue as the Downs confuse with the sky. Across this valley, in which Oxted and Limpsfield are seen one beside the other, rise the wood-darkened hills of the Lower Greensand, and beyond them the hint—no more than that—of the Weald.

For a short distance the Vanguard Way follows the route of the North Downs Way, heading east along the base of the chalk slope and passing through Titsey Park in which a Roman villa was excavated in 1879. Nearby runs the course of the old Roman road from London to Lewes, a section of which is exposed on Ashdown Forest.

Crossing the motorway there follows a relief of woodlands on the northern slope of the Greensand Ridge, then through Limpsfield Chart and onto a rough track with a few fine houses alongside it and you find yourself on the southern side of this narrow ridge. The Weald is shown then in all its glory—seen at its best across a garden wall. There are hurricane-ravaged beech woods on the left, with several cottages strung along their lower edge. In a house at the head of a nearby slope lived Edward and Constance Garnett who, at the turn of the century, held literary court there. Through these woods and across this hill came Conrad, Wells and Galsworthy, D H Lawrence and W H Hudson, Edward Thomas, Belloc, 'Supertramp' W H Davies and a great many more.

The rough track leads down to Trevereux Manor, in whose pond Hudson discovered natterjack toads. Then, with big views over a lush countryside cut away to the east, you cross a stile out of Surrey and into Kent, and come to Crockham Hill.

Days 2–3: Crockham Hill to Blackboys

For YHA members Crockham Hill makes a convenient overnight base in the Victorian

Before the Vanguard Way escapes the clutches of Croydon, it sneaks into the colourful extravagance of Coombe Woods Centre.

country house-turned-hostel overlooking the Weald, but for non-members, nearby Westerham or Edenbridge have hotels and private bed and breakfast houses. Although only a small village, Crockham Hill boasts glorious views from its sunny terrace and an interesting past which goes back to Iron Age times, while more recently it has had its fair share of writers and statesmen, revolutionaries and women of vision. Octavia Hill, the great housing reformer and one of the founders of the National Trust, came to live on Crockham Hill and is buried in the churchyard there. One of her final acts was to secure nearby Mariners Hill for the Trust, and just below this hill stands Chartwell, another National Trust property and home for forty years of Sir Winston Churchill, and passed on the route of the Greensand Way.

South of the village a series of footpaths go along rabbit-happy woodland edges and across open meadows with the High Weald ridge making a prominent peak directly ahead at Dry Hill. It is thought probable that one of the earliest of all Wealden trackways led between Crockham Hill and Dry Hill, for there were Iron Age en-

campments on each of these high points. Certainly the London-Lewes Roman road already mentioned came this way, although after passing through Crockham Hill and the site of today's Edenbridge it would have gone to the east of Dry Hill. The Vanguard Way however, veers to the west of Edenbridge to cross one of the Medway's main tributaries on which stands the white weatherboarded Haxted Watermill, dating from 1680, and soon after goes alongside the site of a one-time Norman stronghold, Starborough Castle.

A bridle path then leads pleasantly between hedgerows, gradually gaining height now with views growing in the north where the Greensand Ridge and North Downs limit the horizon. The track ducks into a wood, exchanging far views for birdsong and shade-loving plants, then enters an orchard. The path wanders up among the apple trees, bees working frantically in the blossom during late spring, the trees heavy with fruit later in summer, a great open vista of low valley and distant hill, of tree and meadow and the silent wash of cloud shadows dashing over corn fields

below, suddenly revealing itself and making this a highlight of the walk. On the crown of Dry Hill stands a marker indicating this as the 24-acre site of an Iron Age encampment of about 500 BC. A lovely place to be when the sun is shining, back against a tree with a jigsaw of Kent and Surrey spread out to the north with all the morning's walk—and half of yesterday's too—thrown open to the sky. Then southward, with more orchards, more green acres of wood and meadow, a farm and a pond—and another county; Sussex.

There are one or two fine cottages, tile-hung and head-down in trim gardens bright with rose and honeysuckle; a short stretch of lane, then more footpaths delving into a secret land of spinney, pasture and parkland; an imposing house lording it over a broad view; then more cottages and into a long, slender wood with a view between the trees to Weir Wood Reservoir trapped in a bowl of far-off hills. In this wood⸴there are bluebells and orchids. Go in spring to catch the fragrance of a world fresh and eager to greet summer round the corner, to study leaves newly unfurled and silken, with the welcome call of the cuckoo or the staccato drilling of a woodpecker for company.

Before you know it you'll be in Forest Row.

In the past Forest Row was an important staging post for the changing of horses drawing coaches on the London to Eastbourne road. Today it is motor coaches and cars that busy this road, while Forest Row itself manages to retain an air of untroubled calm. On my journey along the Vanguard Way I was looking for a café in the village when a local, studying my rucksack, asked where I was going. 'Seaford Head,' I told him.

'Do you find hitch-hiking easy?'

'I wouldn't know. I'm walking.'

'Walking? Where to—the next bus stop?'

'No. To Seaford Head.'

'Seaford Head? My God,' he said, 'there's a madness about!'

Ashdown Forest hugs the village boundaries. It takes only a few short minutes to wander up a side street and onto the Forest, which at this point is used as a golf course. The route crosses the golf course, dodging one fairway after another, over little streams, in and out of birch groves, the bracken and heather-covered acres stretching far off. Winding uphill a narrow road is met on the outskirts of Coleman's Hatch, and beyond it a further stretch of wood-clad heath and a track which leads to the meagre hamlet of Newbridge with its lane fording a stream that eventually flows as another minor tributary of the Medway.

Our route adopts the course of one of many rides over the Forest. It climbs uphill on a long pull to gain a lofty viewpoint a little west of a stand of pines known as Gills Lap Clump. One of the finest of all the panoramas of Ashdown Forest is to be had from here and following the last uphill section it is tempting to throw off the rucksack and sprawl in the heather for a few minutes of relaxation. Nearby, beside the B2026 which traverses the Forest from north to south, there is often an ice cream van well supported by day visitors to this lovely spot, and refreshment here is hard for a walker to resist.

Continuing over the summit of Ashdown

Forest the route takes in King's Standing Clump which, according to tradition, is where Edward II hid whilst hunting deer. A broad spur projects south-eastwards from this and the path wanders along its crest for about half a mile, enjoying lovely views as it does so—especially off to the hint of the

Off the North Downs escarpment the path leads along a tunnel of trees at Titsey.

South Downs in the distance. The spur runs out, the path contours the slope, then descends to a stream and a black ooze of bog where the Medway is born, before heading up the opposite slope and leaving the Forest near the Crow and Gate pub on the edge of Poundgate.

Field paths, warm with soft country all around, lead to a woodland and the woodland leads in turn to houses beside a farm. The path wanders boldly through a garden, between holly bushes, right beside a house and onto a track.

There follows one of the loveliest sections of the whole walk; a green rolling meadowland, ringed with trees, with shadows held tight in narrow vales and with intimate ledges of hillside exploited by bluebells in May. There are long views and secret scenarios that can only be known to the walker of footpaths. A finger post directs the way to High Hurstwood, a huddle of toy houses and a church across the meadows with a deep-cut stream in between.

Kissing gates link several footpaths out of High Hurstwood and after a bewilderment of lanes, tracks and field paths you find yourself at Pound Green to the east of Buxted. A couple of miles to the south-east lies Blackboys, reached by a choice of routes, depending whether the walker wishes to stay overnight at the simple Youth Hostel there. (This hostel consists of a set of timber hutments originally built to house refugees from the Spanish Civil War, and stands on the edge of pleasant woods a little north of the village.)

Days 4–5: Blackboys to Seaford Head

It's 15 miles (24km) from Blackboys to Alfriston, and on the way there is a distinct air of expectation as the Downs grow out of the horizon to lure you on. Towards Berwick some of the footpaths may be a little obscure but by consultation with the map and guidebook no great difficulty should be experienced.

The day begins easily enough with a stuttering of meadows, hedge-lined footpaths and country roads working a zig-zag route east of the Wealdway's line towards the village of Chiddingly. Once again the Vanguard Way takes you through the otherwise private garden of an isolated house where the owners have actually made a feature of the footpath by covering it with an archway of roses. It leads into a strip of woodland, then out of this to follow more

hedgerows with a long view of the South Downs several hours' walking away. Soon Chiddingly's elegant stone spire calls across the meadows—as it has called a scattered congregation for seven hundred years. A few paces from the church stands the local Post Office Stores, and beyond that the Six Bells pub. A little off route is the curious brick-built Place Farm, formerly known as Chiddingly Place, which incorporates part of a Tudor mansion owned by Sir John Jefferay, Chief Baron of the Exchequer for Elizabeth I. The church contains a fanciful, though partly disfigured, monument to the Jefferay family.

When the Wealdway crossed through Chiddingly it went roughly in an easterly direction before cutting south again. The Vanguard Way, however, heads south-westwards across an open landscape speckled with sheep, then through the briefest of woodland snatches outside Golden Cross. The Downs crouch like sheepdogs ahead; you branch off to the south now through more sheep lands, pass beside handsome Limekiln Farm with its duck-reflecting moat, its cowl-less oast and its flowering trees, and into a low, wind-scoured countryside that formed a substantial agricultural estate for the Romans more than 1600 years ago.

A long, die-straight lane becomes a long, die-straight track which turns boggy and water-logged after heavy rain. Happily the

worst of it consumes only a relatively short stretch and within a few more paces you escape a little south-east of the hamlet of Chalvington. More fields, rising now to Mays Farm which crowns a slope of green and gazes over a considerable acreage of farmland to the gap breached in the South Downs by the Cuckmere. Unseen from here Alfriston lies tucked in that gap and on the far side, Wilmington.

Across more fields you come to another house with a sparkling pond, and the path strays through this garden too. Down then to Berwick Station which lies a few minutes' walk away from Arlington Reservoir. A couple of miles of open country lie between the station and the tiny hillside village of Berwick but having reached the twelfth-century church of St Michael and All Angels on its nob of hill with fine chestnuts in a grove nearby, you find yourself caught suddenly on the fringe of the Downs. Their curves and smooth slopes are moulding all around and the path to Alfriston follows a veritable switchback course over successive hills before coming onto the narrow lane which swings down into this much-sung village, busy with the crowds of day trippers.

The popularity of Alfriston is easy to understand; it has history and an elegant charm; it has the Cuckmere and the Downs, flint-walled houses and ageing timbers. Alfred the Great is said to have hidden nearby from the Danes and the name of the village is thought to have its origins in one of Alfred's warriors. (In 1086 it was first mentioned as *Alvricestone*, meaning Aelfric's Farm.)

Overlooking the Cuckmere River St Andrew's church, with its shingled broach spire and flint walls, dates from the fourteenth-century. Nearby, and dating from the same period, is the small timber-framed Clergy House with its thatched roof. In 1896 the National Trust bought this for £10—its first acquisition. Elsewhere in the village there's the George Inn, a one-time smugglers' haunt built in 1397, and several

fifteenth-century buildings which include the Star Inn with its heraldic figures and a carved lion said to have been the figurehead of a Dutch ship which foundered in Cuckmere Haven.

The Cuckmere itself winds sleepily below the village and through the gentle green valley for the last few miles of its journey from the High Weald to the sea. The Vanguard Way follows along its left bank as far as Litlington, then scrambles up onto the Downs, sharing for a mile and a half the route of the South Downs Way. At first our path greets the sky; there are big views and a hint of the sea. Then you drop into a cleft by Charleston Manor, an historic building with a huge double tithe barn boasting 177 feet of tiled roof, skirt a hedgerow, then climb a series of steps into Friston Forest. This extensive woodland is something of an anomoly on the usually-bare South Downs and covers an area of almost 2000 acres. The land was bought as a catchment area for the Eastbourne Waterworks Company, who in

turn lease it to the Forestry Commission. Through it there are several woodland paths and rides, including the South Downs Way, Forest Walk and Exceat Woodland Walk.

The Path descends again, this time to the tiny village of West Dean. Alfred the Great supposedly built a palace here in AD 850, although if he did there's no sign of one today. What are seen, though, as you walk through on the route of the Vanguard Way, are a few attractive old houses, a duck pond and the dark mass of Friston Forest rising ahead. To regain the Forest entails climbing more than 200 wood-strengthened steps.

A short woodland path is followed, then out of the shadows to big skies, across a stone stile with the slope of the Downs falling away towards Exceat, and the classic ox bows of the Cuckmere snaking through water-meadows below. Out to the south the Downs fold into Cuckmere Haven—and there sparkles the sea. It seems a long way from East Croydon's tower blocks.

Down to Exceat; along the road to cross

Left: **Haxted Mill, now a watermill museum on the outskirts of Edenbridge.**

Below: **Berwick, near Alfriston, on the edge of the South Downs.**

the river, then southward on the right bank among bushes and low stumpy thorn trees, waders crying on the mudflats, gulls circling overhead, the smell of the sea, the taste of salt on your face, a squint of sun on low pleated waves. At the chalk-walled Haven you veer right beside coastguards' cottages and amble up the cropped grass path through Seaford Head Nature Reserve to the clifftop perch that marks the climax of the Vanguard Way; a walk that has led from suburbs to sea.

Left: **Ashdown Forest forms a high ridge with extensive views. Gills Lap Clump overlooks a northern vista.**

Below: **Between Alfriston and Cuckmere Haven, the Cuckmere river curls itself with numerous ox bows. The path leads alongside it through a Nature Reserve.**

WALK 6: *The South Downs Way*

On the first day's walk over the Seven Sisters, you hug the cliff edge and peer onto Beachy Head lighthouse.

Distance: 102 miles (164km).

Time Required: 6–7 days.

Type of Walk: An easy downland walk with few steep ascents or descents. Waymarking is exemplary, as are stiles and gates found all along the route. The walk uses a mixture of paths, tracks and country lanes. Several Youth Hostels are ideally positioned along the route to ease accommodation problems. There are few camping possibilities but plenty of b&b establishments.

Start: Eastbourne, East Sussex.

Finish: Winchester Cathedral, Hampshire.

Maps: O.S. Landranger series 199, 198, 197, 185.

Guidebooks: *The South Downs Way & The Downs Link* by Kev Reynolds (Cicerone Press). *A Guide to the South Downs Way* by Miles Jebb (Constable). *Along the South Downs Way to Winchester* written and published by the Society of Sussex Downsmen.

102 Miles (164km) from Eastbourne to Winchester

There is something rather comforting and friendly about the South Downs. They're rolling hills yet soft hills, green and gentle hills with dry scoops at their heart, but sliced by the waves of a restless sea where they face out to France. Seen from the north they swell one after another in a lengthy wall behind which lies the Channel. Sheep crop slopes on which ancient man first worked at a primitive form of agriculture and along their crests the smooth texture of turf-thatched chalk is roughened here and there with prehistoric burial mounds, pitted from long-forgotten flint mines or palisaded and ditched against an enemy dead these past two thousand years.

Exploring the Downs one is constantly

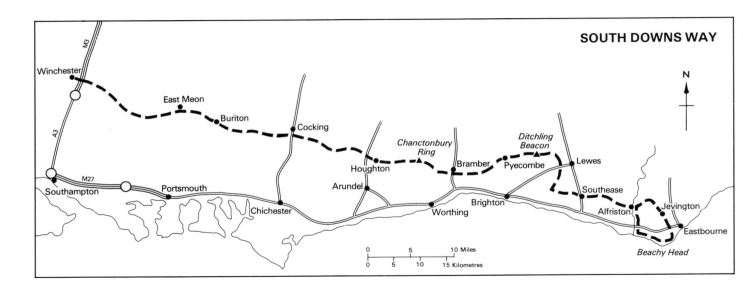

SOUTH DOWNS WAY

reminded of the past, while the present becomes a glory of larksong and huge panoramas. Rabbits and hares share the morning pathway. Cowslips in spring cast a pale yellow shadow on meadowlands that should be green and orchids bathe the day with their extravagant spikes of purple. Wandering the South Downs Way gives a rich kaleidoscope of experience and breeds a fresh respect for the first settlers of this waterless land. It *is* waterless too, for chalk being a soft and permeable rock, rainfall is quickly absorbed, so the few streams that are met along the way are all found deep in the valleys and practically the only surface water of note on the Downs themselves will be discovered in the many dewponds, or artificial puddles, expressly created for the purpose of trapping moisture. (It is with this dry state in mind that the Society of Sussex Downsmen, in conjunction with the Countryside Commission and local authorities, have provided drinking water taps in strategic places along the route for thirsty walkers and riders.)

While early man settled on the backs of the Downs and used their crests as a natural highway, from Roman times onward the hills were mostly left to large flocks of sheep and villages were built at the foot of the scarp slope where springs and streams gave a regular supply of water. Then, instead of maintaining tracks along the crest, new highways were built below, in the valleys and along the bed of the Weald, and only those routes that actually crossed the Downs were used with any regularity by traders; just shepherds and farm labourers having

cause to keep the old east-west trackways open.

Two hundred years ago there were around 200,000 sheep grazing the eastern portion of the South Downs, but now prairie-like fields of corn wave in the summer breeze and ewes and their lambs are contained in fenced areas of pasture where once they roamed on open land under the watch of a shepherd and his dog. The very nature of the Downs is changing, ever evolving. But whilst one imagines lawn-like slopes of grass being the original clothing of this land, that is a misconception, for experiments show that without grazing or ploughing the Downs soon revert to woodland. It was man, then, who first cleared the tree cover of the South Downs for agriculture. Then he turned the Downs from arable to pasture, while it is modern farming practices that are responsible for returning that pasture back to grain once more.

Yet this matters little to the South Downs Way walker. The mixture of arable, meadow and woodland produces a rich variety of landscapes through which to wander, and the ribbons of chalk path, flint track and narrow lane underfoot maintains that variety and allows an easy passage over the succeeding miles.

Those miles amount to about 102, now that the official route has been extended to Winchester. Originally the Countryside Commission approved an 80 mile (129km) Way from Eastbourne to Buriton on the Sussex/Hampshire border, but this admittedly-pleasing village was seen as an

unsatisfactory conclusion to a long walk and the historic cathedral city of Winchester was deemed a far happier destination for any pilgrim with the sun on his brow and the breeze in his hair. So Winchester it now is. One hundred and two miles (164km) of pleasure; from the sea to the city.

Day 1: Eastbourne to Alfriston—Seven Sisters Route

The South Downs Way was the first officially approved long-distance path to be designated a bridleway as well as a walking route, but since it was not possible to create a bridleway across Beachy Head and the Seven Sisters, the first stage has an inland alternative. It is difficult to know which is the better since both inland and clifftop routes have many scenic splendours and those with sufficient time at their disposal are urged not to discriminate but to walk both in due course. One has the sea and a helter-skelter of clifftop baize, the other plunges you into an embrace of downland green with far views, a flint-walled hamlet and a treasury of the past in hilltop barrow and sweeping slope of pasture.

The Seven Sisters route draws the rambler out of the discreet seaside town of Eastbourne and onto the lofty, crumbling clifftop of Beachy Head where you peer down onto the lighthouse more than 500 feet (152m) below. From here to Cuckmere Haven evidence of the chalk structure of the Downs is dramatically and clearly displayed, for it appears as though a huge knife has sliced through the downland 'cake' exposing its ingredients to the wind, frost, rain and sun. Together with the regular pounding of the waves that weaken the cliffs below, these agents of erosion are chewing away at the land so that the distance between Sussex and France is slowly but steadily increasing. Sussex is losing out.

All this must be borne in mind as you stride along the clifftop to the former lighthouse of Belle Tout and down to Birling Gap, for there's little future for the long-distance walker who steps too close to the edge. Up here you'll no doubt meet more people than on any other countryside stretch of the walk, for there's a road that comes right onto the cliffs and everyone wants to taste the sea air, sniff the breezes and gaze at this much-loved scene. Wandering across it with a rucksack on your back and a week's journey to Winchester ahead is one of the best beginnings possible.

There are refreshments available at Birling Gap, and crowds too, but these are soon left behind on the climb to the first 'Sister',

known as Went Hill. Next comes Bailey's Hill, Flagstaff Point, Brass Point, Rough Brow and Short Brow. The final cliff in this switchback succession is Haven Brow with its view of the wide gap of Cuckmere Haven set out below.

This river mouth is a rarity, for of all those in Sussex it is the only one without a port; a steep slope of shingle through which the Cuckmere sifts its way into the Channel, it has the Seven Sisters walling it to the east and the continuing cliffs of Seaford Head to the west. The Cuckmere, although the shortest and smallest of the four Sussex rivers to breach the Downs, is a real river of character and the path drops from Haven Brow to its raised bank and follows it inland as far as Exceat Bridge near the eighteenth-century barn that houses an exhibition devoted to the Seven Sisters Country Park.

At all times of the year the final stretch of the Cuckmere, from Exceat to the shingle banks at the Haven, makes a pleasant short

walk, and whenever the sun shines (in winter as well as in summer) the paths are busy with ramblers and family parties out to catch the sea breezes and a morning's exercise.

A few paces from the Country Park Centre the way climbs steeply to a wall where you enter Friston Forest along a path that is also taken by the Vanguard Way. It soon descends on more than 200 timber-braced steps to West Dean, an attractive hamlet with age in the walls of its cottages, but then climbs out again straight away to a northern stretch of the same forest. Beyond and below lies Charleston Manor that dates from the Domesday Book, but the footpath leads on beyond it along a hillside towards Litlington, and from there by way of a lane, path and footbridge into Alfriston.

The charming street in Alfriston at the end of Day One on the South Downs Way.

Day 1: Eastbourne to Alfriston—Inland Route—via Jevington

The official start to this bridleway route is an untidy corner off Paradise Road on the edge of Eastbourne but one soon ascends among ilex and beech to emerge on the lip of the Downs with a view over the town and beyond that to the Pevensey Levels. You then wander northwards across Eastbourne Downs golf course to Willingdon Hill where, to my mind, is the real beginning of the South Downs Way. Ahead, as far as the eye can see, the hills roll out a welcome. Some are tree-lined; some are bare green or striped where hay has been cut; some are hedged and others open. One gains an impression of space, and larks rise singing.

Willingdon Hill once bore a windmill. It's now little more than a slightly raised mound with nothing much to indicate its former use. There are crossing tracks nearby and a pair of old stone markers that were brought here from the Barclays Bank building in Eastbourne after it was bombed during the last war. One such marker directs the route down a rough track to Jevington.

Jevington sits tidily in a dry wedge of a valley, its flint and brick cottages typical of the Downs, its lovely old Saxon church standing in a graveyard speckled in spring with daisies, forget-me-nots and bluebells. There is an air of quiet contentment about Jevington; one of the little gems of the Downs. Along a line of horse chestnut and elder the path climbs past the church to Holt Brow and a broad open grassland with a faint trail leading onto Windover Hill, one of the busiest archaeological sites in Sussex. History lies all around with burial barrows and ditches and refuse pits from Stone Age flint mines. But the best-known historical feature of the area remains unseen from the path. Immediately below, and etched in white brick, stands England's largest 'chalk' figure, the Long Man of Wilmington which is so beautifully seen from the route of the Wealdway. Since the South Downs Way passes along the crest of the Downs above his head, he remains anonymously hidden from us, although Wilmington village is clearly visible at the foot of the slope.

Beyond Windover Hill a clear chalk track winds round the head of Ewe Dean and descends among blackthorn and elm trees to Plonk Barn, which is not a depot for cheap wine but a private residence apparently named after the planks from which the original barn was built. Opposite this a path

leads across the Cuckmere by way of a footbridge, and so into Alfriston.

It's an easy day's walk from Eastbourne to Alfriston but as the first stage of a long journey this is no bad thing. There's plenty of accommodation available of varying standards and prices, including a Youth Hostel downstream a little and virtually opposite Litlington. In the village there are food stores, pubs and restaurants, and the National Trust's first acquisition, the Clergy House, standing next to the church.

Days 2–3: Alfriston to Botolphs

Dodging the crowds of visitors who daily throng Alfriston's street, the long-distance walker is only a few minutes from the open spaces and gusting breezes of the Downs. Whilst Alfriston has much of interest, it is good to be wandering on once more, and the crest, once gained, rewards with a splendid vista of deep-patched Weald on the one hand, and scooped coombes leading to the sea on the other.

All along this first line of hills are ancient tumuli, some clearly evident, others less so. Below Bostal Hill a winding road formerly used for car rallies brings picnickers and hang-gliding enthusiasts to a car park with a view. Continuing, the way climbs onto the grassy brow of Firle Beacon—crowned with a long barrow and a trig point—and then veers slightly leftward towards a pair of radio masts on Beddingham Hill nearly 2 miles (3kms) away. This is sheep-grazing country while below, in the shadow of the Downs, huddles the compact little village of West Firle, known simply as Firle. The elegant Firle Place, standing next to the church, was the ancestral home of the Gage family; a charming house of grey stone tucked among beech woods.

Up here, with the breeze in your hair and the distant drone of space in your ears, you share the Downs with yet more prehistoric sites. The long barrow on Firle Beacon is merely one, for there was an Iron Age village nearby, and west of Beddingham Hill a Bronze Age collection of huts and workshops. North of the escarpment there was an Iron Age hillfort on Mount Caburn, occupied for some three hundred years until the arrival of the Romans. The conquistadors from Rome crossed the Downs somewhere up here along a trade route they established to transport grain from their Wealden agricultural estates to the coast where Seaford and Newhaven stand today. So, as you tread the springy turf and gaze on

broad horizons, you can almost hear the tramping steps of those predecessors who were the first-ever wanderers of the airy crests of these South Downs, and imagine what life must have been like for them.

There's another car park between Firle Beacon and Beddingham Hill where enthusiasts come to fly their radio-controlled model aircraft, yet one soon loses company with the buzz of tiny motors, and before long the flower-bright slope of Itford Hill offers a quiet place to sit for a few minutes, to absorb the joy of birdsong and the gentle pendulous heads of cowslips waving about you. In the valley below runs the Ouse, second of the Sussex rivers to be crossed, and one that in the past held an important role in the livelihood of downsmen. It was into this river too that Virginia Woolf, defeated by mental illness, threw herself in 1941. Her body was washed up against the piers of the bridge over which you walk into Southease.

Southease is a seemingly lost hamlet among a bower of trees standing a little diffidently away from the right bank of the River Ouse, from which villagers used to earn their keep. For this was once a fishing village of some account and according to the Domesday Book, rent of no less than 38,500 herrings would have been paid to the Norman Lord of Lewes. Today, Southease consists of a few cottages and a distinctive round-towered church overlooking a green. There's not a herring nor fishing boat in sight.

Half a mile or so of road walking brings you to Rodmell, but there's a recommended diversion one could make through a valley named Cricketing Bottom which leads to the tiny hamlet of Telscombe, snug in a fold of the Downs, where an overnight may be spent in the simple yet comfortable Youth Hostel next to the church. It is one of those

Right above: **Eastbourne Pier is an obvious place to begin the long walk to Winchester—down on the beach with a tide seething.**

Below: **Walking over the Seven Sisters sets the tone of the South Downs Way, for you can see so clearly the depth of chalk over which almost the whole route will go.**

gentle outposts worth seeking; a cluster of buildings divorced from the rush and bustle of the world, with hills all around, sheep bleating, horses sneezing, flowers waving. Trapped in a liquid evening shadow, Telscombe's hostel holds something of the very best about Youth Hostelling. Somehow the magic remains.

Mill Hill overlooks both Cricketing Bottom and Rodmell. From it the way journeys along an exposed track over Front Hill and Iford Hill, larks rising from the flint-cluttered corn all about you, then swings to the very scarp edge at Swanborough Hill where a vista north and east takes in the full glory of contrast; steep hill slope and the tartan patchwork of the Weald spread far off. Villages line the flat ground below, sheep bend to their task of cropping the downland neat as a tilted bowling green, and there are coombes easing southward into a mysterious anonymity where once fisherfolk brought their wares from Brighton on the old 'Juggs Road'. The path follows the line of 'Juggs Road' on a loop round the side of Castle Hill but then deserts it to wander north, passing alongside a woodland called Newmarket Plantation, and across the busy Brighton road outside Lewes.

Much of the countryside has now been put to the plough. Arable has replaced pasture, but before too long there is a resumption of green turf and the fluff of distant sheep. An inner downland valley returns the South Downs Way walker to the northern lip of the escarpment at Plumpton Plain, a misnomer if ever there was one. Again the route wanders westward with glorious views over your right shoulder and you come to Ditchling Beacon, saved by the National Trust, protected as Nature Reserve, yet trampled by honeypot motorists who gather on the 813-ft (248-m) summit— around which the outline of an Iron Age hillfort can be seen—to gaze on a broad panorama. It is indeed grand, but there are other grand views on this walk to enjoy in solitude, and were it not for the temptation of an ice cream from a van in the car park, I'd have chased ahead to avoid the crowds. A mile farther west you pass the Keymer Post and stray from East Sussex into West Sussex, and another mile later come to the Clayton Windmills, Jack and Jill.

Once the South Downs were a-flurry with windmills; not so now. But Jack and Jill remain as popular features that are easily and affectionately recognised from the Brighton train. They stand side by side a

The Clayton windmills, Jack and Jill, are prominent features on the South Downs Way.

little north of the crest; one a private residence, the other, Jill, in the care of a protection society and open to the public. Jill, the smaller mill, originally stood in Patcham near Brighton where she was built in 1821 but she was then hauled bodily onto the Downs by a team of oxen to work alongside Jack.

A track leading down beside a golf course takes you to the village of Pyecombe where the famous shepherds' crooks were made, then up again and over West Hill to Saddlescombe hiding below Devil's Dyke. From West Hill the Clayton Windmills make a pleasing sight across the valley behind but the path soon plunges down a steep grass slope, through an enclosed track and out to a farm and a row of cottages at Saddlescombe. Fighting a scrub-and-tree-

confusing route onto the back of Devil's Dyke, where the earth ramparts of an Iron Age hillfort are clearly seen, you will then find yourself once more on the northern scarp edge, and on a clear and easy chalk track following a switchback course over successive hills. The last of these is Truleigh Hill with its cluster of untidy official buildings, a farm or two and a flat-roofed Youth Hostel standing right beside the track. The track leads on, then makes a grassy descent into the valley washed by the

River Adur. Across this you come to the little hamlet of Botolphs.

Days 4–7: Botolphs to Winchester

Like Southease on the Ouse, Botolphs once busied itself with fishing, but the sea drew back from the valley and left it literally high and dry. The village all but died and practically all that's left now is a mellow Saxon church, some humps and bumps in the fields where former dwellings stood, a farm or two and a handful of houses. A lane leads uphill out of the valley and a track takes you onto the Downs again.

Now the Downs are spreading out. They're broadening as they move inland away from the sea. At first there are lovely coombes sweeping cloud shadows in distorted journeys across the pattern of corn or grassland. Then there are the great earthworks—off our route—of Cissbury Ring; a massive fortress built in about 250

Near Firle Beacon the walker experiences the wide open spaces typical of the South Downs.

BC, in which some 60,000 tons of chalk were dug and thrown up to form the ramparts, and around ten thousand logs used as an additional wall of timber. It's a staggering place where the past holds gallantly on to the present. That past is truly epic too, for in a corner of Cissbury's ring lie the remnants of a flint mine dating from about 3390 BC. From Cissbury a trackway leads back to the route proper of the South Downs Way which it meets at Chanctonbury Ring, for many the very symbol of the Downs and roughly halfway point along the original Eastbourne—Buriton route.

For two hundred years the beeches which, alongside the sycamore and oak, make up Chanctonbury Ring, created a prominent mushroom of foliage on the hilltop above Wiston House, home of Charles Goring who, in 1760, planted them. But the hurricane that ripped across southern England in the early hours of October 16th 1987, wrought havoc amongst these noble trees. Fifty per cent of the woodland grove was uprooted, and many of those trees that remained upright had limbs torn from them. From afar one would not suspect it but as you draw closer, so you see the empty spaces and bowls of exposed soil where not so long ago magnificent tree specimens stood proud. A

victim of the wind, is Chanctonbury Ring; yet it remains a magical place nonetheless, with the site of a Roman temple in its very centre.

A mile or so west of Chanctonbury Ring another busy road is crossed in a deep cut on the edge of Washington village, but the Downs are quickly regained at Highden Hill, striding along easy tracks over grass and beside cultivated fields for half a dozen miles (10km) or so. I came across here one spring day, on a section totally devoid of shelter, when a sudden storm broke. Lightning streaked the sky and thunder shook the ground beneath my feet. That lightning made fence-posts of fire. Rain lashed from an evil sky. But there was a certain magic in that storm and in my exposed position that raised my perception of the walk, and my appreciation of the gifts we too often take for granted was given a fresh boost.

On Rackham Banks a view opens to the north and west and you gaze off to the sunlit watercourses of Amberley Wild Brooks, to the River Arun dragging itself through the lowlands, and across the Arun Gap to the continuing Downs. It's an enticing view and you're soon swinging down the slope towards the river whose bridge, by Amberley Station, takes too much traffic for the walker

Above: **The Clergy House in Alfriston was the first property acquired by the National Trust. They paid £10 for it in 1896.**

Below: **Jevington churchyard in springtime is a mass of wild flowers.**

Beyond Coombe Wood, for example, the pathway takes you to the edge of Houghton Forest and then veers away from it, leaving the massed greenery as part of a distant theme that refuses to go away. It encroaches again west of Bignor Hill where you cross the line of the old Roman Stane Street, but it is not consciously imposing until you've reached Woolavington Down and find that the next 4 miles (6km) to Cocking are almost entirely surrounded by woods; outliers of Charlton Forest. This is deer country and it's worth walking quietly, ears tuned to the woodland peace. Eyes are upon you.

Below Manorfarm Down the little village of Cocking is a delight, and surprisingly untouched by the traffic that cuts through it. It was here when the Normans arrived, as was the church. Then the settlement was valued at '. . . 6 serfs and 5 mills yielding 37 shillings and sixpence'. Round by the church a clear chalk stream bubbles its way from the turf to flow north into the Rother, while the walk resumes westward, once more along the crest of the hills with woods standing back and a long view across them to the spire of Chichester Cathedral, and far beyond to include even the Isle of Wight on a clear day.

Making a loop round Treyford Hill there's a group of Bronze Age burial mounds—dating from around 1600 BC—known as the Devil's Jumps, where a number of bronze implements have been found. Passing these you enter Phillis Wood among lovely mature green-trunked beeches, but then you must watch carefully for a marker indicating a change of direction, otherwise you'll miss the way to isolated Buriton Farm and up to Pen Hill with its lovely panorama.

Sometimes it's good to sprawl on a hilltop and give yourself up to the day. Alone on Pen Hill I did just that; threw off my rucksack and shirt and lazed in the warm April sun listening to the arias sung by half a dozen skylarks that were no more than minute specks in the blue vault above.

Rabbits loped across the track below me; a pheasant crackled, distant sheep tested the acoustics of the Downs, then a cuckoo hiccupped from the woods. There were flowers in the field margins and blossom on the blackthorn. It was so good not to have to be anywhere else but here!

Immediately west of Pen Hill stands Beacon Hill with its hilltop Iron Age fort but the true way skirts this and comes back to the northern scarp edge on Harting Downs.

to find pleasing, accustomed as you have become to the empty openness of the Downs. But the next village, which is Houghton, leads gently along a country lane and returns you to a trackway climbing towards Coombe Wood.

Until now the eastern Downs have been largely wood-free but the western half of the walk is to become more and more enclosed by trees. The very nature of the walk undergoes a subtle change, although the changing pattern of the landscape evolves slowly, gradually, as you wander into it.

The cropped downland grass here is starred with flowers, while the views north are imposing and memorable. In the valley below lies South Harting, and between it and Buriton, a distance of less than 4 miles (6km), you leave West Sussex and enter the county of Hampshire.

As stated earlier, Buriton marked the official end to the original South Downs Way. That has now been extended to Winchester; an additional 20 miles (32km) of variety and scenic pleasures. First comes a walk through the Queen Elizabeth Forest, a large part of which is absorbed into a Country Park. (There are plenty of deer roaming freely through this forest, and it's worth stepping quietly, ears and eyes alert.) Then, having ducked beneath the monstrous roar of the A3 trunk road, you come to Butser Hill Ancient Farm where a demonstration site shows how life would have been led in Iron Age times. Experiments in Iron Age agricultural methods, crops and materials are being conducted to the north of lofty Butser Hill—highest point on the South Downs—in an area rich in ancient trackways, Bronze Age burial mounds, Celtic fields and defensive dykes. It's a fascinating place and worth delaying the onward march to study it.

Butser Hill is a popular place, for it's accessible to the motorist, but it doesn't take long to plunge once more into the empty Downs as you wander across Tegdown and Hyden Hills along a true green lane, before emerging onto a stretch of country road walking through the inshore Naval training establishment of HMS Mercury. Wether Down is next, and a sunken track that leads from it sloping down to Coombe Cross. The Downs here appear to have lost any real continuity of purpose. In the valley below Henwood Down isolated hills rise about you, circling the tilted farmlands. There appears not to be one single ridge line any more, although it is all fine walking country still. And on Old Winchester Hill you tread the earthworks of an Iron Age hillfort with cowslips in the grass and a vast panorama plunging in every direction. This is a National Nature Reserve with downland plants and a rich assortment of butterflies. Descending from it, through a little woodland, you come to another chalk

The River Meon is a lovely chalk stream crossed towards the end of the walk.

stream which is followed down to the sparkling River Meon.

Half a day's walk leads from Exton to Winchester. Fields of corn or golden rape, broad acres of downland grass, hilltop views and lonely farms; flint walls and bowers of leafshade; a winding of country roads, a die-straight line of hedged green lane cutting across Ganderdown. Ganderdown leads to Cheesefoot Head. From there to Telegraph Hill and, escaping rifle ranges, you drop down a flint track to the neat hamlet of Chilcomb. And then to Winchester itself; city of architectural splendour. King Alfred's town; a river and a cathedral; watercress beds and archways of glory.

Should a long walk have a more fitting end?

59

WALK 7: *The Downs Link*

Baynards Station is now a private residence, but to the walker wandering by, it appears ready to greet the 12.15 from Guildford.

Distance: 33 miles (53km).
Time Required: 2 days.
Type of Walk: An easy walk on mostly firm paths following the line of a former railway. The only hills to contend with are at the start, all others levelled by the construction of embankments or cuttings. The walk links the North Downs Way with the South Downs Way; it also crosses the Greensand Way and the Sussex Border Path, and shares part of the route of the Wey-South Path.
Start: St Martha's Hill, near Guildford, Surrey.
Finish: Botolphs, near Shoreham by Sea, West Sussex.
Maps: O.S. Landranger series 186, 187, 198.
Guidebook: *The South Downs Way & The Downs Link* by Kev Reynolds (Cicerone Press). *The Downs Link* (a slim route guide produced by the three councils that devised it, and available from West Sussex County Council, County Hall, Chichester PO19 1RL).

Walking a Disused Railway

By the time Britain's network of railways was nationalised in 1948, the countryside was criss-crossed with some 19,000 miles (30,600km) of track; track that had not only reshaped the landscape but had stimulated many otherwise isolated country communities. But between 1952 and 1967 numerous unprofitable branch lines were dismantled—mostly hastened by Dr Beeching's notorious report of 1963—and the working rail system was effectively reduced to just 11,000 miles (17,700km). This demise has had a profound, and in many cases beneficial, effect on the countryside, for wild flowers, animals, birds and insects all profit from the absence of trains on literally hundreds of acres of deserted embankment and cutting, while in many instances walkers and cyclists have gained access to new routes where a number of abandoned railways have been adopted by local councils as recreational facilities. Walking disused railways has subsequently developed as an attraction all its own.

The Downs Link uses one such line on its novel journey from the North Downs Way to the South Downs Way; the line which was built in two sections by the London–Brighton South Coast Railway (in 1861) and the Horsham and Guildford Direct Railway Company (opened in 1865). It strikes through the Weald from the south of Guildford as far as the hamlet of Botolphs near Shoreham, where the South Downs Way crosses the River Adur. However, the walk itself actually begins to the north-east of the old railway, on the North Downs Way at St Martha's Hill between Guildford and Albury, and gives 33 miles (53km) of pleasant wandering with practically no necessity to check the map.

The concept of a trans-Weald walking route to link the North and South Downs is one that has been attempted elsewhere. The Wealdway achieves a similar objective in the east on its journey from Gravesend on the Thames to Beachy Head on the Sussex coast. The Vanguard Way links the bustling suburbs of London with the open glory of Seaford Head, and the Wey-South Path also embraces the two lines of the Downs by following various waterways from Guildford to Amberley. But of all these the Downs Link is the only route which makes a conscious, single-minded effort to join the two officially approved long-distance downland Ways in the south-east.

This is not one of the Countryside Commission's National Long-Distance Paths or Trails. Nor was it achieved by an enthusiastic group of ramblers. The Downs Link is, in fact, the result of a joint development completed in 1984 by three local authorities who owned much of the former railway line: West Sussex and Surrey County Councils, and Waverley Borough Council based at Godalming in Surrey.

The Downs Link is a bridleway as well as a walking route, but in contrast with many another walk shared by horses, this one is mostly firm underfoot by virtue of the tons of clinker ash upon which the old railway track was laid. Now that the track has been lifted, the once-bare bed has been invaded by a profusion of plants, and along embankments and through cuttings trees, shrubs and blankets of flowers have discovered a sanctuary. In their season you'll find bluebells in great drifts, often banked

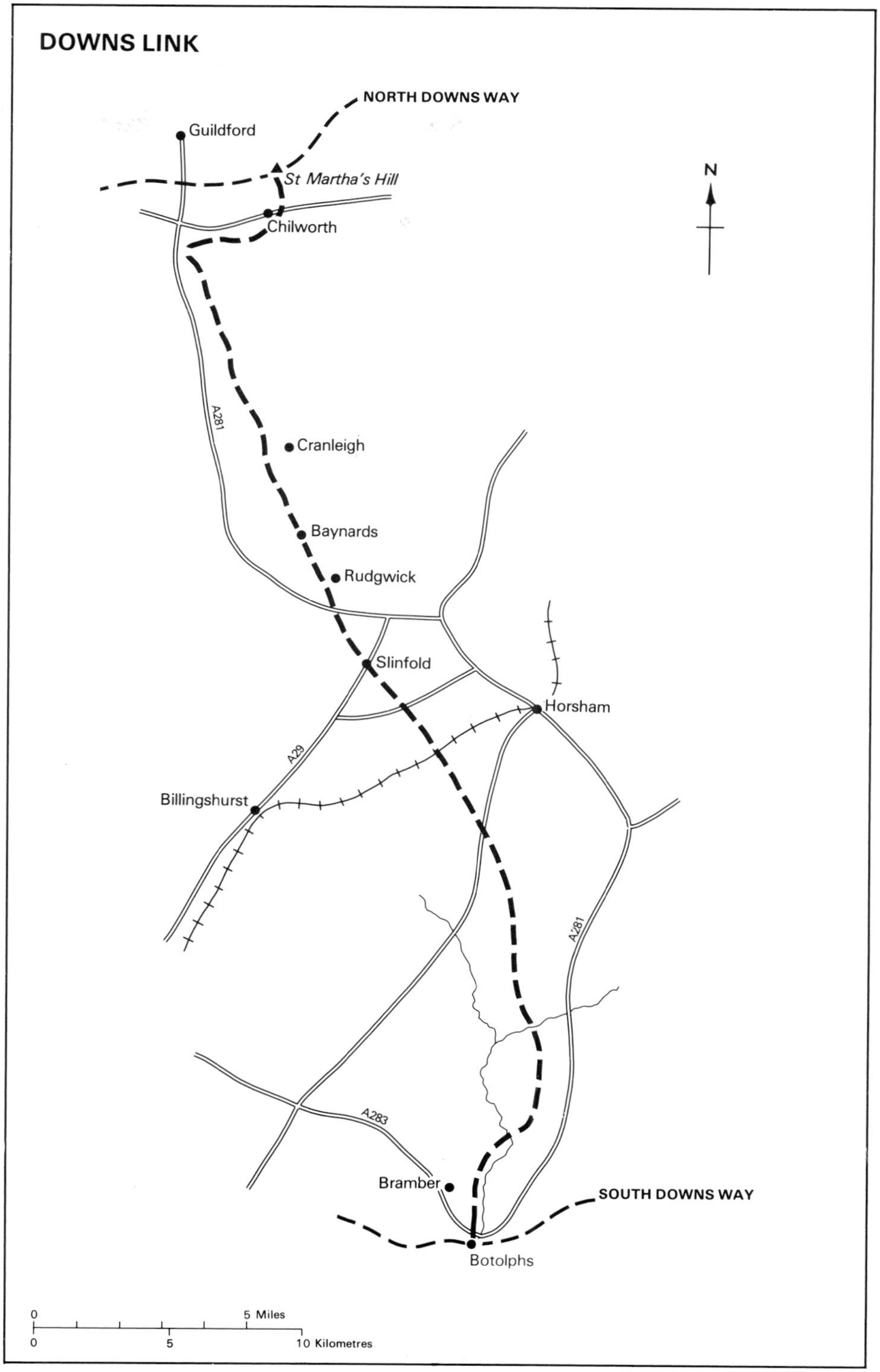

DOWNS LINK

against the pungent-smelling but attractive white stars of ramsons. Purple orchid and cowslip are found towards the southern end of the walk; elsewhere golden saxifrage, herb robert and watercress may be seen. The bright spikes of rosebay willowherb have spread all over the country now, their seeds borne aloft on hairy sails—each plant producing something like 80,000 seeds to be scattered by the winds and birds. Railways

61

aided their spread and along the Downs Link there will be stretches brightened by swards of this attractive, if sometimes straggly plant. The track is also an important wildlife refuge in what otherwise would be either suburban or agricultural settings. Badger setts and the earths of foxes are often seen close by the route, and towards evening rabbits stray onto the open grass-covered pathway. The pathside hedgerows harbour voles and mice, and birds nest in the secret tangle of branch and thorn.

Walking the Downs Link is a nature lover's journey, and since the route creates no real navigational problems, one can concentrate on the rich tapestry that nature weaves along the way. Few who are observant will be disappointed by it.

Days 1–2: St Martha's to Botolphs

I can think of few more rewarding beginnings to a long walk than the hilltop church of St Martha's outside Guildford. You have to walk to get there, making a pilgrimage, as it were, with the reward of magnificent views over countryside through which you'll be striding for the rest of the day. And who would argue with Arthur Mee when he wrote:

> It is hard to think that any village church in England stands so marvellously on a hilltop as

this. Proudly alone it is, keeping company with the trees and the grass and the winds, and a heavenly Surrey view. With a glorious countryside of woods and hills all round, St Martha's has the feeling of being above them all.

It's a sandy hilltop, trees clambering up the slope and attempting to conquer the brow, but not so much as to close off the surrounding land. I've been there in all weathers and have never lost that sense of jubilation as the crown of the hill is gained and the Weald falls away in folds of greenery. On clear days the long, wooded ridge is seen striking eastward, washed with the blue light of distance; on damp days in early spring, mists hang among the trees and squirrels dance in the branches to dislodge droplets of moisture as you wander beneath. The day I set out to walk the Downs Link had something of each. It began clear, but by the time I left the train at Chilworth and found the path to the summit of St Martha's, clouds had gathered and rain was in the breeze. It was like that, on and off, all the way to Botolphs. But there were pleasures to be gained from both.

About 400 yards (370m) east of the church, along the broad sandy track that is the North Downs Way, a wooden finger post set near a stone marker indicates the start of the Downs Link path. It heads directly

down the southern slope among trees and bluebells and with views into the Tillingbourne Valley below. It's a green and pleasant valley with a mild-mannered stream flowing through. This stream, the Tilling Bourne, rises near Leith Hill and on its 10-mile (16km) journey to join the River Wey outside Guildford it endows several of the loveliest villages in all of Surrey with its calm personality. Surprisingly for such a gentle stream, the Tilling Bourne once powered eight watermills and provided the impetus for such industries as tanning, weaving, the manufacture of gunpowder and iron. It also has watercress beds and a lush vegetation where it flows through a little woodland below St Martha's.

Soon after crossing the A248 road just outside Chilworth the path leads into mixed woodlands at Blackheath where, in spring, the flush of new growth gives the air a subterranean liquidity as freshly unfurled leaves paint a thousand shades of green in the dancing air. There are choruses of birdsong, the raucous shrieking of jays, the pad of foxes, and grey squirrels everywhere among the trellis of overhead branches. A lovely patch of woodland it is, with open spaces of heath and gorse, slender birch and broom, and a deeply sunken trail that takes you out of it among banks honeycombed with badger setts. Then along a track to pass one of Surrey's finest moated Elizabethan houses, Great Tangley Manor.

After Wonersh Common, heading westward, the route leads alongside meadows with grand views across the valley on the right towards St Martha's and to the left up onto Chinthurst Hill. Instead of crossing Chinthurst Hill the route winds round its northern side, in places rather muddily in an enclosed groove of a track with overhanging hedges and trees, but then emerges to Old Chinthurst Farm, crosses a minor road linking the villages of Shalford and Wonersh, and at last reaches the bed of the former railway beside the overgrown remains of the Wey and Arun Canal. The Canal was built 200 years too late to be of much value and it is ironic that the railway

Blackheath Woods are alive with birdsong and a kaleidoscope of shades of green in springtime.

Above: **St Botolph's church marks the southern end of the Downs Link.**

Right: **Autumn paints fronds of bracken with extravagant colours.**

which caused its early demise now joins it as another of Surrey's industrial antiquities.

There are two bridges here, one above the other. One was built to cross the Canal, the other to take traffic over the railway. Cross the first, smaller, bridge and then bear left to follow the line of the former Guildford–Horsham railway.

Almost at once there's an air of adjacent urbanity, despite the trees lining the way and the fact that few houses are to be seen. Below the track flows Cranleigh Water, a tributary of the River Wey which makes a most attractive feature—especially where it rushes over a weir. Then you come to Bramley and Wonersh Station, an incon-

gruous platform and a signboard, with the former railway station buildings now taken over by a builders' merchant. A short stroll away from the path, along the lane to the left, would bring you to Wonersh village, a one-time centre of the cloth industry.

Wandering along an embankment now you look down onto the backs of Bramley's houses with a pleasant little stream washing through their gardens, and leaving the last of this half-hearted urban fringe, one is rejoined by the comparatively sluggish green flow of Cranleigh Water. Open country lies ahead and the path heads through flowery banks and beneath a bridge that takes the Greensand Way to Shamley Green. Now off the hills and into the Weald proper, we may be thankful on a wet day for the firm bed of the old railway, for Wealden clay is particularly notorious hereabouts. Cobbett complained about it on one of his *Rural Rides:*

> I was warned of the difficulty of getting along, but I was not to be frightened by the sound of clay . . . where a wagon could go my horse could go. It took me, however, a good hour and a half to get along these three miles. Now mind this is the real Weald where the clay is bottomless; where there is no stone of any sort underneath.

Cranleigh Water veers away from the route, scooping its way in a bed of 'bottomless clay' only to return later in a squiggle of ox-bows beyond Run Common. A couple of miles or so on the route curves gently and brings you to the edge of Cranleigh, said to be England's largest village, and one whose name is derived from the cranes that were bred at nearby Vachery Pond for the table of royalty, in the days when these leggy birds were considered a delicacy fit for a king's palate.

Cranleigh, one-time basket-making village, one-time Wealden iron village, grew in importance when the Wey-Arun Canal was opened. It received a second boost with the coming of the railway, for its station was the main one on the line between Horsham and Guildford. That station site has now been absorbed by a shopping precinct, and practically all you see of it as you wander on is a railway signal standing rather forlornly beside the path.

With open countryside replacing Cranleigh's tenuous spread, the track pushes through a cutting whose lining trees link their branches overhead in a guard of honour. Then you emerge from the cut and come onto an embankment a short distance from unseen Vachery Pond, one of Surrey's largest sheets of water and one which is thought to have been a hammer pond in the days of the all-important Wealden iron industry. During the early years of the nineteenth century it was also used to maintain water levels in the Canal. It lies off to the left with woods on three sides but with a footpath that skirts its southern edge and offers an interesting diversion from the main route. (There are many such diversions available from the Downs Link, which makes it a fine walk to be tackled in isolated sections.)

Beyond Vachery Pond the track sneaks past a lesser pond on the right, banked with rhododendrons, and then through woods smoky with bluebells and along yet another embankment taken over by primroses growing in extensive clumps, and with wild clematis scrabbling up to the branches of neighbouring trees. I find something very soothing in nature's determination to resurrect a wild garden on land that man once shaped to his own devices, then finally abandoned when it lost him money. First came the surveyors, eyeing the land for exploitation. Then came the navvies who shifted the heavy clay by the soggy ton and spread their clinker ash to provide a sturdy bed for the great shining tracks. Then for a hundred years the peace of this countryside would have been regularly shaken as the massive steam-driven locomotives thundered their way to and fro. And now? Now there's birdsong in spring. And wild flowers with butterflies on them through the bleached days of summer. A countryside restored, revitalised, accessible. We walk on a die-straight course, on the level track that is now more often used as a highway for the creatures of the land than as a long-distance walking route, and are reminded of nature's resilience. Left on her own she sows seeds of glory and the sensitive walker grows rich from her selfless, quiet industry.

Out of the woods you pass along the bottom of a few gardens, come to the Thurlow Arms pub and reach the spruce buildings of Baynards Station, looking ready to greet the 12.15 from Guildford, but a quarter of a century after the last train stopped here.

In his *Portrait of Surrey,* published in 1970, Basil Cracknell bemoaned the fact that Baynards Station was just three short years along the road to dereliction. He reported grass growing along the track, the station platform littered with bric-a-brac and the name-plate missing. Today all this has changed, and the station is probably in better condition than at almost any time in its history. Of course it is a station in name only now, for the buildings have been adapted as a private residence. But the name-plate is back, there are doors marked for Porters and Lamp Room and the platforms appear ready to receive passengers for the next steam train. Whoever has worked this change must surely be a railway 'buff' for none but a true enthusiast would have flourished such love on it, and one of the outer walls now bears a plaque proclaiming that the building received an award in 1985 from the Surrey Industrial History Group. We can but applaud this glad restoration.

The Thurlow Arms pub was built by a one-time owner of nearby Baynards Manor, a great Tudor house which stands well back to the east in Baynards Park, whose gates are passed a few paces beyond the station.

South-east of the station the railway used to disappear into a tunnel, but since the line's closure this tunnel has been filled in and the path now makes a slight detour along the edge of South Wood where wood anemones battle with bluebells for superiority, and rhododendrons blaze later in May. In the middle of the wood you pass out of Surrey and into West Sussex, cross the route of the Sussex Border Path and come to the brick-making village of Rudgwick where refreshments are available at a pub, and accommodation may be found at a nearby hotel.

It's 5 miles (8km) from Rudgwick to the sprawling buildings of Christ's Hospital School which, standing to the south-west of Horsham, marked the southern limit of the single-line Guildford section of the railway. And those 5 miles are mostly open country miles, with some of the broadest views of the whole route. There's a Nature Reserve near Slinfold, more typical brick railway bridges to pass under, and the crossing of a major Roman road, Stane Street.

When the track was laid outside Rudgwick the railway inspector was unhappy with the steep gradient to the station, so he insisted on easing the slope by raising the embankment. One of the side-issues of this demand is the curiosity of a two-tiered bridge over the River Arun, the upper bridge being erected to carry the railway. The river is a sluggish waterway here, but its banks are lined with wild garlic and on either side a peaceful landscape stretches away among hedgerows and spinneys. Crab apple trees, old and gnarled and past their best, grow alongside the track as you stride towards Park Street Nature Reserve, with its numbered posts marking a nature trail. Then, just before arriving in the neat residential street of Slinfold, you pass beneath the brick arched bridge carrying the A29 on the line of the Roman Stane Street and wonder at the traffic that marched this way nigh-on two thousand years ago, heading from Chichester to London. The legions of Rome left their mark indelibly on the landscape of Britain as surely as have Dr Beeching's dismantled railways. Ruler-straight routes of passage marking the shortest distance between points A and B.

A study of the map of this area illustrates the impression stamped by Rome. There's Roman Station (or Roman Gate), and Roman Woods near Stane Street's junction with an alternative north-bound route. It is said that a bell, on its way from Rome to York during the occupation of Britain, fell into marshy ground near Slinfold and was lost, while north-west of here the remains of a Roman brickworks were discovered, as well as a length of pavement 30 feet wide.

Slinfold is but a brief interruption of countryside and you're soon wandering again through low landscapes of meadow and spinney with distant hills capped with crew-cut woodlands brash against the sky.

One of the benefits of walking railways is the ease with which major roads are crossed. Bridges remain intact, so one simply passes either beneath or over the scurrying traffic and almost immediately becomes swallowed again by the countryside. The A264 south of Broadbridge Heath sends its traffic roaring overhead and moments later you resume into the peaceful land with a tower seen rising ahead above meadows and trees. This is at Christ's Hospital School, but instead of striking directly along the line towards it, it becomes necessary to leave the old railway track and take a quiet country lane for perhaps a mile among big fields and beneath a huge, stretched sky. There's no hardship in this, especially as you suddenly have a long view north across a complex of meadow, field and woodland to the blue line of the Greensand Ridge, where Holmbury Hill and Leith Hill stand out as the major points along it.

Christ's Hospital is the famous Bluecoat School, founded by Edward VI, that was transferred here from its original site in

London in 1902. The building is a rambling mixture of architectural styles set in well-mown grounds, and the Downs Link path edges alongside its playing fields to rejoin the bed of the old railway at Itchingfield Junction. Once more you resume the walk through a short patch of countryside with views growing of the South Downs ahead, before diverting again to pass through the village of Southwater where there will be an opportunity to buy drinks and snacks for the way ahead, from a convenient general store.

In times gone by Southwater was an important brick-making centre and although this industry has now departed, the flooded clay pits that were formerly a part of this industry have been adopted as a country park. They lie a short distance off the path as you leave the village, duck beneath its bypass and take once more to a countryside of gentle, open fields and pastures lined with hedgerows, dotted with spinneys and woodland shaws. Trackside woods are flush with wild flowers, as indeed is the track itself. Bugle, yellow archangel and primroses make a bright pattern of blue on gold along one stretch of embankment, with white buttons of stitchwort punctuating the base of hedgerows.

A mile beyond the little hamlet of Copsale an embankment takes you over one of the tributaries of the River Adur, a river that will be a regular companion now until the end of the walk. Sometimes that river will be flowing close by, sometimes snaking through

First sign of the former railway that is adopted by the Downs Link, is this double bridge over the sluggish River Wey.

a neighbouring field marked by a grassy bank or distinctive line of trees. A number of minor streams have eased their way from Wealdon ridges to form the Adur. They come from furnace ponds, parklands and wood-crowded hills, sidling along the edge of pasture and plough-turned field before joining forces to break through the wall of the Downs at Upper Beeding. Those Downs are becoming more evident in the south and having passed the overgrown platforms of the now-missing West Grinstead Station, Chanctonbury Ring clearly shows itself as a neat arc of trees on the horizon.

Wandering through a low cutting here in spring you may be greeted by the colourful spikes of the early purple orchid. It's a lovely stretch of the track, springy underfoot, studded with flowers and with the South Downs growing out of the landscape. I came along here on a calm evening with twilight beginning to slide from the hills. It had been raining earlier and the light now was pure and crystal clear. A lone blackbird was warbling the Last Post. Ahead of me the track slid green and inviting between those low grass-smoothed banks where dozens of rabbits had emerged to feed, safe—they'd assumed—from interruption. There were does and bucks and their young crouching,

One of the benefits of walking a disused railway is the firm footing brought about by hundreds of tons of ash laid down to take the sleepers.

nibbling, cleansing, hopping, each one innocent of my presence as I squatted against the bank and watched. The blackbird continued to warble, but there were no other sounds, apart from the light thud of rabbits' paws and the soft settling of moisture into the land. It was a scene of utter peace and tranquillity and I felt an overwhelming sense of privilege at being alone to catch this glimpse into nature's private world—no matter how *ordinary* such scenes

may be. Because of this walk my life had gained something rather special.

Partridge Green is a well-contained village on a dog's-leg of roads, and it's necessary to leave the track of the railway here for maybe half a mile, then resume across a wide plain of pasture sliced with watercourses and with solitary farms addressing the empty acres. This is one of my favourite parts of the whole walk. There is a sense of space, and with the rising Downs half a dozen miles (9km) away, the knowledge that one landscape merely eases into the next, no matter how different the two may be. Each has its own quality, its own essential flavour, and it would be wrong to compare one with another. For those of us

who love the countryside, and enjoy wandering through it, there will always be something new to discover.

In this low green plain the Adur is building its strength to make a final bid for the sea. The track crosses it and we are teased with alternatives. The Downs Link maintains its association with the one-time railway and curves towards Henfield before sweeping back south-westwards to Bramber. But there are footpaths on both banks of the river and it would be feasible to follow this all the way to Botolphs. That, too, would be a grand way to finish the walk, keeping an eye open for the wildlife that exploits the river and its banks, as well as the damp water meadows around. There's not much in it, mileage-wise; just two options, both worth tackling. Better not choose between them; find time to tackle both!

So, following the railway's line you come to Henfield, pass along its western edge and return to the open pastures with cattle grazing and ducks enjoying the reed-lined dykes and streams. Near the old timbered Stretham Manor you once more cross the Adur where the Romans crossed in the first century AD. (They had a road running along the base of the Downs which linked some of their agricultural enterprises, and of course they had an important settlement at Chichester which needed to be supplied.)

Across the river you leave the track and take to a narrow farm lane. This delivers you to the village of Bramber where its singular digit-like remains of the flint-walled castle, built in 1083, stand upon a mound of earthworks, probably Saxon in origin. The castle was built by William de Braose to guard the gap in the Downs where the Adur breaks through. But when the castle was in use, it was the sea that used to flow here and ships would sail inland beyond the South Downs. Nearby Steyning, in fact, had a port until the fourteenth century, and Botolphs, where the walk ends, was a prosperous fishing village with its own salt industry until the Middle Ages.

The last brief stretch of the walk takes you across the A283 and onto the line of the old railway, drawing close to the river once more and then linking with the South Downs Way a few paces from Botolphs' simple little church, in a hamlet that lost the sea and became tied to the land. The sea now lies beyond the Downs, while the Downs themselves, rising all round, invite you into their embrace—for further exploration.

WALK 8: *The Thames Walk*

Cleeve Lock, upstream from Streatley.

Distance: 156 miles (251km).
Time Required: 10–12 days.
Type of Walk: A level and easy walk on a mixture of towpath, footpath and pavement. The paths are mostly good, being clearly defined, although in places there is little sign on the ground, yet they are obvious enough with the river as your guide. The actual walking time could be easily doubled by those tempted to visit many of the places of interest along the way.
Of all the routes in this book, the Thames Walk is ideally suited to those who choose to tackle it in dislocated stages. Access by public transport is easy for much of the route.
Start: Putney Bridge, London.
Finish: Thames Head, near Kemble, Gloucestershire.
Maps: O.S. Landranger series 176, 175, 174, 164, 163.

Guidebook: *The Thames Walk* by David Sharp (The Ramblers' Association).
Other reading: *Ordnance Survey Guide to the River Thames* (O.S./Robert Nicholson Publications). *A Thames Companion* by Mari Pritchard & Humphrey Carpenter (Oxford University Press).

Following London's River to its Source

The Thames is a peaceful companion. A river that has eased its way out of the Cotswolds and across the bulk of southern England for so many thousands of years that it has given up all pretence of haste, it has little in common with those fly-by-night upstart mountain torrents that are boisterous with turmoil and spray. Certainly, the

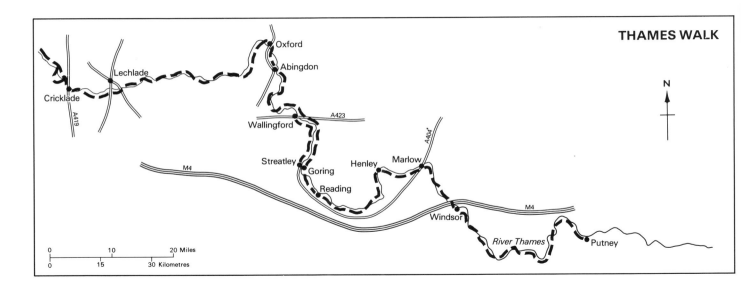

Thames has its moments of middle-aged tantrum as it boils across several weirs or floods low-lying meadows in winter, but these are only momentary lapses from grace. For the most part it is well-mannered, slow moving and gentle. A peaceful companion indeed.

To walk upstream from London to the Cotswold foothills alongside the river all the way is an impossible dream, since sections of the one-time towpath have been hi-jacked by various developments over the years, but the route outlined here will give many days of pleasure as you work your way from city to town, from town to village and from village to open countryside as green and inviting as many a lowland region of Britain. Through it all the Thames flows sedately and casts its own personality of calm upon the landscape.

The Thames Walk is an unofficial one, a route publicised by the Ramblers' Association and one that may be seen almost as an interim measure, while the 'official' Thames Path proposed by the Countryside Commission grinds its cumbersome journey through a bureaucratic wilderness in order to gain Ministerial approval, and from there—hopefully—to an eventual reality on the ground. A series of footpaths, linked with long reaches of old towpath and the odd diversion along a minor road, will lead to 156 miles (251km) of walking along the best parts of the river bank. When the Countryside Commission's route finally comes to fruition, it will be nearer 180 miles (290km) from the Thames Barrier at Greenwich to its source at Kemble. By then one or two new

footbridges will have been built across the river, as well as over tributary streams or ditches, and access agreements will have been settled. But that, as they say, is a long time a-coming.

It's been thirty-odd years so far.

Thirty-odd years ago when legislation for the creation of national long-distance footpaths came into being, the idea of a continuous route along the Thames was raised. There were, after all, traces of towpath leading from Putney Bridge to Lechlade, but as that towpath formerly crossed from one bank to another by way of ferries that now no longer exist, the proposed route for walkers would have been brought to an abrupt halt in a number of places. Moreover, the cost of repair following years of towpath neglect was assessed to be rather too high, so the plan was all but forgotten. Then in 1977 the Southern Area of the Ramblers' Association resurrected the idea and even carried out a complete survey of the route in conjunction with the River Thames Society. The report resulting from that survey highlighted various problems and suggested the creation of new river crossings and stretches of newly made footpath.

In 1980 the Thames Water Authority gave its general support to the principle of a continuous Thames Walk, and four years later the Countryside Commission itself publicly announced its intention to create a long-distance route alongside the river. In 1985 Jenny Blair was appointed Project Officer, and the proposals arising from her study were put to the Secretary of State for

the Environment in 1988 for his official sanction.

It is an easy walk, a level walk, a walk that is accessible for much of the way by public transport—at least from London to Oxford—and one that has almost as many tempting diversions as it has miles. It will suit the stroller looking for an hour or so's exercise every bit as much as the long-distance strider eating the miles. In fact it is the ultimate in walks for those with only an odd weekend to devote to it. The River Thames is unhurrying and leisurely and one could return time and again to its banks over a number of years and always find a welcome in its gentle character.

To walk the whole route in one outing will require around ten to twelve days, although it could be achieved in less by those with no desire to stray here and there to poke into additional corners of interest. There's plenty of accommodation available in the river's lower reaches, although London prices will inevitably dominate. There are several Youth Hostels spaced along the route within a mile or two of the actual path, as well as various bed and breakfast establishments.

The 'official' route is expected to begin at Greenwich. However, this 'unofficial' walk starts at Putney Bridge and goes upstream through Richmond, Windsor, Henley, and on between Goring and Streatley where the river breaks through the chalk of the Chilterns. It continues along the Thames Valley to Abingdon and Oxford, then out among low meadows to Lechlade where the river becomes more narrow and sinuous, to Cricklade and finally among farmland in search of the springs that traditionally mark the source of London's river.

For those who know the Thames only by reputation, this walk will be an eye-opener. There is so much to see, so much to do. There's such a rich tapestry being woven by the river; a nation's history is intertwined from the very start and it continues on more than half the route to the hills that spawn it. But that's not all. There's a soft and benevolent landscape too. It's not lonely. It's a peopled land, and if they're not actually sharing the river or the river bank with you, they'll never be far from it. They and the ducks and geese, the swans and coot and moorhen, the voles and fieldmice, butterflies and dragonflies.

Winter mists fail to hide the splendour of Windsor Castle across the river.

Days 1–5: Putney Bridge to Goring

Those who were brought up amid Boat Race fever will recognise details at the start of this walk, for the initial 4 miles (6km) or so to the Ship Inn at Mortlake follow the course of the annual race between Oxford and Cambridge Universities. The first such race, held in 1829, was not rowed here at all but at Henley. Then it was moved to the stretch of river between Westminster and Putney, but there was so much river traffic that the race had to be transferred to the Putney–Mortlake course in 1846. It has been raced here ever since.

The towpath begins on the right bank heading upstream. It's a busy place of barges and boathouses, with the eights and skulls of both the London Rowing Club and Westminster School often seen practising their sport with great vigour. It's distinctly urban, of course, but soon there will be surprising touches of the rural where old reservoirs and wasteland areas are popu-

lated by waterbirds. On the opposite bank Hammersmith is reached by an ornate and colourful bridge, but you ignore this and continue on the right bank. Beyond Mortlake the river persists in its snake-like writhings as you pass alongside the Royal Botanic Gardens at Kew and the Old Richmond Deer Park. Richmond Lock is the first of many; the next is at Teddington where the nearby weir is not only the largest and most spectacular on the river, but it also marks the boundary between the tidal and non-tidal Thames.

At Kingston, 13 miles (21km) from Putney Bridge, you must cross the river and follow Barge Walk round the sweeping curve that gives a more cautious approach to Hampton Court Palace than is offered by the optional short cut directly across the park from Hampton Wick.

Hampton Court is known throughout the world, for the world comes to Hampton Court. It's an imposing building and a result of Cardinal Wolsey's driving ambition. Born

mountain cranesbill *(Geranium pyrenaicum)*, a plant native to the Pyrénées, growing along some of the banks. Seen in its traditional mountain setting one would hardly expect to find it in an urban environment beside the Thames. But such is the adaptability of Nature.

At Weybridge the river is joined by the Wey Navigation, one of the earliest rivers to be worked as a canal. This ran between Weybridge and Guildford, with an extension as far as Godalming and a rather short-lived route to join the Arun in Sussex. This canal link between the Thames and the south coast closed over a hundred years ago.

The north bank is rejoined at Chertsey and then it's back to the south side by way of Staines Bridge. Cooper's Hill rises ahead with its dignified memorial to all those airmen who died in the Second World War. Below it spreads the meadow of Runnymede where King John met his barons in 1215 to set the seal to Magna Carta. Nearby too, is the Kennedy Memorial, built on an acre of land given to the American people.

Historic associations seem to run in groups and as the miles are devoured so the gleaming fairytale turrets of Windsor Castle come into view. The walk dodges from one side of the river to the other, and the castle looms one moment and hides shyly the next—but only momentarily, for the town is dominated by its overpowering presence. It was Henry II who built the castle between 1165 and 1179, but successive monarchs have contributed to its steady growth, and probably none more so than Queen Victoria who spent more than a million pounds on its refurbishment.

Royal Windsor is not a place to scurry through, even were that possible with a

Left: **From the arches of the Town Hall, one of Abingdon's several churches is clearly seen.**

Right above: **Abingdon stands on the right bank of the Thames. One of the town's occupants stretches its wings before taking the plunge.**

Below: **Seen from the river, Oxford's city skyline is one of the finest in southern England.**

the son of an Ipswich butcher, Wolsey was a gifted man who, by the time he was forty, had created for himself an income of £100,000 a year. In 1514 he began to build the grandest private house in all England, thus upsetting Henry VIII who later brought about his downfall. It was Henry then who took over the house, added the Great Hall and made it a Royal Palace, spending more money on it than on any other building. Wren made some additions on behalf of William III, but structurally

little has been done to it since.

Although a fee is charged for entrance to the Palace, access to the park, gardens and courtyards is free. There is a restaurant and a cafeteria here, open daily from Easter to September.

Immediately after the Palace the walk recrosses the Thames to its south bank, and heads upstream to Molesey Lock, past some reservoirs at West Molesey and on to Sunbury Locks. Walton on Thames comes next, and it is here that one may discover the

rucksack on your back and the milling crowds of tourists thronging every street. It's very much a dawdler's town, while on the opposite bank stands Eton with its world-famous College, founded by Henry VI in 1440. Between Windsor and Eton the river is white with swans as, indeed, it appears to be along so many reaches. Long regarded as a royal bird, Thames swans, in fact, belong not only to the Queen but also to the Vintners' and the Dyers' Companies. Between Blackfriars and Henley, which is the limit of the Swan Keeper's jurisdiction, the Crown owns about 500 swans and cygnets, and these are marked in July at the annual Swan Upping.

Below the castle the Thames Walk crosses from Windsor to the Eton bank, and after cutting along Brocas Street and behind more boathouses, you head out along open meadows on the grassy towpath with fine views back towards the castle, now seen suspended above the town. Beyond Boveney Lock there is a broad open stretch of walking along the river bank in what is known as Thames Field. The village of Dorney, worth a diversion to see, stands off to the right, while ahead roars the M4 motorway. Just before passing beneath this extremely busy highway, Monkey Island is seen on the opposite bank where the Third Duke of Marlborough built a fishing lodge and pavilion in 1744.

By the time the walk reaches Cookham you'll have grown used to locks and weirs, will have seen much of historic interest and beauty, and will now be enjoying more peaceful acres and a lessening of London overspill. A rural aspect, uncluttered and unhurried, begins now to emerge with greater insistence. On the left bank rise the delightful beech woods of the Cliveden estate whose magnificent landscaped gardens and historic mansion, now in the hands of the National Trust, have been a venue of political intrigue and scandal on more than one occasion. On the terrace of the first house (there have been three fires destroying successive houses) the Duke of Buckingham killed the Earl of Shrewsbury in a duel in 1668, while Lady Shrewsbury looked on disguised as a page.

The present house, with its forty-six bedrooms, was designed by Sir Charles Barry in 1862. William Waldorf Astor, the American hotelier who later acquired and restored Hever Castle in Kent, bought Cliveden from the Duke of Westminster for $6,000,000 in 1893. During the 1930s guests at the weekend house-parties were dubbed the 'Cliveden Set' and accused of plotting appeasement with Nazi Germany. Then, in the summer of 1963, the house again hit the headlines when the scandal of the Profumo affair, which began here, rocked the Conservative government.

Oxford—silent witnesses to river life look down from their nineteenth-century perch on Folly Bridge.

A woodland path takes you away from the river near the site of the former My Lady Ferry (last of the ferries operated by the Thames Conservancy), and brings the walk into the attractive, well-preserved village of Cookham.

A little farther upstream and you come to Marlow, a bustling, Georgian place with a fine suspension bridge and a weir overlooked by All Saints Church. It was here that Mary Shelley wrote *Frankenstein* while living in West Street with her poet husband. Marlow occupies the north bank of the river and has much to offer, especially if you're in need of refreshment, but it is only briefly visited on the walk before a return is made once more to the southern side by way of Tierny Clark's suspension bridge.

It's a morning's walk from Marlow to Henley, all of it on the right bank with the river making its customary twists and turns, with little islands and trees dipping, birds calling, the Chiltern hills moulding among bowers of leaf to the north. There are three locks to distract and delay you should river craft be working through. At Hurley Lock a pair of wooden footbridges take you over the cut and away from the village. Shortly after passing Frogmill, with the river on another curve, you see the Gothic curiosity of Medmenham Abbey on the opposite bank where the notorious and eccentric Sir Francis Dashwood (1708–81) gathered members of the self-styled Franciscans of Medmenham, erected an inscription over the door proclaiming *Fay ce que voudras* ('Do whatever you like'), and acted out obscene parodies of Catholic rites there.

Then, also on the opposite bank, you will come to one of the best-loved sights of the Thames; a large, white, weatherboarded mill beside a weir. This is Hambledon Mill, thought to date from the sixteenth century and in use until 1958, the final twenty years of its working life being powered by a water-driven turbine. Given time it is well worth crossing the river at Hambledon Lock and wandering the mile or so to Hambledon village tucked in a fold of the Chiltern hills. A classic composition of flint and brick, a fine village green and a fourteenth-century church, Hambledon is considered by many to be one of the loveliest villages in all of Buckinghamshire.

Resuming the walk on the right bank the towpath leads round by Temple Island and along Henley Reach, the straight line of the river that is the course for Henley Royal Regatta, held each year during the first

week of July. Should you need a bed for the night, there's Youth Hostel accommodation in Henley, otherwise the alternatives could be rather pricey.

From Henley to Sonning, a distance of about 6 or 7 miles (10–11km), the walk follows the left bank of the Thames, then returns to the south bank by way of the eighteenth-century Sonning Bridge where the river is split into three channels. Heading upstream the towpath takes you through meadows with Reading's industrial sprawl seen ahead. Up and over the 'horseshoe bridge' where the River Kennet joins the Thames, and very soon you tread the waterfront of Berkshire's major town. Half a day's steady walking will bring you to the gap in the Chilterns where sits Streatley on the right bank and Goring on the left. Across the bridge which joins the two comes the Ridgeway Path. Under the bridge goes the Thames Walk, but for Youth Hostel accommodation you'll need to cross over into Streatley. You've come to the halfway mark on the walk, and the upper reaches of the Thames will lead on into a more peaceful, more deserted series of landscapes. Streatley is as good a place as any to take stock of the situation.

Days 6–12: Goring to Kemble

It is possible to walk on either side of the river for the 6 miles (10km) or so between Goring and Wallingford, but in both cases it will be necessary to stray away from the bank for a short distance. In the past there were at least three ferries operating on this stretch of the Thames and their demise makes it impossible today to follow the towpath all the way.

On the right bank (Streatley side) the towpath is rejoined after a brief diversion to avoid the Swan Hotel, then you wander among trees and across open grassland meadows to Cleeve Lock, and beyond that as far as the Beetle and Wedge Hotel at Moulsford. Large houses with trim lawns block any further existence of the towpath here, but in times past this was the site of one of the sixpenny (2½p) ferries leading to the continuing path on the opposite bank. From the Beetle and Wedge it is necessary to make a diversion along the busy A329 for a little over half a mile and then return to the towpath again at the former Little Stoke ferry. From here it's fairly straightforward walking along the bank as far as Wallingford.

If you decide to follow the left bank from

Goring, however, much of the route is shared with that of the Ridgeway Path. At South Stoke there's refreshment to be had in the lovely flint-walled Perch and Pike pub in the narrow main street, but soon after passing this you cut down a track to the towpath once more, which you rejoin opposite the Beetle and Wedge. Along the low-lying meadows as you wander towards Little Stoke and North Stoke, Moulsford's small but attractive church is glimpsed half-hidden across the river among trees.

Under Brunel's railway bridge the way soon brings you to Little Stoke ferry where yet again the towpath exchanges banks and, in lieu of an easy crossing, you have to remain on the left bank and then cut away from the water at North Stoke. Among trees and bushes you suddenly find yourself going through the churchyard and out again beside black barns and a handsome pink house, through the grounds of Carmel College and then, leaving the Ridgeway Path as it breaks away eastwards on its journey to Ivinghoe, continue to the north to Crowmarsh Gifford which gazes across the river at Wallingford.

For something like two thousand years Wallingford has been an important Thames crossing. On the right bank the Saxons fortified the town. Then the Normans built a castle to defend the site but this was destroyed in 1646 by Fairfax. There are few remains of it left today and those that are to be found are on the wrong side of the river to be explored from the route of the Thames Walk.

Abingdon is the next important town on the river, 14 miles (23km) upstream of Wallingford, but on the way to it a short diversion into the old Roman town of Dorchester, once the centre of England's largest diocese, is well worth the time given to it—especially the great abbey church with its wonderful Jesse window. But later, when you arrive alongside the river below the town of Abingdon, you will know that here is a place with plenty to delay you too.

Although once the county town of Berkshire, Abingdon now finds itself in Oxfordshire. A lovely old market town, it grew around a seventh-century abbey, but the most memorable features today are the church of St Helen's, whose spire marks one of the first signs of Abingdon, the bastille-like jail by the bridge—now a leisure centre—and the many-arched Town Hall that was built by one of Christopher Wren's masons. This marks the centre of the town and is now home to a museum of local history. But of more immediate importance to the walker passing through will be the refreshment places found just a short stroll uphill from the river. There is also a good bus service from here to Oxford.

An afternoon's easy walking will take you to Oxford on the west bank all the way. This is where you will no doubt have more river company than anywhere since leaving London, for there are crews in training, sweating against their oars, and their cycle-bound coaches pedalling along the towpath and calling instructions as they do. At Radley you pass college boathouses but nearer to the city there are many more—boathouses on both banks and no shortage of boats skimming through the waters between.

The outskirts of Oxford are a little 'tatty', but as you are drawn ever-closer along the towpath, so you have one of England's finest city skylines—all spires and domes and turrets—etched as a sun-catching profile across the levels of Christ Church Meadow beyond the river. Matthew Arnold called it 'sweet city of dreaming spires'. And this is just what it seems from the Thames towpath.

Is it possible, I wonder, to walk on by? I think not. Oxford is not the city to allow you to sneak away, however much Cotswold anticipation lures from the west. But you cannot 'do' Oxford in a sprint round Christ Church Quadrangle; nor with a cursory glance from the tower of St Mary the Virgin's church; nor along the backwaters of the Cherwell; nor the Ashmolean Museum between breakfast and elevenses. There's a Youth Hostel here and it would be sensible to book in for a couple of nights or more and spend time exploring this magical city before heading out on what will be the final third of the walk. (Of all the routes in this book, the Thames Walk has so many temptations to stray from the 'straight and narrow' that it would take a very single-minded walker indeed to remain true to the path all the way.)

Fifty miles (80km) remain to be walked between Oxford and the source of the Thames; two very full days, or three or four reasonable stages with the river becoming narrower and less emphatic as it writhes among the broad green meadows of Oxfordshire and, from Lechlade, those of Wiltshire and Gloucestershire. As far as Lechlade the river is navigable for Thames cruisers and it was there that barges loaded with Cotswold stone for building would traditionally set out on their journey to London. But Lechlade is still nearly 30 miles (48km) from Oxford—along the Thames. The crow flies a considerably shorter journey, while the river meanders in a sinuous northerly bow away from the city before correcting itself.

A little way upstream from Oxford you wander past Godstow Lock, and it was in July 1862, on one of his outings on the river with the three daughters of Dean Liddell of Christ Church, that the Rev. Charles Dodgson (Lewis Carroll) came here, and actually composed the story of *Alice's Adventures in Wonderland* as he rowed.

> Full many a year has slipped away since that golden afternoon, but I can call it up almost as clearly as if it were yesterday—the cloudless blue above, the watery mirror below, the boat drifting idly on its way, the tinkle of the drops that fell from the oars, as they wavered so sleepily to and fro, and . . . the three eager faces, hungry for news of fairyland, and who would not be said 'nay' to—from those lips 'Tell us a story, please' had all the stern immutability of Fate.

Beyond Godstow Lock you pass Kings Lock at the northern-most part of the Thames where the river twists back, and it is not long after this that you have a view of Crassington church spire growing out of the countryside on the north bank. You then reach Wytham Great Wood. Owned by Oxford University, the wood, which covers some 600 acres in all, comes right down to the river bank. Beyond the wood is a wharf stream on the north side of the river which used to take barges carrying cargo to and from Eynsham. Then comes Eynsham Lock and the stone-balustraded triple-arched Swinford Bridge, built in 1769 on behalf of the fourth Earl of Abingdon to replace a ferry. Swinford Bridge is one of only two remaining toll bridges on the Thames and the crossing fee of 2p is received still by descendents of the Earl who built it.

The Thames is nervous among ox bows now; there are reservoirs near Pinkhill Lock that pump water from the river—one of these can hold 1000 million gallons—and, in a dry summer, pump it back again to restore the levels and supply downstream waterworks. Farmoor Reservoir is stocked every year with rainbow trout, and its banks are busy with fishermen.

At Bablock Hythe the towpath crosses to the north bank and, if you've timed your arrival right, you may call the publican at the Ferry Inn, who offers a half-hourly ferry service during opening hours, to take you over. (The alternative is to cross the river 2 miles (3km) downstream at Pinkhill Lock and follow a footpath from there.)

There are riverside meadows, green and smooth as you tread more and more remote countryside; the Thames narrowing but writhing still; farms seen across the fields, and villages with a spire here, a tower there. There are weirs and locks and hump-backed bridges, and anglers perched quietly on the margins of the river.

A day's walking from the Bablock Hythe ferry brings you to a teasing view of Lechlade across the low meadows, its graceful spire beckoning as you approach St John's Lock, formerly the upper limit for Thames barges. The towpath, which has been on the north bank since Radcot Bridge, now crosses to the south bank, while Lechlade itself is on the far side, but reached by a footpath from the bridge above the lock. If you need refreshments, leave the towpath here and visit this soft golden grey Cotswold town.

Three hundred years ago Matthew Baskervile visited Lechlade and found a fair by St John's Bridge. (This fair was established as early as 1234.) He wrote:

> It is a great fair for Cattle & Cheese, & here you meet with brave sage cheese no place elsewhere in England shews the like, much diversified in figures, green and white, as to round chees, and some in shape of Dolphins & Mermaids, as Countrey Carvers display them in Cheesfats.

Beside St John's Lock the reclining figure of Old Father Thames makes a pleasing picture. Originally made to adorn the Crystal Palace, the statue was later rescued from its burned-out ruins and taken to Thames Head, where it lay in a cage by the ash tree that guards the spring-fed pool which, by tradition, is the source of the Thames. It was more recently brought to St John's Lock for protection under the watchful eye of the lock-keeper.

Crossing the river at Lechlade is another of those Thames toll bridges, this one dating from the eighteenth century and known today as Halfpenny Bridge. The old toll house can still be seen beside it.

Upstream now the river becomes too shallow for boats and a mile from the town sees the end of the towpath. Because of this the Thames Walk is forced to stray away from the river and along the busy A361 for more than a mile to Upper Inglesham. The

Near Lechlade the Thames winds through low-lying meadows to St John's Lock.

Countryside Commission has recognised this unfortunate diversion by proposing a new footpath be created along the right bank between Inglesham church and Upper Inglesham, and we may hope that this improvement comes to fruition before too long. Upper Inglesham, however, does offer the opportunity to find accommodation in the small, 200 year-old stone cottage that is the Youth Hostel. It is the last hostel on the walk, and its position gives you one final day's walking of about 20 miles (32km) to reach the source.

You return to the river at Hannington Bridge where the Romans once crossed and, keeping to the south side, follow footpaths across farmland and then along a lane to Castle Eaton, a small village set beside the infant Thames. A mile or so from Cricklade a footbridge takes you across to the north

bank and along the riverside among hunched anglers, back to the south bank and into the town.

It's a neat little town with a character all its own, built on a slope with the former Roman road of Ermine Street passing by. In low-lying watermeadows flocks of snipe are said to spend the winter, and from here the Thames becomes yet more shallow, with bulrushes growing along its margins. North Meadow is a splendid place, an ancient meadowland and a Nature Reserve famed for its Snakeshead fritillaries. Our path goes through it.

Twelve miles (19km) remain to be walked, much of the way alongside the shrinking stream, but diverting from it in places in lieu of convenient footpaths. It's a countryside route, with the Cotswolds rolling to the north and the west, with one or two villages to visit: Ashton Keynes, with golden stone, and streams running gaily through the streets; Somerford Keynes where some of the highest mills on the Thames were worked when the river's meagre channel was cut and improved to

increase the flow. (There are no working mills left on the Thames today.)

There are flooded gravel pits all around Somerford Keynes, but you break away from them to pass Upper Mill Farm, and on to Ewen with Kemble a short distance to the west (with its rail link to Swindon or Stroud). A footpath takes you from the Ewen-Kemble road alongside the stream to the A429 and the last bridge on the Thames. A wedge of farmland between two major roads is the site of one of the Thames springs, marked by a windpump, but you continue ahead and cross the A433 (the Roman road known as Fosse Way leading from Bath to Cirencester), wander through a gentle broad valley and come to the stone block that announces your arrival at Thames Head, the source of the Thames.

Maybe the ground will be dry, and you'll feel cheated and somewhat mystified. But look back at the discoveries you've made since leaving Putney Bridge, and acknowledge that the Thames Walk had many lessons to teach. And many pleasures to share.

WALK 9: *The Ridgeway Path*

The Ridgeway path crosses the Thames between Streatley and Goring.

Distance: 89 miles (143km).
Time Required: 5–6 days.
Type of Walk: A long-distance walk following the line of chalk hills stretching across Wiltshire and off to Hertfordshire. It is an ancient trading route which passes a number of impressive prehistoric sites that give the walk its essential character. There are few difficulties to be encountered. The tracks are mostly broad and clear—although they can become sticky in wet weather.
Start: Overton Hill on the A4 near Avebury, Wiltshire.
Finish: Ivinghoe Beacon, Buckinghamshire.
Maps: O.S. Landranger series 173, 174, 175, 165.
Guidebooks: *The Ridgeway Path* by Sean Jennett (HMSO). *The Ridgeway Path* by H D Westacott & Mark Richards (Penguin).

Ridgeway Information and Accommodation Guide by D Venner (published by, and available from: Oxfordshire County Council, Dept of Planning and Leisure Property Services, Speedwell House, Speedwell Street, Oxford OX1 1SD).

Walking through History from Overton Hill to Ivinghoe Beacon

One gains an impression of space on this walk, at times almost more profoundly so than on many of the others included within these pages. That impression is not entirely unwarranted either, despite the proximity of towns and villages, major roads and the interruption caused by the crossing of the

Thames between Streatley and Goring. For along the Ridgeway the walker treads an elevated path which overlooks the plains of Wiltshire, Berkshire, Oxfordshire and Buckinghamshire—not forgetting too, part of Hertfordshire. Walked at the end of autumn when the fields are bare and ploughs turn the earth beneath a pale sun (later to set into an afternoon's misted horizon bleeding behind you to a chorus of jackdaws and starlings), you'd find it hard to believe that one of the world's largest cities is but a relatively short distance away to the east.

There is little scenic drama along these Downs. The character of the Ridgeway lies elsewhere. The Downs, after all, are not mountains, although their flanks may at times appear as steep as mountain slopes. They have neither jutting crags nor shapely summits but they're certainly not without individual features of an unchallenged loveliness that will excite the perceptive rambler and greatly increase the day's pleasures. And is there anything wrong with the fact that many of these features are there by the hand of man? I think not. The Ridgeway is, after all, a natural highway and from time immemorial man has used it as such. It would be astonishing if he had not left behind him anything more than Neolithic footprints.

It is impossible to lose sight of the fact that the Ridgeway forms a highway. As is true of many another downland ridge featured in this book, it projects from the hub of an important stone civilisation, represented here by the awe-inspiring, massive circles of upright stones at Avebury. All around Avebury—at Silbury Hill, at West Kennett and East Kennett Long Barrows, and at Windmill Hill to the north of the village—the enormity of the past is inescapable, and history follows like a dark shadow as you work your steady way north-eastwards.

The 85 miles (137km) from Overton Hill to Ivinghoe Beacon represent only a small, yet important, portion of a much longer, more extensive route paced by our Neolithic forebears. That extensive route cut a trail right across England's bottom right-hand corner, from the Devon/Dorset coast to the Wash of East Anglia, forming the means by which a rich variety of cultures were brought to ancient Britain from continental Europe. The trail of the Ridgeway through Wessex is today more or less defined by a meandering line extending south of Overton Hill to Lyme Regis, and the Ramblers

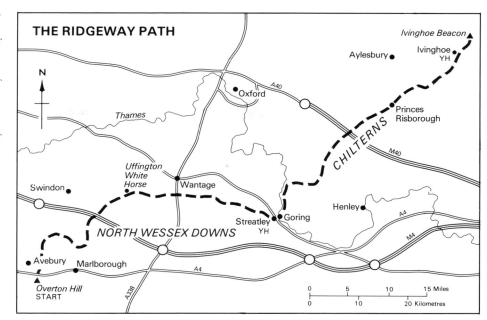

THE RIDGEWAY PATH

Association is currently campaigning for this extended route to be adopted as another officially designated long-distance path, called the Wessex Ridgeway. (A guidebook to this route, *The Wessex Ridgeway* is available from the R.A.)

At the other end of the Ridgeway Path to the north of Ivinghoe, the *Icknield Way* continues to Thetford on the Suffolk/Norfolk border, and from there to the Norfolk coast along a Romanised section known today as the *Peddars Way*. Combining these assorted Ways into one monstrous walk would create a path nearly 400 miles (644km) long. For our purposes, though, be it sufficient to concentrate on the section known as the Ridgeway Path which, since its opening in 1973, has become one of the most popular of all our long-distance routes.

This popularity has its setbacks. It's an accessible route; some might say almost too accessible for its own good. The mostly open chalk downland section between Overton Hill and the Thames is along a bridleway shared by cyclists and riders. There are tracks, or green roads, that are available to motor vehicles (not just farm vehicles), with the result that at times confrontations have inevitably occurred between walkers and trails riders whose mutual rights of passage have been difficult to accommodate. Beyond the Thames, however, the path is a much more piecemeal affair which strays along the base of the Chilterns for a while then, near Princes Risborough, it returns to the hilltops

among beech woods before trees become more sparse again near the end of the walk. Not all of this half of the Way is designated bridleway or green road, so walkers are mostly left to wander the footpaths alone and without fear that the peace of the countryside will be assaulted by the scream of highly-tuned engines.

To say that the Ridgeway is a 'dry' walk may seem strange coming from someone who experienced no shortage of puddles or muddy patches during an autumnal journey! But dry it is—both from the point of view of surface streams and availability of drinking water. Walkers are therefore recommended to carry sufficient liquid refreshments with them on each stage of the route, although there will be opportunities now and then to top up at a pub or village shop with something stronger than just water.

Four or five days should be adequate time for active, long-distance walkers to complete this route, but as with most journeys, he who wanders with an enquiring mind will gain most from this series of landscapes if the march of time is not allowed to dictate the pace. I would therefore recommend taking maybe five or six days over it, although there are enough temptations to stray from the straight and narrow (or, as it may be, wide and winding) trail, so that a week would not be too long to stroll from A to B. And then you'd still be sure to have missed something of interest.

commencing his journey, by treating Avebury to an act of pilgrimage too. Few could fail to be moved by what they find there.

First the stone avenue; like markers of some prehistoric racecourse, these dual lines of upright stones stretch to the south-east of the village, and if approached from the Overton Hill area, are the first obvious signs to catch the eye. On their own they would be worthy of remark but as they merely lead to greater wonders, one tends almost to dismiss their significance from mind—and this is understandable, since the stone circles to be shortly discovered as you wander north along the avenue represent one of Europe's most impressive sites and the mightiest circle henge in the British Isles.

Go there early in the morning when all is peace and quiet, with just a few sheep grazing in the long, dawn shadows that fall from the sarsens, and where magpies bounce in the frost—and you can almost hear the pad of Neolithic footsteps. Whispers of the past come flooding with the rising of the sun, and you'll be captured by the magnificence of our ancestors' achievement. Are these huge open circles (religious symbols of their time) any less awe-inspiring than the great Christian cathedrals of the Middle Ages? I doubt it. Each is a product of intense dedicated labour to which we can only turn and marvel.

Pottery finds suggest that Avebury's stone circles were begun between 3000 and 2000 BC when perhaps three circles were created as well as the stone avenue. But imagine with what ingenuity these monstrous sarsen stones, ninety-eight of them and some weighing up to 40 tons, were dragged from the Downs and then raised to their present positions. And then consider the effort required by the Beaker People to excavate the huge ditch around the circles, enclosing nearly thirty acres in all, and to create the massive bank above it. From the top of this bank one gains an astonishing view of

Above: **Pitstone Windmill (National Trust owned) brightens the low-lying countryside below Ivinghoe Beacon.**

Below: **At once the Ridgeway Path scores its way across a bald and open landscape.**

Whilst the official start to the Ridgeway Path is on a track running alongside a transport café on Overton Hill a couple of miles or so from Avebury, none but the most blinkered of walkers would set out from here without having first paid homage to the original Ridgeway ramblers of some five thousand years or more ago. Since Avebury's wonderful and well-known stone circles and stone avenue would no doubt have been a focus of any journey along these Downs in the far distant past, the modern walker ought to spare an hour or two before

Right above: **The hamlet of Woolstone nestles below the Downs near the White Horse of Uffington.**

Below: **The flint-walled pub, the Perch and Pike, stands in the village of South Stoke, a short walk from Goring on the Thames.**

Avebury; an impression that will last for many a long Ridgeway mile.

Days 1–3: Avebury to Streatley

The Ridgeway begins as a broad flinty track scored along the crest of the bare Downs. This is Richard Jefferies' country without question; the land he knew and loved as a boy and which inspired in him a deep understanding of the natural world. There are vast panoramas, a huge sky, beech-clad knolls that disguise Bronze Age round barrows but offer scant protection from the breezes that come unchecked across the plains below. Wind- and water-proofs are a must for this walk. Avebury lies in a bowl out of sight to the left but after a couple of miles you come to a crossing track known as the Herepath, another ancient track, which leads down into that bowl. (If you begin your Ridgeway journey at Avebury's stone circles, it would be feasible to short-cut Overton Hill and use the Herepath for access to the route.)

Now you're on the edge of Fyfield Down, a National Nature Reserve and a prehistoric landscape littered with sarsens, those remnants of a vast layer of sandstone laid down some twenty to thirty million years ago as a covering to the chalk of the Downs. These sarsens are sometimes called 'Grey Wethers' although their colouring varies in the changing light. A barrow was constructed here as an experiment in the early 1960s in order that archaeologists could monitor changes caused by erosion and vegetation and it is amusing to speculate on a possible debate between historians of some futuristic civilisation as they discuss the particular reasoning behind this twentieth century barrow!

Over Hackpen Hill the hillfort of Barbury Castle appears ahead, and beyond that, beyond Swindon's blotch, spreads a hint of the lovely Vale of the White Horse into which a magnificient view is later gained. There is another white horse carved in the chalk below Hackpen Hill, though it is not actually seen from the path. It's a copy of the famous White Horse of Uffington and was made in 1838.

At 880 feet (268m), Barbury Castle has a commanding view and, although the historic line of the Ridgeway passes to one side of it, our modern route goes right through it. This Iron Age fort covers almost twelve acres. It has two ramparts and ditches, and after the Romans had left it was refortified by the Britons in order to defend the Thames valley. On the downland slopes below the hill an historic battle (the Battle of Bera Byrg) was fought in AD 556 against the invading Saxons, in which the Britons were defeated.

Since the historic Ridgeway has been engulfed by a modern road, the Countryside Commission's route creates a diversion, swings away in a southerly loop and exploits the line of yet another ancient route along the chalk crest of Smeathe's Ridge. This makes a delightful stretch of walking and it leads to Ogbourne Down and from there on a steady descent to the tiny, one-street village of Ogbourne St George.

The Ridgeway proper is rejoined at Fox Hill on the northern side of the M4 motorway, but between Ogbourne St George and Fox Hill you pass several strip lynchets and ancient ditches, and the Iron Age hillfort of Liddington Castle that was one of Richard Jefferies' favourite haunts. This great nineteenth-century natural history writer (one of the finest and best-loved of them all) was born at Coate on the outskirts of Swindon, and he often climbed the slopes of Liddington Hill from which he drew so much inspiration. There is a plinth on the hilltop bearing a plaque to record the affection with which he is held today.

More Saxon-made strip lynchets are seen almost a mile from Fox Hill, but the track is now mostly blinkered and contained by hedges on a straight line running parallel with the Icknield Way that follows the lower, northern slope of the Downs. The track is muddy in places, even days after rain, and it is not always possible to avoid some of the larger puddles because of the constricting hedgerows.

Wiltshire is left behind and you enter Oxfordshire. Then you cross a minor road above the pleasant village of Ashbury, and a mile later come to Wayland's Smithy. Wayland was blacksmith to the Saxon gods, and the 'smithy' here is a huge long barrow, thought to date from about 3000 BC. It is all of 180 feet (55m) long, 48 feet (15m) wide at the front end and about 20 feet (6m) at the rear. When I arrived there, hoping to take photographs of it, the place was swarming with two school parties, the children making notes and measuring the site with welly-booted strides under the direction of their enthusiastic teachers. I could well appreciate their enthusiasm, although mine was kept in check by frustration caused by my inability to get a pupil-free shot of it!

Leaving Wayland's Smithy the track takes you beyond a small wood and out to the glory of the grassy Downs. This grassland is welcome after so much plough-turned expanse, and coming close to the northern edge the views are tremendous as you gaze out over the Vale of the White Horse and into a patchwork of meadows and fields picked out by lines of trees and hedges. This is one of the loveliest parts of the walk and it is understandably popular. The White Horse of Uffington, the very symbol of these Downs, is picked out in chalk on the steep northern slope, but you cannot see it from the Ridgeway, nor with ease from many places below. A number of theories have been put forward as to its origin (like the Long Man of Wilmington on the South Downs and the Cerne Abbas Giant in Dorset), and the latest, most acceptable suggestion is that it dates from the Iron Age because of similarities in the shape of horses depicted on coins of the period. There has been a lot of weeding, then, to keep the horse white for over 2000 years, and the day I was there a workman was busy with a strimmer keeping the outline untroubled by a grassy mane.

Traditionally the 'scouring' of the White Horse was the duty of villagers whose parishes along the spring line at the base of the Downs formed the Hundred of Hildeslow, and over the years it became an event celebrated with games and fairs. In 1780 it is said that 30,000 people came for the scouring. And Thomas Hughes, who was born in Uffington in 1822, described the event of 1857 when cheese-rolling was one of the main attractions.

Perhaps the best view to be had from here is from the lip of the Manger, that curious, narrow, steep-sided coombe that directs one's attention to a nestle of village and spinney and the broad stretch of the lowlands beyond. Woolstone lies down there below the Manger; a shy collection of cottages and pub sunken into the roots of the land and with the Downs creating a protective wall behind. The Romans were in Woolstone, and in the remains of their villa was discovered a black and white mosaic.

Above the White Horse is Uffington Castle. This is yet another Iron Age hillfort on the very edge of the Downs, with one or two sheep pens wedged in its surrounding ditch at crazy angles. The Ridgeway Path continues eastward from it, mile upon mile of broad open spaces, open to the wind and the sun; a kingdom set aside from the lowlands of industry and conurbation. It makes for easy, carefree walking, and when you gaze out over the Thames valley on a clear day you can make out the line of the Cotswolds beckoning from afar.

Two hours, or half a dozen miles (10km), beyond Uffington, the track brings you to Segsbury Camp, otherwise known as Letcombe Castle, one more in the long procession of Iron Age hillforts built along the Ridgeway as if to emphasise yet again the importance of this downland route through history. Shortly after passing this you come to the A338 where it crosses Angel Down. Wantage lies some 3 miles (5km) down hill to the north, an attractive little town that was the birthplace of King Alfred, and 2 miles further along the walk, an unofficial long-distance path called King Alfred's Way crosses ours on Wether Down. Just before

This beech-crowned hillock is passed early on the first day of the Ridgeway Path.

coming to this path, however, you pass an imposing monument to the local benefactor and hero of the Crimean War, Robert Loyd Lindsay, Baron Wantage.

By direct contrast to the great number of archaeologically interesting constructions along the Ridgeway, one becomes aggravated by the distant presence of the cooling towers of Didcot Power Station ominously smoking amid a horizontal landscape. Those lofty white chimneys confront the scene with a display of arrogant disregard for the lie of the land. They are on show for miles, making no attempt to blend with the landscape or to shield themselves from view, and their presence down in the Vale persists over more than a day's steady walking. Nearer to hand the proliferation of brick that makes up the Harwell Atomic Energy Research Establishment complex is another blot on the landscape, the more so because of the empty grandeur of the open Downs to which you've grown accustomed. (On a long walk such as this, architecture often takes on a fresh significance, especially

when that long walk travels through unknown countryside. The walker adopts a greater sense of architectural awareness, as buildings are seen as part of the countryside itself—buildings are extensions of the land, not simply houses or offices or even research establishments and power stations.)

With the introduction of turnpikes on main roads in the eighteenth century, the Ridgeway was used as a drove road, with cattle and sheep journeying along it from Wales. Wantage was an important market, but so was East Ilsley a couple of miles (3km) south of the route along the A34. A fortnightly sheep fair was held there until early this century, and 100 years ago as many as 80,000 ewes and lambs would be sold in a day.

Two hours beyond the A34 you come striding down the slope beside a golf course and into the flint and brick solidity of Thames-side Streatley, which marks the halfway point of the walk and the end to the Ridgeway proper. Behind you now the Berkshire Downs. Ahead rise the Chilterns

81

where the continuing route adopts the Icknield Way after a meandering low-level preamble, and as a consequence the very character of the walk changes, though without detracting from its charm.

Days 4–6 Streatley to Ivinghoe Beacon

Streatley and Goring face each other across the Thames with a certain prim respectability. The river has carved a swathe through the ridge of chalk at this point and imposed its own personality upon the twin towns, investing them with colour and unsuspecting gaiety, a bright interlude on the long walk. There's accommodation here, some of it rather up-market, but there's also a Youth Hostel in Streatley only a few paces off the route where ramblers are welcome and rucksacks taken for granted.

The Thames sweeps round a bend and divides to create an island or two. River craft are moored on the right-hand side of the trestled bridge as you wander over; some

may be waiting to pass through Goring Lock, bright with flowers off to the left. There's a weir, ducks and swans, and willows dangling their branches over the water. And there is always someone just 'messing about in boats', as Kenneth Grahame put it.

All in all the Thames crossing makes a welcome interval for the Ridgeway walker; a marked contrast to what has gone before and what is yet to come on the way to Ivinghoe Beacon.

On the Chilterns side of the river you turn north and wander upstream for 5 miles (8km), sometimes on the very bank, sometimes—as in South Stoke—a short distance from it; yet the atmosphere of the Thames prevails. Out of South Stoke the path takes you beneath the red brick arches of a railway bridge designed by Brunel in 1840, and half an hour later you come to the little village of North Stoke which is linked to the hamlet of Ipsden on the Chilterns slope by a quiet bye-road. The churches of

both parishes once belonged to the Abbey of Bec in Normandy. As the route leads through North Stoke churchyard, it would be worth spending a few minutes exploring the church itself; a simple place of cool, 600 year-old echoes.

It may be possible to gain the Chilterns ridge from North Stoke by taking the road to Ipsden and beyond, but the Ridgeway Path actually continues to head north for a further mile, straying through the grounds of Carmel College (a Jewish Public School) and then breaking away to the east where you rise at last to follow the remains of a Grim's Ditch (or Grim's Dyke)—the name given by the Saxons to an extensive earthwork. There was one beside the Ridgeway to the south of Wantage, and another, of semi-circular shape near Wigginton outside Tring. In his Ridgeway guide Hugh Westacott suggests that these ditches were created as territorial boundaries, while others put forward forceful arguments for their being defensive earthworks like Offa's

Left: **Below the White Horse of Uffington, which is unseen from the path, lies this curious scooped hillside known as the Manger.**

Above: **Avebury church is virtually surrounded by the magnificent stone circle, but it is a splendid building in its own right and worthy of a visit before setting out along the Ridgeway.**

Right: **Ivinghoe Beacon marks the completion of the Ridgeway Path, but from it extends the ancient Icknield Way.**

Dyke. As you wander along Grim's Ditch you can speculate on the reasons for yourself and, maybe, conclude that both purposes could be equally valid!

At the end of a 3 mile (5km) run of the ditch, during which you gain some more height, you come to the tiny village of Nuffield in whose churchyard lies William Morris, Lord Nuffield, the philanthropist and founder of the British motor industry. You cross Nuffield Common with its golfers and wander an undulating course over a rucked countryside to reach a delightful coombe with Swyncombe's squat little Norman flint church, dedicated to St Botolph, nestling within it. The Chilterns embrace you. Friendly hills they are, with clutches of beech wood, and after crossing another of their ridges the path brings you down the slope of the escarpment to the Icknield Way at last, and you follow this for the next 9 miles (14km).

The market town of Watlington lies off the route about a mile to the north, while Watlington Hill rises over the Way to the south with its distinctive carving in the chalk described by H J Massingham as being 'like the ghostly shadow of a church spire lying along the hill'. Massingham said it had been carved as a pointer for the summer equinox some two and a half thousand years ago. But Massingham was wrong. Or at least, partly wrong. It was, in fact, created by Edward Horne in 1764 who, seeing from his window Watlington church outlined against the hill, decided it would look better with a spire—so he had one carved on the hillside to suit his fancy.

On the other side of Watlington Hill, but not on the Ridgeway Path itself, Christmas Common is a reminder of the Civil War, for it is said to derive its name from a Christmas truce arranged there in 1643 between Royalists and Parliamentarians. The whole area is one of the most popular of all for walks on the Chilterns, as well as being among the loveliest sections of the eastern Ridgeway Path which traverses below. The chalk downland, with its spinneys and ragged sprouts of blackthorn, gives fine views, while in summer the butterflies for which the Downs are known, add another dimension to a day spent in the outdoors.

Beyond Watlington Hill the path is crossed by the ancient track of the Ruggeway, now used as part of an unofficial long-distance path which links the Chilterns with the Cotswolds. The Oxfordshire Way is 65 miles (105km) long, and was the creation of the Oxfordshire group of the Council for the Protection of Rural England.

Remaining under, rather than on top of the hills, the path continues towards the concrete ribbon of the M40 which takes a slice out of the Chilterns to the right. Like the Ridgeway, the Icknield Way (Upper and Lower) was similarly used as a drover's route to London and as you wander along it at about 3 miles an hour (5kph), it is tempting to contrast the enormous difference in the speed at which sheep and cattle would have been driven on the long journey from Wales a hundred years ago, with that of the great lorries thundering along the motorway today. What would those patient drovers of old make of our world of the late twentieth century!

The upper and lower routes of the Icknield Way run parallel lines with very

At the northern end of the Ridgeway Path, Ivinghoe Youth Hostel provides welcome accommodation for walkers.

***Avebury's stone circle is one of
Europe's finest ancient monuments.***

little between them. At Chinnor the lower
route is swallowed by the B4009, while the
upper route, which is followed by the
Ridgeway Path, picks its way between chalk
quarries and goes along the edge of Bledlow
Great Wood. After this the Ridgeway and
the Upper Icknield Way part company for 3
miles (5km) or so before joining forces again
for a very short stretch—and for the last
time—on the southern outskirts of Princes
Risborough.

It's about 18 miles (29km) from Princes
Risborough to Ivinghoe Beacon, and on this
final leg at last you return to the hilltops for
long views and big skies. There is a steep
climb onto the hills among beech woods,
down to The Plough inn, then up again to
the Chequers estate, country home to
successive Prime Ministers since it was
presented to the State in 1922 by Lord Lee
of Fareham. The house dates from the
sixteenth century (although the estate is
much older), and was built by William
Hawtrey. But walkers on the Ridgeway Path
see little of it since the public right of way
makes a curve at a respectable distance, and

heads through more mature beech woods
onto the popular Coombe Hill where the
Ridgeway Path was officially opened in a
ceremony on 29th September 1973.

Coombe Hill, at 832ft (254km), is the
highest point on the Chilterns, a Site of
Special Scientific Interest and in the care of
the National Trust, to whom it was presented by the same Lord Lee of Fareham who
gave Chequers to the nation. On the hilltop
stands a much-damaged monument
dedicated to the 148 men from the Chilterns
who died in the Boer War, and below to the
east lies the small town of Wendover, which
Robert Louis Stevenson described as lying
'well down in the midst [of the plain] with
mountains and foliage about it'.

Between Coombe Hill and Wendover you
cross Bacombe Hill with its fine views.
Again, in his *Essays of Travel*, Stevenson
wrote of these:

> 'The great plain stretches away to northward,
> variegated near at hand with the quaint
> pattern of the fields, but growing ever more
> and more indistinct until it becomes a mere
> hurly-burly of trees and bright crescents of
> river and snatches of slanting road, finally
> melting away into the ambiguous cloud-land
> over the horizon.'

The continuing route takes you along
Wendover's main street before returning to
the hills once more where you remain for

half a dozen miles (10km), some rather
soggy but improving with distance. Down
then through Wigginton on the edge of
Tring, and across the dry valley sliced by the
old Roman road of Akeman Street (now the
A41). The Grand Union Canal washes
gently through the valley, imparting an air
of indolent reassurance, in calm contrast to
the trains that rattle through nearby Tring
Station.

Again you climb onto the hills, firm in the
knowledge now that the long walk is nearly
over and an hour and a half should get you
to the top of Ivinghoe Beacon. Turlhangers
Wood sees almost the last of the beeches with
which you've grown so familiar, and beyond
Aldbury Nowers you've mostly open
downland with more large vistas to enjoy.
These are regrettably spoiled by the brazen
Pitstone cement works, but if you arrive, as I
did, on the summit knob of Ivinghoe Beacon
just in time to watch the late autumnal sun
stain the western sky, those chimneys and
stark buildings somehow manage to create
an exclamation mark in a half-swallowed
landscape. They seemed to me to emphasise
that this was my journey's end, while in the
misty north-east I knew that ancient
trackways would continue for many a day
yet the line that was begun 5000 years and
more ago. There's something immensely
reassuring in that.

WALK 10: *The Cotswold Way*

Distance: 102 miles (164km).
Time Required: 6–7 days.
Type of Walk: A long-distance walk with a difference. It does not shun habitation like so many other walks, but specifically seeks out some of the loveliest of Cotswold villages and small towns nestling below the hills. As a consequence the route is very much an up-and-down one. Much of the way follows the western scarp edge on well-defined footpaths and bridleways. Waymarking is mostly good. In inclement weather some of the tracks are likely to be muddy and, in places, waterlogged.
Start: Chipping Campden, Gloucestershire.
Finish: Bath, Avon.
Maps: O.S. Landranger series 150, 151, 162, 163, 172.

Guidebooks: *The Cotswold Way* by Kev Reynolds (Cicerone Press). *The Cotswold Way* by Mark Richards (Thornhill Press and Penguin—2 separate books). *A Guide to the Cotswold Way* by Richard Sale (Constable). *Cotswold Way Handbook* (written and published by Gloucestershire Area R.A.).

Broad Views and Dainty Villages—from Chipping Campden to Bath

My arrival in Bath came at the end of a damp October day. A heavy overcast sky had eliminated twilight and brought on early evening as I wandered through the elegant city streets making for the Abbey and the ancient Roman baths at the conclusion of the Cotswold Way. Along a

Above: **An hour from the end of the walk Prospect Stile gives a view of Kelston Round Hill. The path skirts round its left flank.**

Right: **Beyond Birdlip the Cotswold Way spends a morning delving through mixed woods with sneak views teasing here and there.**

86

Above: **The ornate Jacobean gatehouse in Church Stanway.**

Below: **The old Market Hall in Chipping Campden.**

lumière—just for me.

I stopped in my tracks then, transfixed by the scene. My feet were cold, wet and a little sore. I was hungry from wandering 26 miles on a cheese roll and a Mars bar, and was growing tired. But the sight of the Abbey had me spellbound. Out of the shadows and into the light, it held me there with its symbol of peace and hope and beauty. Behind me stretched over 100 miles of wandering through a friendly, scenic, much-loved part of Britain, and this was a magnificent finish to it. The Cotswold Way ended for me as memorably as it had begun. And in between? Well, in between there had been plenty of variety and colour, history and romance, challenge and reward; something, in fact, of everything. A walk, it was, of beauty.

The Wolds are mellow uplands lying roughly north-south, with a sharp western face and a south-eastern slope that drains away gently, tilted towards the upper valley of the Thames and the Oxfordshire plain. Along the western scarp edge a series of footpaths and bridleways have been linked together to create the Cotswold Way; a switchback, to-ing and fro-ing, climbing and falling, stuttering route it is. One moment you're wandering high along the lip of the hills, the next you're heading down from them to visit a village or small town set against their ankles. Then up again, zig-zagging back and forth to catch the best the Wolds can offer. The Cotswold Way is a little over 100 miles (164km) in length, but by virtue of its meandering course you could probably create a more straightforward walk from Chipping Campden to Bath requiring little more than half that overall distance. But that would be cheating!

Other long walks in this book aim almost specifically to avoid centres of habitation. They seek out the more remote corners of southern England and shy away from towns and villages except where these are totally unavoidable. Not so the Cotswold Way. Much of the character of this route belongs to the lovely village streets with their weathered stone cottages; to the small market towns whose prosperity grew from the importance of Cotswold wool in the Middle Ages; to the efforts of man in the landscape. Each of these today helps conjure the very essence of the Wolds. But if the essence of the Wolds is owed in part to man in the landscape, another part of the walk's character belongs to the huge views from the escarpment that look over a vast lowland

deserted arcade my boots trod worn flagstones while overhead hundreds of sparrows chattered excitedly. All light had drained from the sky. The streets were emptying of people, the arcade had only its sparrows and me.

Then I heard music, and turning a corner saw an elderly bearded busker standing in the shadows playing Mozart on his violin, while directly ahead Bath Abbey rose from the darkness into the white brilliance of floodlighting. The Abbey had its own *son et* plain, in places punctuated with individual outlying hills that once were part of the main limestone block of the Cotswold scarp, in places lit by the broad windings of the River Severn.

It's an historic walk, as are most included in this book, for it is almost impossible to tread the Cotswolds and remain unaware of that lengthy succession of the ages of man. There are long barrows dating from the New Stone Age, round barrows of the Bronze Age, hill forts of the Iron Age and signs of Roman occupation, not only in Bath at the southern end of the walk, but elsewhere in sheltered coombes where wealthy citizens, serviced by the legions of Rome, had their villas some 1500 years ago.

In the late Middle Ages around half a million sheep grazed the Cotswold pasture-lands, 'large flocks of sheep, with the whitest wool, having long necks and square bodies.' Today you can walk for miles without seeing one, for many of the farms have turned their lands over to arable. But there are rabbits and hares, and in the beech woods sign of badger and fox. There are pheasants too. Pheasants by the hundred. If the South

75
Old milestone propped against a Cotswold wall near Tormarton.

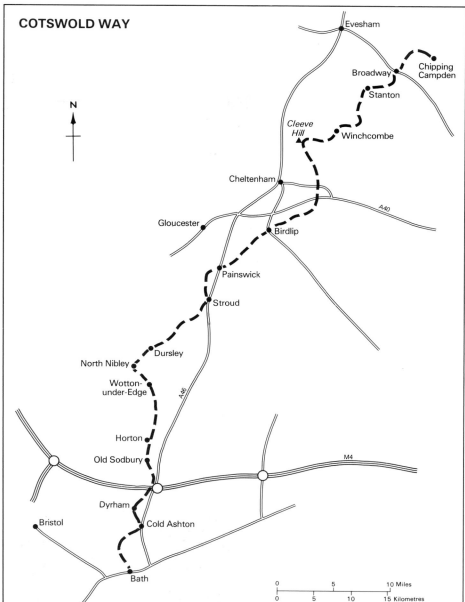

COTSWOLD WAY

Downs are loud with larks, the Cotswolds are a-flutter with pheasants.

Day 1: Chipping Campden to Winchcombe

The route begins full of promise in the lovely old market town of Chipping Campden, as fine an introduction to the Cotswolds as one could hope for. The sandy coloured stone, the uniform gables, the leaded windows of the houses all bring a conformity of design that is most pleasing to the eye, without tending towards unnatural quaintness. In the wide and spacious High Street stands the Jacobean Market Hall—once Campden's focus of attention. Then there's the Town Hall, the Woolstapler's Hall and Grevel House, home of William Grevel, England's foremost wool merchant in the late fifteenth-century. Campden's foundations of prosperity are obvious; Cotswold sheep, known as Cotswold Lions, gave the town its standing and its townsfolk their wealth.

Officially the walk begins in the High Street but it would be better to begin by the Parish Church of St James, which was built

bridleway rising uphill to reach the sudden scarp edge at Dover's Hill where the first memorable views of the walk are to be enjoyed. Here you gaze over the flat Vale of Evesham and out to the Malvern Hills in the west. It is an expansive panorama and one that will be recaptured in part now and again as the walk progresses.

Dover's Hill is named after Captain Robert Dover, a somewhat eccentric and wealthy lawyer who organised 'Olimpick Games' here at Whitsuntide 1612, opening the events on horseback wearing a suit supplied by James I topped by a feathered hat. These games included leap-frog, wrestling, skittles, tilting the quintain, singlestick fighting and shin-kicking and, apart from the interruption of the Civil War—one of the last battles of which was fought on the slopes of the hill—they continued annually until 1852 when they were stopped by the enclosure of the Parish of Weston-sub-Edge. The games were revived in 1951, and the site is now in the hands of the National Trust.

Leaving Dover's Hill a series of field paths lead to the Broadway-Chipping Norton road where a rather well-designed topograph stands on an attractive picnic area. A short distance from this, after passing through a spinney and across a meadowland scooped into numerous strange hollows, you come to the foot of Broadway Tower. This major landmark was built in 1800 by the Earl of Coventry who lived at Croome Court, Worcester. It stands upon a grassy knoll on the very edge of the escarpment and commands a spectacular view over the Vale of Evesham. The Way now descends from the tower towards the Vale, heading alongside a chequerboard of fields with the scarp slope curving off into the distance.

Broadway lies below at the foot of the slope, enticing with its promise of refreshments. But if ever a village could be said to display the sign of exploitation, it is this. Basically Broadway is a delight of mellow stone buildings typical of Cotswold vernacular. A wide street (hence Broad way), a village green, the Wolds rising above; there's no shortage of features to appreciate here. But everywhere there are notices and metal signs advertising this product, or that antique shop; commercialism runs riot, and is made even worse by the non-stop procession of cars grinding nose-to-tail through the street, while others are parked seemingly on every verge.

Immediately beyond the green the Cotswold Way turns into a side street and begins

Left above: **Stanton is one of the classic Cotswold villages. It's almost too neat to be true.**

Below: **Broadway is a splendid place cursed by traffic and too many visitors.**

Above: **Coming down to Stanton the path goes past this pond, with the Vale of Evesham in the distance.**

in the fifteenth century in response to a bequest by Grevel. Next to it stands a curious gateway flanked by square lodges. These are all that remain of Campden House, a mansion built by Sir Baptist Hicks around 1615, and burnt to the ground thirty years later by Royalist troops in the Civil War. Opposite there's a fine row of almshouses, also built by Hicks, and these adequately represent the essential Cotswold architecture.

There is so much to see and to admire in Chipping Campden that it is all too easy to forget the real purpose for being there. But once you've managed to drag yourself away, the route leads along a back lane and on a its climb back onto the hills. A stony track leads along a narrowing crest. One or two former quarries, long deserted and grassed over, are passed; there are consistently wide views; rabbits scamper across the path seeking cover; the occasional horse comes trotting along. It's a most pleasant stretch of walking but at Shenbarrow Hill where there was an Iron Age hill fort, it is necessary to desert the Wolds again, this time to visit the charming little village of Stanton tucked shyly below at the base of the slope.

Stanton is almost unbelievably pretty, its street lined with near-perfect cottages, unspoilt by overtly modern applications that mar so many similar houses in other villages and towns. As you wander down the street one almost expects to find a film crew on the corner shooting a period piece for the big screen.

It takes but a few short minutes to pass through Stanton and along an easy traverse of the lower slope of the hills, with a soft landscape drawing you on. There are distant green ridges topped with woodlands, isolated domed hills standing proud of the otherwise level plain, and before you've walked far you enter Stanway Park among avenues of stately chestnuts. Stanway (once known as Church Stanway to distinguish it from Wood Stanway nearby) consists of little more than a seventeenth-century manor, a church, a stone-roofed tithe barn and a rather ornate Jacobean gatehouse. In all it has the air of a feudalistic hamlet lost among ancient, dappled trees. Wood Stanway, on the other hand, appears to be a livelier place altogether. Its collection of seventeenth and eighteenth-century cottages and farms are protected by the curve of the Wolds, and the surrounding farmlands laid open to the west. Above the hamlet the hills loom steeply and the Way heads onto them once more, then along a track from Stumps Cross to reach the hill fort of Beckbury Camp before sloping down again beside orchards to the remains of Hailes Abbey. The Abbey ruins can be seen over a fence from the path which now follows a Pilgrims' Way across the fields to Winchcombe.

Days 2–4: Winchcombe to Wotton-under-Edge

Winchcombe is a handsome town wearing a tidy facade. It occupies the valley of the little River Isbourne which flows from Cleeve Hill in the south-west. Hills rise on three sides, giving it a certain amount of protection. An ancient place, is Winchcombe, with a colourful history that requires more than a single night's stopover to unravel. For the Cotswold Way walker the town is important, however, for its wealth of bed and breakfasts, its pubs, restaurants and shops.

Despite your eagerness to resume the walk, before leaving Winchcombe it is worth

Archways and imagination are all that remain of Hailes Abbey.

making a short diversion to look at the gargoyles round the Parish Church of St Peter. There are forty of these, and they are considered to be among the very best examples of the art in all of England.

Almost opposite the church, Vineyard Street takes you across the Isbourne, out of town, and very soon past the entrance to Sudeley Castle, one-time home of Katherine Parr, Henry VIII's widow. A little way beyond the castle entrance a series of footpaths lead across several fields, past Wadfield Farm and along a track towards Humblebee Woods. Hidden among a group of wall-enclosed conifers nearby is the site of a Roman villa. From here there is a lovely view looking back into the valley with Winchcombe and Sudeley Castle both nestling among trees.

Belas Knap is the next object of interest. Standing high on the crown of a hill above Humblebee, with woods on one side and open fields on the other, is a splendid Neolithic burial chamber measuring some 180 feet (55m) by 60 feet (18m) and 13½ feet (4m) high. At its northern end is a false portal with two horns lined with dry-stone walling. There are two chambers along the eastern side, one on the west and another at the southern end, and these are reached by way of shallow passages walled with stones laid in an almost identical fashion to the many drystone walls seen all along the Cotswold Way.

A field path, then a farm track, lead across a wide, exposed landscape from Belas Knap to the barns of Wontley Farm, and from here a change of direction takes you to Cleeve Common, an open moorland-like region of bracken and gorse and a maze of tracks cutting away in all directions. The waymark of a yellow (or blue) arrow with a white spot will be seen on low wooden posts across the Common as your guide. It's a useful guide to have too, for the present route makes a circuit of Cleeve Hill and is not shown on the Ordnance Survey map (1984 revision) and, much of it being around the 1000ft contour (305m), the mist often comes swirling on a damp day to add confusion. Perhaps that is why the line of cliffs along the western edge of Cleeve Hill is known as Cleeve Cloud! (Another suggestion is that Cloud is derived from 'clud', meaning a rock mass.)

Cleeve Hill, Cleeve Cloud, there are so many lovely names to conjure with along the Cotswold Way. Thus far we've had the intriguing Belas Knap, but there are even better to come: Birdlip and Hetty Peglar's

Tump, Uleybury, Nibley Knoll and Old Sodbury, Painswick and Wotton-under-Edge. Each one draws riches from the English language and paints pictures in the mind.

There are more Iron Age hill forts here, but there's also a golf course and a trig point with a topograph nearby indicating major

The lofty spire of Painswick Church is seen from many miles away.

features in a broad panorama, and in the village of Cleeve Hill a little below the golf course there's a Youth Hostel.

Heading south now the Way skirts Cheltenham's sprawl by diverting into the back-country of the Wolds, through woods and along a short stretch of road walking (that seems much longer than it really is), before returning to the edge of the escarpment at Charlton Kings Common near Leckhampton Hill. From here you almost peer down the chimneys of Cheltenham, but the best chimney of all is the Devil's Chimney, a limestone stack standing proud of a lower terrace of the escarpment. It is, in fact, a remnant of a former quarry.

Country lanes and trackways, in places rather soggy in wet weather, alternate with beech woods as you approach Crickley Hill Country Park. Here you come to evidence of yet more hill forts and camps; the first was Neolithic and dates from about 4000 BC, followed by two Iron Age camps. A large viewing platform has been erected with a variety of information panels depicting the history of the area.

The Way then leads erratically southward along the scarp edge, into woods again and out to Birdlip Hill a little below the village that sits at a traffic-mad road junction. It's woodland almost as far as Cooper's Hill, but the path keeps mainly to the edge of the trees and fine views are presented between them out to the broad sweeping Vale of Gloucester. Near at hand, where pheasants stray from the woods, fields slope down to the blue dazzle of Witcombe Reservoir, and as you briefly veer northwards you can gaze across the bay created by the curving ridge, and back to Crickley Hill, which was passed a couple of hours or so earlier.

A sudden steep rise leads onto Cooper's Hill, a promontory glade with an extensive panorama limited only by the crowding trees that frame it. Brockworth lies immediately below, with Gloucester stretching out its tentacles as if to contain it. There's a maypole on Cooper's Hill which is hung about with ribbons on the Spring Bank Holiday, and a cheese-rolling race is held down the precipitous slope. This ancient ritual is, or was, repeated at Uffington on the Ridgeway, but its origins are confused by Time and no-one really knows what it is supposed to represent—although that does not put an end to speculation.

Leaving Cooper's Hill behind, the route goes through Brockworth Wood, a National Nature Reserve in which there's a confusion of tracks. Cotswold Way signs fortunately keep you on the right trail. Below the wood stands the Benedictine Prinknash Abbey, an ugly modern building more like a city office block than a monastery in a peaceful setting. A mile further and you come to Painswick Beacon (or Painswick Hill, as the O.S. has it), a place of green undulations where golf is played round what was once an Iron Age

A beech-lined path leads off the Wolds and down to Horton.

camp. The actual route skirts the Beacon to the south, but on a clear day the hilltop is worth a diversion for the view, which includes Gloucester to the north.

The golf-course route leads to Paradise. Well, of sorts. Paradise is the name of a hamlet on the outskirts of Painswick. It nestles on the eastern slope overlooking a valley that has woods on the far side, and it is in this valley that Painswick, a gem of a Cotswold town, is to be found. Painswick's building stone is grey, its houses fashioned onto streets, its tall, graceful-spired church is elegant and set back behind avenues of neat trimmed yews and table tombs. There is an air of self-esteem about the town. The cloth trade inspired its fortunes, and today as you wander through, it is comfortably un-crowded and surprisingly peaceful.

You leave Painswick along Edge Road opposite the splendid lych gate on the corner of the churchyard, and are soon among fields once more. These take you down to a stream, and climbing the far side near Jenkin's Farm it is worth pausing for a moment to capture the view of Painswick apparently slumbering in its bed of greenery. The Wolds make a gentle backdrop, creating here a soft and tranquil landscape that is seen to even better effect on Scottsquar Hill—reached by way of a colourful slope of silver birch. The hill has been quarried in the past, and on the short stretch from the hilltop to a narrow road beyond, the quarry dips are a tangle of undergrowth through which the path has to fight its way. On the road a signpost directs a continuing track to Haresfield Beacon. This track takes you through more woodlands, now and then opening to sudden vistas of enchantment; farms and cottages occupying the land with toy-sized stature.

It is at Haresfield Beacon that you have one of the finest viewpoints of the whole walk. You reach it through broad-leaved woods, passing as you do a stone commemorating the lifting of the siege of Gloucester in 1643, and then over a crown of turf on Ring Hill to the narrow projection of the scarp edge where a trig point marks the Beacon itself. This is another hill fort site that was adopted by the Romans, and among the Roman finds unearthed here was a hoard of some 3000 coins.

But it is the view that will remain vividly in the memory. A huge and magnificent panorama, it exploits every direction but that to the east. The River Severn draws a great meander, and sunlight picks out the

Gloucester and Sharpness Canal nearer to hand. Off to the west the Forest of Dean clogs the horizon, while the Cotswold Edge, hiding the sprawling brick town of Stroud, leads the eye to outlying hills.

South-east of Haresfield Beacon there's a second splendid promontory, a neck of meadowland bearing a topograph. From it the Way crosses to a National Trust car park, then plunges into yet more woods on the north-western edge of Stroud's industrial intrusion. To avoid Stroud the route manages to remain mostly among fields until, once over a railway line, it brings you briefly onto the A419 at Ryeford. The River Frome and the Stroudwater Canal (built in 1779) are crossed in perhaps the saddest area of the whole walk, yet it is not long before wooded Pen Hill above King's Stanley and Middleyard clears the mind and gets the lungs working hard again.

Stanley Wood hugs the northern slope of Pen Hill. The path through leads among as fine a collection of stately green-boled beeches as any found along the length of the Cotswold Way. It is a delight of a switch-back course, up and down and then contouring with ease; out through a coppice to a sloping meadow above Woodside Farm, then back among trees again. The route is clearly marked and it takes you up onto the scarp edge at Frocester Hill where you pass the Nympsfield Long Barrow before gaining yet another magnificent view, with the curiously detached flat-topped Cam Long Down seen ahead to the south-west. The

The Devil's Chimney, above Cheltenham, is a remnant of a former quarry.

Cotswold Way crosses over the crown of this hill, and you will tackle it within the next couple of hours.

Between Frocester Hill and Cam Long Down the route passes close to two more sites of great archaeological interest. The first is Hetty Pegler's Tump, an almost perfectly preserved long barrow of the Severn-Cotswold period, with a door kept locked to help its preservation—although the key is available from a cottage a short walk away. The other site is Uleybury Hill Fort on the scarp edge. It's a massive, thirty acre site, one of the finest promontory hill forts in the country, and it has never yet been fully excavated.

Now follows a steep descent of the scarp slope to Hodgecombe and Springfield Farms, both tucked tight against the foot of the hill, then along a track to begin the sharp ascent of the green turf-smoothed Cam Long Down and Cam Peak beyond it. Both these hills, being distinct outliers, give impressive 360 degree panoramas, and from them the Cotswold Edge displays many features that have been familiar thus far along the walk.

Dursley lies below Cam Peak, and as you dodge through the town you see some of the best and some of the least worthy features of its juxtaposition of ancient and modern. The

*A commemorative clump of trees
above Wotton-under-Edge.*

old Market House, set on columns of stone
and with a statue of Queen Anne standing in
a recess above the east end, is one of the
obvious landmarks to aim for. You then cut
through a shopping precinct and make for
Stinchcombe Hill by way of May Lane and
Hill Road, taking care not to be led astray
by similar waymarks to those of the Cotswold Way.

On Stinchcombe Hill there is another golf
course and yet more fine views, but you
quickly plunge down again into a deep
valley; passing near Stancombe Park and
coming soon to charmingly-named North

Nibley through a tunnel of a track with an
odd doorway (dated 1607) half-hidden in a
crumbling wall. On Nibley Green below the
church the last battle to be fought in
England between private armies took place
in 1470 between the Berkeleys and the
Lisles. About 2000 men took part and Lord
Lisle, shot first in the face, was stabbed to
death and his retainer army then fled and
was scattered over the surrounding country.
Above the village rears Nibley Knoll, a
prominent hill with a tall memorial tower, a
monument to William Tyndale who translated the Bible into English and who was
thought to have been born nearby. There is
speculation, however, that the Tyndale born
in North Nibley was not, in fact, William,
but another who was not even related.

A sunken track takes you up to it, and
from the projecting lip of the hill you can see
not only the broadening Severn beyond the
Vale of Berkeley, but far off in the west the
Brecon Beacons and Black Mountains, while

to the north Stinchcombe Hill is a reminder
of where you've just come from. Leaving
Nibley Knoll you take to woods once more,
passing alongside the hill fort of Bracken-
bury Ditches and out to another promontory at Wotton Hill where a circular wall
encloses a plantation of trees. The original
trees were planted to commemorate
Wellington's victory at Waterloo in 1815,
but they were felled and used to fuel a
bonfire celebrating the end of the Crimean
War. Others were planted in 1887 to mark
Queen Victoria's Jubilee. The present
clump dates from 1952.

From Wotton Hill a steep descent takes
you into the little town of Wotton-under-
Edge, a name which pictorially emphasises
its position as a 'wood-town' beneath the
Cotswold scarp edge.

Days 5–6: Wotton-under-Edge
to Bath

Wotton dates from Saxon times and by the
seventeenth century it was one of the most
important of all the Cotswold wool towns.
There were several productive mills along
the stream that runs through the town but
the trade they fostered has all but disappeared now. Given sufficient time, it is a
place that rewards a morning's exploration,
while the walk through gives a memorable
glimpse of some of its treasures. The fine,
sturdy church of St Mary the Virgin is one of
the treasures that is actually on the route,
and this is certainly worth a visit. But soon
after leaving the church you find yourself
out of town and in a valley known in its
upper reaches as Tyley Bottom, strolling
beside a lovely mill stream that takes you
through fields to the neighbouring hamlet of
Coombe. From here you break away,
leaving the valley, to climb onto the back of
the Wolds once more.

On the hilltop dry-stone walls run die-
straight to take a track towards the scarp
edge. From it you see across to the Tyndale
monument on Nibley Knoll, then bear away
on a traverse of the slope towards a screen of
trees that will close all views from you. From
now on there will be little of the escarpment
to be seen until you draw close to Bath. The
very character of the Wolds begins to change
and it becomes more akin to downland than
hitherto, with a more rolling, folding aspect,
broad and smooth with slopes less severe
than on the northern part of the walk.

A long, deeply-sunken track walled with
high banks draped with ivy, bursting here
and there with shade-loving ferns and

overhung with trees to complete a 'tunnel' effect, takes the Way off the hills again and down to the edge of Wortley. Field trails draw you on from Wortley to Alderley, crossing a once-important little stream that flows from Ozleworth Bottom squeezed by the Wolds to the east. In the hey-day of the Cotswold cloth industry, this clear, though unprepossessing brook was responsible for powering around a dozen mills; the one from below Alderley served more.

There's not much to be seen of Alderley, the 'clearing in the alders', but what is evident is both charming and peaceful; a few cottages, a small but attractive church, an Elizabethan mansion and a farm or two. Waymarks take you from it along a gentle scooped valley upstream towards Lower Kilcott. It is a lovely walk on an autumnal morning with the tops of the hills rising out of the mists like islands floating on a grey sea. Coming off the fields and onto a lane you pass from Gloucestershire into the county of Avon, then head along the lane beside the Kilcott stream. There's an eighteenth-century corn mill still standing by its pond half a mile along the lane, and shortly after passing this you take to a path that leads eventually to the lofty Hawkesbury Monument, a rather presumptuous tower built as a memorial to General Somerset who served under Wellington at Waterloo.

The route does not go into Hawkesbury but instead flounders along an enclosed track known as Bath Lane—liable to be waterlogged and muddy in wet weather—and on to the edge of the hills again above Horton. Horton Court, an odd but lovely combination of Norman hall and Tudor house, is owned by the National Trust, and on the outskirts of the main village there was once a hill fort. Walking from the Court to the village, fine broad views are given of the low country leading off to the Severn.

Little Sodbury is gained across more peaceful countryside. It is a gentle land, spoiled only by the marching pylons that stride in silver skeletons across the fields. On the hill above Little Sodbury stands Sodbury Hill Fort, gained by a farm approach track and a secretive footpath. Consisting of eleven acres of ramparts and ditches, and now grazed by sheep, the fort was originally built in the Iron Age but it was considerably strengthened by the Romans who used it as a frontier post. The Saxon army camped here in 577, and in 1471 Edward IV and his brother Richard (later Richard III) rested here with their army on their march against

Margaret of Anjou. History is in the very turf as you wander across this great green saucer, and out through steep-banked ramparts on the other side to follow field paths to Old Sodbury.

A mile or so to the south of Old Sodbury you pass through the pheasant-crackling, guinea fowl-scampering, Capability Brown-landscaped park of Dodington House, which is unseen from the Cotswold Way, although standing only a very short distance from it. All appears as nature intended, but on emerging from the park west of Tormarton, you face the horrors of the twentieth-century with heavy traffic thundering along the A46. A diversion through Tormarton itself gives the opportunity for refreshment; almost the last chance before Bath—a good afternoon's walk away. It also allows you to gird your loins before crossing the M4's intrusion and making a break for open countryside once more.

Dyrham seems unaware of the modern world. It sinks among the hills, all mellow stone and leafy wistfulness, and the way to it round the walled deer park of the National Trust's Dyrham House and past some of the finest strip lynchets (terraced fields, possibly of Saxon origin) to be seen anywhere in southern England, leads in a real tease, so that you have no inkling of the village's delights until you come down through the trees, and there it is set before you.

The Wolds are curious formations now, and it is difficult to come to terms with their geography. At Dyrham they drain away to the west, but a couple of miles (3km) farther on, at Cold Ashton, they fold into a bowl to the south. Cold Ashton Manor peers over its hedge-studded wall into that bowl. It's a lovely view, but a finer one is that into which you walk shortly after.

Having wandered through Cold Ashton you cross the Bath road and take to Greenways Lane; a name which prepares you for the gentle beauty of the scene ahead. As the lane curves south-westwards so the countryside unfolds before you. There is no scarp edge here, but a landscape of little hills and valleys. Gentle hills, rolling hills with woodlands on them; the hillsides themselves cut into patterns by dry-stone walls or hedgerows. A spinney here, isolated tree there, casting umbrellas of shadow on the grass. There are one or two farm cottages beside the lane as it steepens and grows yet more narrow. It's all so soft and homely; a kind and welcoming land, so easy to love.

Sparrows chased one another from the

hedges, and high overhead a hawk hung motionless, head down and alert for hint of an unsuspecting meal as I strolled down the lane. And coming down Greenways Lane summed up for me the very best of lowland walking. There was life all around me. Abundant life, but peaceful life. I walked through it, absorbing it, but leaving no trace behind. I did not disturb that peace, yet I took it with me and fed upon it. With gratitude.

A few meadows and a rough track will take you across the valley and onto the opposite hillside where there is yet another memorial, this one to Sir Bevil Granville and commemorating the battle of Lansdown which was fought here in July 1643. Although nowhere nearly as tall as either the Somerset Monument at Hawkesbury Upton, or the Tyndale Monument on Nibley Knoll, this is a rather fussy piece of work surrounded by iron railings, like a barrier of spears.

Hanging Hill is next, and suddenly there's a scarp edge once more, a promontory with big views down to the Avon and out to Bristol. Then yet another golf course to skirt before crossing Little Down Hill Fort beside Bath racecourse. There comes an overwhelming sensation that the walk is nearing its end, and finding the scarp edge again, suddenly there lies Bath ahead and below, slumped in a shallow bowl of hills facing towards the setting sun. Prospect Stile is exactly what its name suggests; a stile with a wonderful prospect. It overlooks the last hill of note on the walk, Kelston Round Hill. On that hill there's a crown of trees. It's a bosom of a hill, soft and rounded and with a broad level land stretching beyond it. A hedge-lined track leads towards it. A temptation. The Cotswold Way accepts that temptation but then surprisingly slips along the edge of the hill and heads for home.

Bath is that home. For 102 miles (164km) you have walked along the very fabric that built one of England's loveliest towns. You have sampled villages fashioned from it, seen elegant houses financed by the sheep that grazed upon it and grown aware of the many ages of man that have adopted it for their home. But for the Cotswold Way walker, with 100 miles and more paced beneath the boots, the streets of Bath spell the real homecoming.

Perhaps, like me, you too will be welcomed by the glory of the Abbey rising out of the darkness into the light. A symbol that all's well that ends well.

WALK 11: *The West Mendip Way*

Crook Peak is easily recognised from Loxton Hill.

Distance: 30 miles (48km).
Time Required: 2 days.
Type of Walk: A medium-length walk along the line of the Mendips, for the most part following the upper plateau, but descending here and there—quite steeply in places. Way-marking is good, but some of the paths and tracks tend to be rather muddy.
Start: Uphill, near Weston-super-Mare.
Finish: Wells, Somerset.
Maps: O.S. Landranger series 182.
Guidebooks: *The West Mendip Way—The Walker's Guide* by Derek Moyes (Mendip Publishing). *The West Mendip Way* by Andrew Eddy (published by Weston-super-Mare Civic Society, 3–6 Wadham Street, Weston-super-Mare, BS23 1JY). (This guide is written for the walker heading from Wells to Uphill.)

On the Limestone Brow of Somerset and Avon

The West Mendip Way is one of the lesser-known long walks of southern England, but in that partial obscurity lies some of its appeal. For those unfamiliar with Somerset's hills, this 30 mile (48km) route from Uphill near Weston-super-Mare to the lovely little cathedral city of Wells, will give an opportunity to explore a charming countryside whose national acclaim is mostly restricted to the tourist honeypots of Cheddar Gorge and Wookey Hole. The Mendips, however, have far more to commend them than simply these.

They stretch from the Bristol Channel in the west to the Wiltshire border near Frome in the east, and may be described as having three separate ridges or tablelands. The first rises abruptly from the Channel as the elongated headland of Brean Down—although just 3½ miles (5.5km) away in the Severn tides the Mendips briefly emerge as the green-capped and cliff-girt island of Steep Holm, an ornithologist's delight. The small western portion continues by way of Bleadon Hill before dropping into the gap forced by the innocent-looking Lox Yeo River where the M5 motorway takes advantage of the natural gateway to breach the hills without having to cut its own way through. Then comes the larger, higher section of Mendip, where a broad escarp-

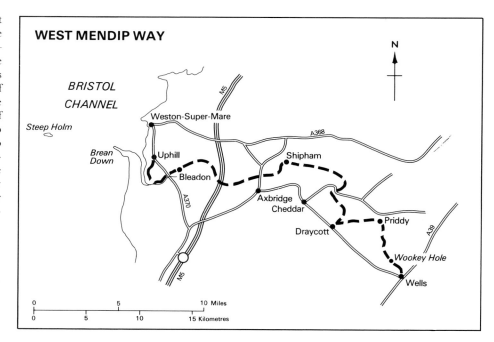

On Bleadon Hill the Romans marched to bring lead from their mines at Charterhouse. When the weather lifts grand views are to be had.

ment curves gently to the south-east towards Wells, while the third portion to the east of the Bristol to Wells road tapers gradually before losing itself in the confusing undulations that ruffle the borders with Wiltshire.

Basically the Mendips are a range of hills formed of mountain limestone and showing rainwater erosion typical of this type of rock, with fissures (known locally as swallets or slockers) and gorges, and pitted with intricate cave systems. Underground are some spectacular formations and features created by the chemical action of rainwater on rock, and a number of these caves offer rewarding expeditions for enthusiasts who flock to them all year round in order to grovel in their dripping darkness. Their highest summits are marked with red sandstone crowns, and seen from the north a full line of hills, some heavily wooded, appear to be dominated by the sandstone ridge of Black Down and its outline of heather-carpeted moor. This is the highest of the Mendips at 1066 feet (325m).

From the south the Mendips reveal their full height when viewed from the low-lying watery plain of the Somerset Levels. But it is on the hills themselves, on the broad escarpment 1000 feet (305m) and more above sea level, that the Mendips give of their best.

On the breezy shelf of this escarpment dry-stone walls create vast grid-lines across field and pasture, and from its lip extensive views gaze out over the flat plains below towards Glastonbury Tor, full of history and legend. It was from this escarpment that King Arthur supposedly contemplated his kingdom of Avalon and from Arthur's Point above Wells, planned the death of the infamous Witch of Wookey. Both Arthur and his queen, Guinevere, are reputedly buried within the grounds of Glastonbury Abbey to the south.

At first glance the Mendips may seem empty hills, but man has been active here for many thousands of years—back into the dawn of pre-history, according to evidence found in some of the caves. (That at Westbury-sub-Mendip has been particularly revealing.) After Stone Age, Bronze Age and Iron Age Man, the Roman occupation had a considerable impact on the region, for at Charterhouse above Cheddar the Romans had one of their industrial centres where lead and silver were being produced in AD 49. Mining activity continued among the hills long after they had left, but for a substantial period the main use of this upland was as a royal game reserve; the Forest of Mendip. There were few settlements on the upper plateau, and when agriculture eventually took over as the primary use of the land, the isolated hamlet of Priddy became the centre of sheep-rearing, and there has been an annual Sheep Fair held on the village green there for six centuries. The dry-stone walls, which give the area an appearance rather similar in places to that of the Yorkshire Dales, are a

The little creek (or 'pill') at Uphill where the West Mendip Way begins.

result of the Enclosures Act of the early 1800s.

Walkers with a sense of history will find plenty of sites of interest as they set out on their explorations. There are long barrows (something like 500 of them have been identified on the Mendips) and earthworks, ring forts and sites of Roman settlement, in addition to the mines and lead works of an industrial era.

Yet those who walk the West Mendip Way are more likely to react to the open spaces, the big views from the edge of the escarpment and the lime-loving plants that brighten the way. There are extremely rare species among the cliffs of Cheddar and Ebbor but on the grasslands typical limestone flowers will be seen in abundance. At 30 miles (48km) it's not a long route, when compared with most of the others in this book, and fit walkers could probably manage to complete it in one day, if so inclined. But those who would rather make it a two-day outing would perhaps best be served by treating the small town of Cheddar as an overnight stop. There's camping, bed and breakfast and Youth Hostel accommodation available there.

The West Mendip Way was devised by local Rotary Clubs to celebrate the Queen's Silver Jubilee in 1979. It is a well-defined route waymarked with oak posts bearing the name of, and distance to, the next village. Underfoot the paths and tracks are deeply rutted in places and muddy after rain where the route combines with a bridleway. There are only two possible refreshment stops along the way without making a diversion from the route, and the open exposed upper plateau can be a cool, windy place, even on bright summer days, so you should carry adequate clothing, food and liquid refreshment.

Then before you set out there comes the problem of deciding which direction to tackle the walk—west to east, or east to west? Whilst there is something to be said for walking towards the sea, having the lure of sun on water drawing you along the line of the hills, similarly there are convincing arguments for heading eastward. Firstly there is the obvious benefit of having the prevailing winds with you. But the second reason clinches it for me. That is to have the splendour of England's smallest city waiting at the end of the walk, with its glorious cathedral making an obvious finale to match that of Winchester at the end of the South Downs, Canterbury on the North Downs

and Bath at the finish of the Cotswold Way.

Day 1: Uphill to Cheddar

Uphill marks the southern limit of Weston Bay but it is constantly threatened by its larger neighbour of Weston-super-Mare spreading towards it, although as yet the village has not been entirely swamped. Uphill has a hill, to be sure; an outlook of a knoll with the redundant Norman church of St Nicholas and the remains of a windmill on top. But apparently that is not what gave it its name. Uphill, they say, is a corruption of Ubba's Pill—'pill' being a West Country term for a creek, or inlet. Hubba was chieftain of a Viking band who was slain in a battle on the River Parrett to the south of the Mendips in AD 878. In those times the sea covered most of the Somerset Levels almost as far as Glastonbury, which would have made Uphill a suitable port. Indeed, the port is said to have been used during the Roman occupation for the shipment of lead and silver from their Mendip mines, and it was used increasingly throughout the Middle Ages. Today there is just a small tidal harbour and a boat-clogged creek jutting from the River Axe.

The walk begins nearby, on the corner of Links Road with a boatyard adding colour and a focus of activity. You cut round the back of the hill to avoid walking through the village and pass Walborough Tumulus, thought to have originated as a protected village settlement. The low-lying marshland of Bleadon Level is rich in birdlife—especially on the River Axe where wildfowl, waders and seabirds chatter and chortle as they stalk the oozing mudbanks and tidal waters for food. But the path soon leads away from the lowlands with Bleadon Hill beckoning ahead.

It is a little over 3 miles (5km) from Uphill to the rather grey, south-facing village of Bleadon, and although the route avoids its centre, you pass a short distance above to cross the western side of Hellenge Hill. Bleadon, however, is worth a brief visit for it has a fine church and a market cross outside the churchyard wall. There is an imaginative legend attached to the name of the village which tells of a marauding band of Danes who moored their ships on the Axe and came ashore to plunder the neighbourhood. All the inhabitants fled to the safety of the hills, save for one poor lame woman who was forced to hide. Whilst the Danes were in pursuit of the villagers, she cast their ships

adrift and, with news that their invaders were marooned, the locals took heart and turned on the Danes whom they massacred nearby. The site of this battle came to be known as Bleed Down, or Blood Down, and this in turn was corrupted to Bleadon. Thus an entertaining tale has come to be associated with the naming of this small village, while the true meaning is no doubt rather more prosaic than legend would have it.

The walk across Bleadon Hill is an easy one, once you've mounted its steep western slope, for you swing along the narrow Roman road with long, intermittent views breaking away to north and south, the slopes plunging away to flat and empty country and the sea showing itself clearly out in the west. With a good light views from this high point include the Welsh coast across the Bristol Channel, and even the Brecon Beacons 50 miles (80km) away. Exmoor and the Quantocks are seen to the south-west; so may Dunkery Beacon be picked out, and the lighthouse at Burnham-on-Sea where the River Parrett discharges into Bridgwater Bay. Nearer to hand rises the splendid hill of Brent Knoll, like a cone centred in the Somerset Levels where once it stood as an island. The lane you wander along is said to have been used by the Romans for transporting lead from their mines at Charterhouse to the port at Uphill, although there is no conclusive evidence to support this theory.

Shortly after passing a picnic area giving more lovely views to the north, the lane curves to the left and begins its long descent. A track continues ahead and, deserting the lane now you take to it. This can be rather muddy and rutted but it improves later as you rise alongside a plantation onto the brow of Loxton Hill at the eastern end of the Bleadon *massif*, and overlook the breach in the Mendip wall caused by the Lox Yeo River. On the far side of the gap stands the conspicuous shape of Crook Peak over which the walk will shortly be climbing. Beside you now is Loxton Wood, a cheery, bird-happy place, and as you drop down the slope towards Loxton village, so you pass out of sight of a cave naturally hollowed from the base of a steep rock wall.

The village of Loxton huddles as a rural backwater on the hillslope, church and farmyard side by side in pastoral harmony. There's another restored stone village cross here, a little like that at Bleadon, and inside the church a magnificent pulpit carved out of a single block of stone dating from the fifteenth century, resting on the figure of a man also carved from stone. According to Arthur Mee, who knew and loved England more profoundly than almost any other man, there are more medieval stone pulpits in Somerset than in any other county. But when he wrote that he was including Loxton's which, thanks to the re-arrangement of county boundaries, has now been annexed to Avon.

Between Loxton and Crook Peak the West Mendip Way has to cross the M5 motorway, then almost immediately over the Lox Yeo River which here forms the county boundary, and you enter Somerset. It's a sharp hard climb onto Crook Peak, traversing slopes of gorse just below the rocky summit which stands at 627 feet (191m) and which in the past had one of Somerset's major beacons on top. More magnificent views are shown from the summit, which makes it worth a short diversion, but the continuing route leads almost due east along the county boundary that has now deserted the river. You walk on, left foot in Avon, right foot pacing Somerset turf, over Compton Hill (named for the village of Compton Bishop below) and Wavering Down following the line of a fence and wall that more or less define the boundary. This is all popular walking country, and justifiably so. Wavering Down catches the sea breeze; an airy refreshing belvedere with a panorama to bring a smile to your face.

The bridleway loses height after Wavering Down and takes you through King's Wood and onto the Sidcot to Axbridge road at Winscombe Hill. On the eastern side of the road is Shute Shelve, a rocky bluff much diminished by successive road improvements, that has a grisly history. A gallows used to stand at the top of this bluff in the days when the road squeezed through a narrower defile than today's. Even before Judge Jeffreys' notorious assizes were held, the Hanging Field on Shute Shelve was a noted site for executions and the remains of those found guilty were often left dangling for travellers to see as they passed below. In the parish records of Worle, a suburb of Weston-super-Mare, the following account records a local murder in 1609 which resulted in Shute Shelve's Hanging Field being put to use:

> Edward Bustle cruelly murthered by consent of his owne wyfe who with one Humfry Hawkins and one other of theyre associates were executed for the same murther and hanged in irons at place called Shutt Shelfe

neere Axbridge. A good president for wicked people.

The continuing route follows Winscombe Drove, an ancient drove road that is deeply rutted in places, rather muddy and overhung by trees, and which leads round the northern flank of Shute Shelve Hill. As you

Above: **Typical Mendip barn built of local stone.**

Right: **The village water pump in Draycott was last used as recently as the early 1970s.**

slide your way through the muddy patches here, spare a thought for peasants of old who would have driven their sheep and packhorses along this same route year in and year out. Doubtless conditions underfoot would have been considerably worse for them, following as they did in the wake of a few score animals.

As you progress towards Shipham, you can see the village of Winscombe below and off to the left. You leave the drove road, bear left to Winterhead Hill Farm, then cut away to drop down towards Shipham Brook which you cross by stepping stones. Having crossed the county boundary for the last time all the remainder of the walk as far as Wells will be in the county of Somerset. Over the stream a steepish climb leads to the southern outskirts of Shipham, a small village with grey cottages lining narrow lanes, whose inhabitants turned from sheep-raising to mining and subsequently became renowned for violence. In the eighteenth century they were said to be so wretched and depraved that Hannah More, friend of William Wilberforce, set out to re-Christianise and educate them.

The path brings you onto an old turnpike road where you bear right, and soon after head left again along a metalled track. A footpath continues, eventually leading among gorse and bracken to a curious region

of humps and bumps known as 'gruffy ground', formed by generations of mining. All around Shipham open pits were dug for calamine, and in the 1790s Shipham had more than a 100 mines in operation. Calamine was a vital ingredient used in the brass and zinc industries of Bristol. Raw calamine was heated in special ovens and reduced to dust, and one such oven remains in Shipham today. Rowberry is another former mining village, tucked under Dolebury Warren twenty minutes' walk away to the north, but off our route. From Shipham you gaze up at Dolebury Camp, a truly impressive Iron Age hillfort with great earthen ramparts that appear to be ready to crash down the hillside.

Following the course of another stretch of Roman road that led to Charterhouse, you wander through the Forestry Commission's Rowberrow Warren on the slopes of Black Down, and out to isolated Tyning's Farm riding centre, with a collection of Bronze Age round barrows nearby. When they were excavated a cremation urn was found in one of them along with several items of jewellery and three pygmy vessels. By contrast with the dark tree-restrictions of the Warren, the countryside now is broad and open to the elements, the farm buildings looking rather vulnerable to the whims of nature, a huge sky stretched over all, while just to the east of the farm lies a depression within which is the entrance shaft to Tyning's Barrow Swallet. A little further along the field beside the continuing Roman road are a number of other caves, the best-known of which is GB Cave. It has passages more than a mile in length and reaching a depth of 440 feet (134m). The main chamber, the largest such in the Mendips, is spectacular, having an impressive waterfall and its roof hung with beautiful stalactites. The entrance to this cave is covered with a concrete blockhouse that is all but hidden from the lane.

Wandering along the lane below Black Down's summit you reach the highest point on the West Mendip Way, then turn away from the Roman road on the entrance drive to Charterhouse Farm. Beyond the farm a path continues down to Cheddar, but the West Mendip Way heads south-eastward with views of the Cheddar Gorge cliffs off to your right, then down into a hollow alongside Long Wood, an ancient woodland under the care of the Somerset Trust for Nature Conservation. Another drove road takes you through the wood, and soon after you pass Black Rock Quarry and go down

through Black Rock Nature Reserve with its orchids and scrub, as far as the road near the head of Cheddar Gorge.

If it is your intention to spend the night in Cheddar, just follow the winding road downhill for nearly 2 miles (3km) under the great looming crags of the gorge, a playground for climbers and home of the extremely rare Cheddar pink (*Dianthus gratianpolitanus*) which is only to be found on these cliffs.

Day 2: Cheddar to Wells

Cheddar is probably the most widely-known of all Mendip towns; known for its cheese, its strawberries, its caves and its gorge. Parts of the town are attractive; parts are bland with bungalow development, but it has a colourful history and plenty to satisfy the wanderer of the West Mendip Way who chooses to rest up here before tackling the final dozen miles (19km) or so to Wells.

Leaving the town you must retrace your footsteps through the gorge, which gives a far better opportunity to study the huge walls than could ever be gained by car, as far as the entrance to Black Rock Nature Reserve. Opposite the gate a rocky climbing path, sometimes rather slippery, takes you among trees and scrub onto the open plateau where a magnificent view across the Mendips and the low-lying valley under the escarpment rewards your exertions. On the edge of the hills you come to a circular dewpond, a typical downland creation formed to trap rainwater for farm animals to drink from. As you peer down into the deep Vale of Avalon, the fields of soft fruit that stretch either side of Cheddar are seen in all their richness, while ahead lies the huge bowl of Cheddar Reservoir.

Having gained so much height from the town it is with a niggle of resentment that you have to lose much of it again—and so soon. The way leads down through Mascall's Wood where a second path breaks away to Cheddar, and round then among the productive acres of a market garden to Bradley Cross. But just as you feel ready to enjoy some level walking, the track starts to climb again, this time towards Carscliff Farm and on to pastureland with yet more superb views.

Now there comes another descent, this time crossing Middle Down Drove and dropping steeply through Batcombe Hollow. The valley lures you with its fruit fields and dazzle of greenhouses, and with Glastonbury Tor making a substantial impact on the wide panorama. Below Batcombe Farm a lane takes you into the village of Draycott on the Cheddar to Wells road and on to a simple but eye-catching memorial to John Card, a local benefactor who died in 1729 after founding the Draycott Charity with a gift to the community of about 100 acres of land. The monument, in local Draycott stone, was erected by Henry Spencer with donations from the public. It is variously known as the Spencer Monument and the Card Memorial. Nearby stands the old village pump, last used in the early 1970s.

Having only just entered Draycott you leave it again by taking to the steep lane that rises behind the memorial, and head up the hillside among strawberry fields. It is the most pronounced climb of the whole walk and you're bound to suffer a little if attempting to complete the route in just one day. The lane finishes and becomes a track. From one copse to another the way leads across the open plateau with big views to enjoy. From here to the lonely little village of Priddy are a number of prehistoric tumuli,

and beyond the village too, two collections of Bronze Age round barrows on North Hill, known as Priddy Nine Barrows and Ashen Hill Barrows, excavated in 1815 by the Reverend John Skinner of Camerton.

Priddy squats in a shallow depression high on the Mendip plateau, a winter-bleak hamlet and a place renowned among cavers for its classic Swildon's Hole, the longest yet discovered among these honeycombed hills. On the triangular village green a small thatched stack of sheep hurdles stands as a reminder of Priddy's importance in providing the venue for a major Mendip Sheep Fair for the past 600 years, since it was moved here from Wells at the time of the Plague in 1348. (The annual fair is held on the green every August on the Wednesday nearest to the 21st). There is a local belief that the people of Priddy retain the right to this Sheep Fair as long as the hurdles remain on the green.

The Romans mined for lead at Priddy and the last such mine here was not closed down until 1908. The ruins of St Cuthbert's

leadworks are still to be seen, but not on the route of the West Mendip Way.

It's only a little over 5 miles (8km) now to Wells on a walk that leads through Ebbor Gorge Nature Reserve, then steeply down the scarp slope to the tourist-frenzy of Wookey Hole. The village has a basic charm with its clear-running River Axe swirling alongside the street. But when queues of cars and coaches clog the village, the walker grows rapidly nostalgic for the peace of the hills so recently left behind. That peace may be briefly sampled again over Arthur's Point where tradition has it that King Arthur surveyed part of his kingdom and plotted the destruction of the Witch of Wookey.

It's all downhill then to Wells. But what a magnificent place in which to finish this walk, with the splendid medieval Vicar's Close, the moated thirteenth-century Bishop's Palace with its swans and lovely trees, and the glorious Cathedral all forming a welcome embrace. A delightful historic city it is, and a worthy focus for the breeze-blown miles of Mendip wandering.

WALK 12: *The Dorset Downs Walk*

Left: **Magnificent Wells Cathedral, one of England's loveliest, makes a fitting conclusion to the West Mendip Way.**

Above: **The almshouses in Milton Abbas are almost alone in having no thatch.**

Distance: 47 miles (76km).
Time Required: 2–3 days.
Type of Walk: Easy walking on mostly good paths, tracks and some country lanes. There is a fair amount of height to be gained and lost as you traverse hill and valley. A number of villages are situated along the route, with shops and pubs for refreshment. The guidebook gives details of bed and breakfast accommodation to be found.
Start: Blandford Forum.
Finish: Bridport.
Maps: O.S. Landranger series 194, 193.
Guidebooks: *A Dorset Downs Walk* by Alan Proctor (Thornhill Press).

Through the Lush Green Heart of a Scenic County

Of the many richly varied counties in the south of England Dorset scores as one of my all-time favourites. It is, after all, a delightfully green and fertile land; a county of golden fields and soft rolling pastures, with cloud-washed downs and wooded valleys and a coastline that stands comparison with any other in Britain. Chalk streams bubble through gentle vales. Villages that bear the charm of past centuries adorn practically every landscape, and there are mellow stone cottages with well-combed thatch and roses over the doorways straight out of Thomas Hardy novels at almost every turn.

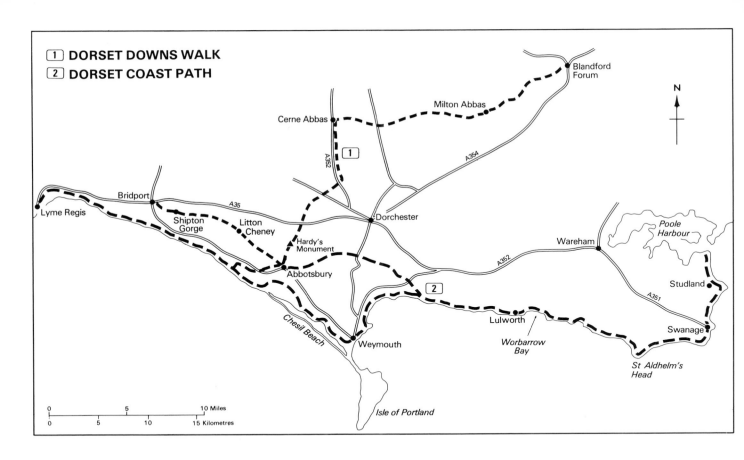

1 **DORSET DOWNS WALK**
2 **DORSET COAST PATH**

It is a great county for the walker. As described elsewhere in this book, the Dorset Coast Path must rank as one of the finest walks of the British Isles. The Purbeck hills too, especially around Corfe Castle, are noted for their splendid prospects, with footpaths running along each scenic ridge and cutting down to woods and folding meadows that lie in their shadow. In the north of the county Blackmore Vale, once a vast forest of oak, is now a neat pastoral countryside of woods and farms defined by a twisted maze of little lanes with footpaths wandering from hamlet to hamlet (there are few villages of any size), crossing streams

Left: **The chalk giant above Cerne Abbas is a potent symbol of fertility, and is clad only in the shadow of passing clouds.**

Right: **The Smith's Arms at Godmanstone is said to be England's smallest inn.**

and low pastures or climbing onto the outlying hills.

And there are the Downs.

The Dorset Downs spread in a broad arc across the county from its eastern border, along the valley of the Stour, and then south-westward to the coast; a series of chalk hills nudging one against another, some bare topped, others wearing chokers of wood or spinney. Tucked against their lower slopes are some of the county's loveliest villages: Milton Abbas, Cerne Abbas, Litton Cheney, Shipton Gorge, each one set on or close by a sparkling chalk stream.

By stringing together a number of paths, trackways and quiet country lanes, a long walk across the Downs which links these villages has been successfully worked out. The route is 47 miles (76km) long. It begins in the little town of Blandford Forum and ends at Bridport near the coast. It's not one of the Countryside Commission's officially sponsored Ways, but a little-known walk without any form of waymarking beyond the occasional standard footpath finger post provided by local authorities. Neither does it have the recognition of the Ordnance Survey as yet, so do not expect to find the route as such identified on the relevant map of the area. There is a recommended Wainwright-style guidebook, however, written by Alan Proctor and illustrated by Dennis Brierley, so armed with this and O.S. Sheet 194 (a tiny section is on 193) the walk becomes a possibility, the dream a reality. It is one to savour.

Days 1–3: Blandford Forum to Bridport

The small market town of Blandford Forum, once a centre for lace making, has grown up on the left bank of the River Stour to the south of Cranbourne Chase. Few of its buildings predate the early eighteenth century, for the town was virtually destroyed by fire in 1731. As a consequence of this the rebuilding programme which '. . . raised this town like a Phoenix from its ashes' has left Blandford with an elegant collection of Georgian-styled residences and public buildings, some of which have unfortunately been overshadowed by more recent developments. The Stour flows below the town, over a weir, through grassy meadows and beneath a fine multiple-arched bridge, beyond which the Dorset Downs Walk begins.

Within a very short distance the bustle of town has been forgotten as you wander across fields and through woodlands with a flavour of the countryside being drawn from the fragrance of wayside plants and the songs of the birds. It's a gentle introduction to the walk, for the real personality of the Downs does not become apparent at once. That will slowly impress itself upon you as you get into your stride and work your way westward.

After almost 4 miles (6km) you come to the village of Winterborne Stickland, one of several little communities to take its name from the stream which flows through the valley. At Stickland the Winterborne is not much of a stream, although it grows slightly more boisterous farther south on its way to join the River Stour on the edge of Sturminster Marshall. The main road through the village (though a minor one at that) follows the stream, and the walk leads along the road for a short distance before climbing through fields to an extensive woodland which spreads across a hill and down its southern slopes. Now you really know you've arrived on the Downs, having left the lower country behind. A track takes you through Charity Wood and into Milton Park Wood, and then you descend the slopes of Hogden Down into the classic, almost overly-pretty street of Milton Abbas.

Set within its own secluded tree-edged valley, Milton Abbas must surely be rated as one of the most perfect of planned villages in all England with two rows of square white-washed and thatched cottages facing each other across a wide swathe of street edged with open plan gardens. At the top of the street is the pub, The Hambro Arms—also thatched. Halfway down is the light, graceful church of St James, which was built with stone taken from an old tithe barn, and directly opposite this stands a row of flint and brick almshouses.

The whole village was planned and built near the site of a previous settlement in 1771 by Lord Dorchester and it has become justifiably known far and wide for its many attractive qualities. As a consequence the village street is invariably busy with visitors' cars on summer weekends.

At the lower end of the village there's a fenced parkland containing a picturesque lake. The walk skirts this at its southern end. A short diversion however, for those with sufficient time and energy, allows a visit to be made via a footpath through the park to Milton Abbey, founded by King Athelstan in AD 932 as a college for canons. After many changes, made over the centuries, the Milton Abbey of today is a public school housed in a gothic mansion. A flight of steps leads steeply through trees from the Abbey Church to St Catherine's Chapel, whose origins date from Saxon times. Up there you're on the edge of the Downs, and a long coombe slips off to the north with woods on the three enclosed sides. The Downs Walk, however, ignores Delcombe Bottom and instead works its way south-westward, heading up onto the broad shoulder of hills that are criss-crossed here with paths, tracks and narrow lanes, and then makes a dog's-leg north onto Coombe Hill where once there used to be a warning beacon. A lovely tucked-away corner of the world, this is.

Then you drop down the side of Coombe Hill above Coombe Bottom, with the church of Bingham's Melcombe ahead. Tracks lead easily into the neighbouring hamlet of Melcombe Bingham, and from there to Higher Melcombe.

All along the Downs there are signs of ancient burial mounds, cross dykes and strip lynchets, and after leaving the private road which leads to the manor house at Higher Melcombe, you pass alongside an earthwork where the hill makes a projecting prow at Dorsetshire Gap, a deep slice carved through the hills. Paths, not always easy to follow, take you west now, across a minor downland lane and over Ball Hill, through a patch of woodland and then across Church Hill, on whose western slopes medieval field systems can be identified.

From the B3143 which you cross north of Alton Pancras, until you come down into Cerne Abbas 3 miles (5km) further on, there is a joy of open views and big skies; an untenanted landscape where you wander with the song of skylarks above and wild flowers at your feet. Distant hills fold into bright patterned valleys. You catch a glimpse of far-off villages; see the glimmer of sunlight on glass but hear nothing save the soughing of the breeze, the lowing of cattle and the melody of birdsong.

Down then to Cerne Abbas, a village of splendid old houses, shops and pubs, a fine church and the ruins of a former abbey that was founded in AD 987 by Ethelmaer, Earl of Cornwall. But perhaps more than the fine buildings, Cerne Abbas is noted for its unselfconscious Giant standing naked on the hillside above the village behind the abbey ruins; a symbol of fertility 180ft (55m) tall, etched in chalk and with a raised club in his hand. No-one really knows how old he is, nor who carved him, though speculation has it that he dates from Roman times.

The River Cerne, which is a delightful chalk stream, flows among trees below the Giant and passes quietly through the village on its journey south among gentle green pastures. There is a footpath which follows the left bank of the stream all the way to its junction with the River Frome outside Dorchester (Thomas Hardy's 'Casterbridge'), and you wander along this path for a little over 4 miles (6km) on what is one of the loveliest sections of the whole walk. On your left shoulder the Downs rise steeply but the Cerne Valley, narrow though it may be, is a fine trench, flat-bottomed with soft turf under foot, with stands of oak and beech, and willows dancing their leaves in the stream.

Below Green Hill you come to the first of a string of tiny lakes—there are several running one into another between Pound Farm and Nether Cerne. Duck, coot and moorhen nest among the forest of reeds and yellow flag. Geese come down to feed. There

are sheep grazing in the meadows that sweep to the water's edge; they share their pastures with the geese.

The hamlet of Nether Cerne holds a pocket of tranquillity. There's not much to the hamlet; just a few cottages, a farm, a squat-towered thirteenth-century church and a manor house standing across the lawn from it. The church of All Saints, with its doorway netted against habitation by swallows, is cared for by the Redundant Churches Fund, while the seventeenth-century manor next door gives the appearance of mellow well-being.

The stream flows on just below the church and the footpath soon rejoins it a little north of the next hamlet, Godmanstone. If for no other reason this will be remembered for having what is reputed to be England's smallest inn, the Smith's Arms. A footbridge over the stream allows the thirsty walker the opportunity for a drink before continuing south to Forston. Here you cross the Cerne, and the A352 road, and leaving the river behind take a path which leads across

Charminster Down.

Later, coming down easy southern slopes, the view to Bradford Peverel church, with Penn Hill behind it, is interrupted by the traffic-busy A37 Yeovil–Dorchester road, but once across this and under a railway bridge, the village is seen clearly across a low meadow. The River Frome winds through this meadow and effectively marks the boundary of Bradford Peverel. The Romans were active here, having built a road and an aqueduct through what is now the village— nearby Dorchester was the Roman city of *Durnovaria*—and on the hills all around there are numerous earthworks and long barrows from an even earlier age.

The Downs Walk continues southward,

Milton Abbas is a classic planned village dating from 1771. A wide street, trim lawns, and manicured thatch on the rooftops. A tourist's delight.

Left: **Pins Knoll is a prominent hill above Litton Cheney with a hint of the sea and the knowledge that the end of the walk is drawing near.**

Below: **There's not much to Nether Cerne, but what there is is picturesque. The church is no longer used, but it is worth a visit.**

Right: **After Litton Cheney you look south across the fields to Puncknowle, and beyond the hill that shelters it lies the sea.**

passing the elegant church of St Mary whose slender spire is topped by a white weathercock, and follows the route of a farm road for some distance across the lush green hills and through strips of woodland to Martinstown, otherwise known as Winterborne St Martin. The River Winterborne here is the South Winterborne, and in parallel with its namesake near Blandford, at least six villages and hamlets along its course take their name from it. Winterborne St Martin has a wide village street, and many of the cottages that line it look as though they ought to be thatched; bald cottages, they seem, in need of a transplant of straw.

With time to spare a 1½ mile (2km) diversion would take you to Maiden Castle, one of Europe's finest Iron Age hill forts with its vast area of terraced earthworks spreading across Hog Hill to the south-west of Dorchester.

Within minutes of leaving Martinstown you are climbing onto the Downs again. Over Grove Hill and Shorn Hill with views growing ever-wider, then along the crest of Bronkham Hill, sharing for a while the line of the inland route of the Dorset Coast Path. Ahead now the Hardy Memorial is clearly seen on the top of Black Down—it has beckoned for many miles—and the track

leads directly to it. It's a noted viewpoint; a 360° panorama reveals an undulating patchwork of meadows and fields, a large proportion of country through which you have walked and a great deal more besides. With the coastline not 4 miles (6km) away, you see beyond a fold of meadows and woodlands to the gleaming lagoon of the Fleet, banked by the Chesil Beach. Portland stands at the far end of the Beach and Weymouth Bay makes a long curve to the south-east. The Isle of Wight can be seen far off, while in the opposite direction the sweep of Lyme Bay leads the eye to cliffs of the Devon Coast.

As for the monument itself, it's a grey shapeless tower, as architecturally inspiring as a factory chimney. Built in honour of that other son of Dorset to bear the name Thomas Hardy, Admiral Sir Thomas Masterman Hardy (1769–1839), flag-captain on Nelson's *Victory*, it was erected in 1844. If nothing else, the 70-ft (21m) tower standing among gorse and heather above what appear to be abandoned gravel pits, serves as a fine marker for seamen—which, for such a man, is an apt memorial. For the walker, though, views are all. Big views over a sweep of rabbit-worried land.

Below Hardy's monument you soon come

to Portesham, the village where he lived as a boy, and to which he returned again later in life. There are some pleasant old cottages in the village but it is saved from being overrun by tourists—who flock to nearby Abbotsbury—by being not quite pretty enough. (There's obviously consolation in being not of the first class!)

Having come within 3 miles (5km) of the sea you climb back onto the Downs outside Portesham and head away from the coast, going north-westward across a region whose past is lost in prehistory. On the way to Tenants Hill you pass to the south of the Valley of Stones, a collection of sarsen stones; then wander beside a long barrow and on the hill itself come to a stone circle. Several footpaths converge here and you now head north down into the valley through which the little River Bride flows. This innocent stream gives its name to a pair of neighbouring villages; Little Bredy and Long Bredy.

Briefly touching Long Bredy you then head across the meadows to Litton Cheney where there is a simple Youth Hostel set in a former Dutch barn that was once used as a cheese and milk factory. The village itself is a charming collection of cottages strung on the southern slopes of the Downs; some thatched with a bubbling chalk stream running past their doors. To the west the line of the Downs sweeps and swirls with individual promontories and prows, and the path takes you up towards Pins Knoll where Iron Age settlers had a primitive farm. From the hills once again you gaze over a soft pastoral landscape to the sea and capture the contrasts that this entails. In some ways this view holds the very essence of Dorset.

The path takes you down into a coombe with a stream running through, then up to the hamlet of Chilcombe; a farm, a pair of cottages and one of the smallest churches in the south. Two miles (3km) farther west lies the village of Shipton Gorge, a busier place than Chilcombe for it boasts a Post Office Stores and a pub. The old village is settled round a farm in a dip but there has been a spell of recent development on the hillside above, from which there are lovely views.

It is then a simple matter of a steady downhill stroll of a couple of miles or so into Bridport. The breeze-blown Downs, the fragrance of drying hay, the aroma of cattle, the songs of the birds all give way to the enclosed world of a lively little town.

Give me the free open space of the Downs. Any time.

WALK 13: *The Dorset Coast Path*

Distance: 72 miles (116km).
Time Required: 5–7 days.
Type of Walk: Scenically spectacular, ever-interesting, but strenuous in places and with much height gain and loss—often on extremely steep grass slopes that can be dangerous when wet. It should be borne in mind that practically all the cliff edges are in a precarious condition and caution should be exercised when the path strays close to them.
Start: Lyme Regis.
Finish: Shell Bay, Poole Harbour.
Maps: O.S. Landranger series 193, 194, 195.
Guidebook: *A Guide to the South Devon & Dorset Coast Paths* by Roland Gant (Constable). *South-West Way: Book 2 Penzance to Poole* by Martin Collins (Cicerone Press).

From Lyme Regis to Poole Harbour

Dorset is shrinking. Anyone who tackles the Coast Path will soon recognise that as an indisputable fact. There are cliff falls, landslips and crumbling edges for almost the whole length of this walk as erosion works its ceaseless toil. There are sea stacks that once were part of the mainland but now stand divorced and surrounded by the tides; marooned nesting sites for countless birds.

Waves dazzle in the sunlight. They crash and roar by storm, surge and sift again along the gravel banks and sandy coves, nibbling at high tide against the base of towering cliffs, creating hollow caves and 'doors' that act as thoroughfares for cormorants and

Above: **Near East Fleet, the Coast Path walker is close to the turning point which leads to Weymouth.**

Right: **Looking west along the Dorset coast from Hanbury Tout.**

gannets, undermining tons of turf-topped rock and soil that sooner or later will be discharged into the sea.

Dorset is shrinking. The Coast Path is ever changing.

But what a coast it is! Of the four separate sections that combine to create the South-West Peninsula Coast Path, the Dorset stretch from Lyme Regis to Poole Harbour—72 miles (116km) in length—is the shortest and, in places, among the most scenically dramatic of them all. Since few walkers, no matter how keen, will find time to tackle the whole of the South-West Peninsula in one go, it seems an ideal opportunity to focus a chapter on the Dorset section. For it can be accomplished inside a week's holiday without too much difficulty and there are sufficient coves, villages and small towns along the way to entice the long-distance walker to take a lengthy rest here and there, to dawdle on sites of geological interest, to study the birds, flowers or butterflies—or simply to stretch out on a sun-warmed clifftop in sheer delight with the tremendous views spread before you. Without doubt the walking here is among the very finest to be experienced anywhere in southern England.

But do not be lulled into an illusion that coastal walking is an easy exercise of sea-level perambulation. The cliffs of Dorset rise and fall with surprising severity. Indeed, in thirty years of mountain activity I've rarely come across such steep paths as those of the Dorset Coast. In mountain country, paths are almost universally eased by contouring or zig-zagging. Not so on the Dorset Coast. Here the paths go straight up and straight down again on a breathless helter-skelter course, sometimes alleviated by a lengthy series of timber-reinforced steps. However, the distance between each individual step is rarely of the right proportion to match one's stride, so they are often more of a hindrance than an aid. Fitness, then, is a prerequisite for enjoyable coastal walking, and if you're not fit by the time you start, you certainly will be at the finish!

Accommodation is no problem on this walk, there being plenty of guest houses, hotels, Youth Hostels and camp sites along the route, or accessible from it. However there are two Ministry of Defence firing ranges that interrupt the path, but these are usually open during school holiday periods and at weekends. At Tidmoor Point, west of Weymouth, sentries are posted at either end of the ranges when firing is in progress, and

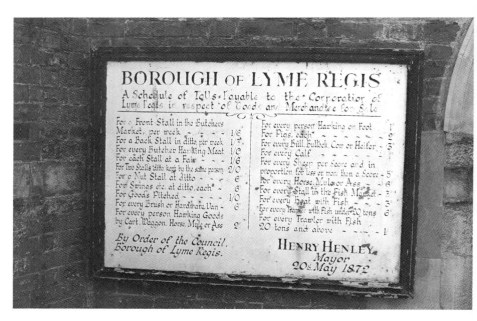

they will either make alternative suggestions or give permission to cross when firing stops. But east of Lulworth there is a more demanding 7-mile stretch (11km) of Coast Path that heads through MoD ranges, and before setting out on this section it is advisable to check that it is safe to do so by telephoning the Range Control Office at Bindon Abbey (0929) 462721—extension 859 or 189.

Days 1–3: Lyme Regis to Weymouth

With Devon nudging its western limits, Lyme Regis is the first Dorset settlement met by those tackling the complete South-West Peninsula Path. An historic and not unattractive town at the mouth of the River Lim, it has an unimposing yet neat little harbour created by the Cobb, a semi-circular breakwater of stone construction dating from the thirteenth century, that gives just sufficient protection from the weather to shelter small vessels. Several times during the reigns of Henry IV and Henry V the town was burned in raids by the French, but it still managed to supply the fleet with two fully manned ships to face the Spanish Armada. In 1685 the Duke of Monmouth landed in Lyme prior to the Battle of Sedgemoor, and the town has also featured in the fiction of Jane Austen *(Persuasion)* and more recently, of John Fowles *(The French Lieutenant's Woman)*.

The steep streets come down to an eastward view dominated by the flat-topped

cliff of Golden Cap, highest on the south coast of England at 618ft (191m), but almost immediately upon setting out on the walk to it, the path has been diverted northwards to avoid a landslip above Black Ven. As an alternative you cross Timber Hill and walk into Charmouth before resuming the Coast Path proper to the east of the River Char and head up to Cain's Folly where the cliff edge is a-crumble of red soil. From it you gaze along the coast to Golden Cap and the sparkling sweep of the bay. Stonebarrow Hill is a short way off to the north-east and in a car park nearby the National Trust has an information centre from which the Golden Cap estate is given considerable publicity. So much of this corner of Dorset is now protected from further development by the National Trust who have jigsaw-like been acquiring stretches of unspoilt coastline since the launch of Enterprise Neptune in 1965.

The beach below Cain's Folly is a favourite with fossil hunters, as is Black Ven, for when great lumps of cliff break away, they often bring down with them the fossilised remains of sea creatures upon which no man has ever set eyes before.

Down from Cain's Folly you pass isolated Westhay Farm, cross a pair of meagre streams and begin the climb to Golden Cap which, like others nearby, is a cliff of blue lias clay topped by a golden-tinged sandstone that glows in the evening sunlight. On its broad summit, on which a lookout station was perched during the Napoleonic

Wars, one knows a sense of space and freedom. The sea dominates all to south, east and west, but inland Dorset's rolling hills conceal comfortable coombes with farms and little villages and isolated homes. It's a warm and hospitable landscape—an exiled Englishman's dreamland. It is the landscape of Thomas Hardy and one can so easily imagine characters from his much-loved novels inhabiting those soft coombes.

Seatown, the little huddle of cottages, huts, pub and caravan sites reached by a steeply plunging pathway from Golden Cap, is part of Hardy too. In *The Mayor of Casterbridge* Henchard came to the fair with

*Left: **Toll board in Lyme Regis.***

*Below: **Weymouth at Bank Holiday time comes as a culture shock after the days of peaceful, almost solitary walking.***

his wife and there sold her whilst the worse for drink.

From Seatown the path continues along Ridge Cliff and Doghouse Hill with more fine views inland but from Thorncombe Beacon (507ft/155m) there's a particularly memorable view back to Golden Cap and the curve of Lyme Bay spreading into Devon. On the eastern slopes you descend through fields to Eypemouth (or Eype's Mouth) where another of those half-hearted Dorset hill streams manages to lose itself in the shingle of the beach. Eypemouth, incidentally, is reputed to be one of the finest beaches along this coast for swimming.

Just under a mile of walking over West Cliff brings you down to the little protected harbour of West Bay at the mouth of the River Brit. Bridport which takes its name from the river, lies a short distance upstream, a one-time rope- and net-making town of some repute. Until the coming of the railway in 1884, West Bay was known as Bridport Harbour. From it Bridport rope

was transported to Naval shipyards round the coast but today the harbour trades in fish; shingle and sand are exported and timber from the Baltic unloaded here. The village is a curious mixture of fish stores, industrial buildings, shops and holiday complex, with a towering red cliff rising steeply from the beach. This is East Cliff, one of the steepest climbs for the Coast Path walker so far.

There's a golf course right on the very top of the cliff, the fairways almost reaching the edge along which the path goes. You've barely caught your breath from the climb onto it before the path plunges steeply into a cleft and straight away climbs once more, only to drop again to Freshwater Caravan Park, one of those regimented summer estates with neat little gardens and mown lawns that nonetheless detract from the natural grandeur of the wild coast scenery.

Burton Cliff offers escape. From it you gaze along the 17 miles (27km) of Chesil Beach to Portland; a great shingle pathway,

a reef constructed by the rush of tide, the excavations by undercurrents over millions of years of unremitting labour. Much of Burton Cliff is falling away. On the beach below amonites are often picked up. Others, perhaps, will be gathered by the tides and rolled along to join the Chesil collection.

Burton Bradstock is an attractive village of stone cottages, some thatched, standing back from the sea. A lane leads from it to a National Trust car park on the shore's edge. Burton Beach, and Cogden Beach which runs against it, mark the beginnings of the geological conundrum that is Chesil. As this

long pebble bank stretches off towards Portland, so it grows in height and width and at the same time the stones that form it are found to be bigger than those at the western end. No-one really knows why this should be, except that this grading is probably due to the pounding waves and swirling currents.

As the Coast Path tackles Chesil Beach—happily not too far, for it makes uncomfortable walking—so you find it is rich in plant-life. Thrift spreads in dense carpets of pink. There's sea-kale, sea-spinach and sea-beet; there are patches of mallow, white

yarrow and the bright heads of the yellow sea-poppy relieving the monotony of shingle. On the landward side tall reeds disguise stretches of marsh. Burton Mere is a bird sanctuary, a small and somewhat ragged-edged freshwater lagoon, and the official path goes along its left-hand side, returning to the pebble beach a little farther on by way of a wooden footbridge over a seething ditch.

Near West Bexington an alternative inland stretch of Coast Path cuts away in order to avoid Weymouth. It rejoins the main route at Osmington Mills after a 17 mile (27km) diversion, having visited the lofty Hardy Memorial above Portesham—the memorial is not to Thomas Hardy the novelist, but to Nelson's flag-captain on HMS *Victory*—and White Horse Hill with the huge chalk figure of George III riding to Weymouth.

West Bexington is extremely popular with sea anglers, and along the beach on either side lines are strung out beyond the broiling surf, the shingle slopes broken by mushrooms of protective umbrellas. An easy track takes the walker for another couple of miles before breaking away on a hedged farm track towards the ruins of St Catherine's Chapel standing on a hilltop overlooking Abbotsbury.

The reason for this short inland diversion is to avoid the much-visited Abbotsbury Swannery and in order to continue the path on the mainland side of the extensive lagoon called the Fleet, which from Abbotsbury to Portland makes a waterway between the land and the pebble reef of Chesil Beach. The Swannery is one of those well-loved

Left above: **The village of West Lulworth has a number of pretty thatched cottages, so typical of Dorset.**

Below: **The Smugglers' Inn at Osmington Mills.**

Right above: **Lulworth Cove is surely one of the best-known features of the South Coast. An oyster shell created by the regular pounding of the waves.**

Below: **The wide expanse of Weymouth Bay is coloured with sailboards.**

attractions that draws crowds of tourists on bright summer days. It has been here since at least 1393—when there were no tourists—and there are more than 500 mute swans today exploiting the rich feedings to be had along the Fleet on the eel-grass that grows there.

Abbotsbury itself is a village well worth visiting but the Coast Path studiously avoids doing so by skirting it to the south on a breezy ridge over Linton Hill. Towards the eastern end of this grassy ridge there's a welcome sign attached to a finger post. It announces that morning coffees and afternoon teas are served at Clayhanger Farm a short distance downhill. The farm stands isolated from neighbouring farms or villages in a landscape of green, and with the blue line of the Fleet glinting in the sunshine.

South of Langton Herring you come down to the water's edge near a Nature Reserve protecting the breeding grounds of numerous wildfowl and follow along the vegetated margins of the Fleet, round inlets

and saltings, shoulder-high with bushes and with waving fields of corn or barley on the inland side. That plans were laid to build a nuclear power station here—on Heritage Coast—is another monstrous illustration of the insensitivity of some of those in positions of authority. It's a 'lost' corner for much of the way, in total contrast to the crowded promenades of Weymouth soon to come; in marked scenic contrast to the western cliffs of the previous two days, and with those beyond Weymouth Bay. Walking along the shores of the Fleet is an interlude worth savouring for itself.

Days 4–6: Weymouth to Shell Bay

Weymouth, with its honeypot gaudiness, is the only place on the Dorset Coast Path that is neither an Area of Outstanding Natural Beauty nor designated Heritage Coast. Taken for itself, in isolation, it is no worse than many other seaside resorts, and better than some. But after the glories of the walk

from Lyme Regis, and especially coming on the heels of the remote inlets of the Fleet, it strikes the walker a hammer-blow of noise and bustle from which he will be anxious to escape.

It is only 12 miles (19km) from Weymouth to Lulworth, but in those 12 miles the walker experiences a revelation of glory with some of the most magnificent and spellbinding coastal scenery to be found anywhere. Not just in Britain—but anywhere in the world. It matters not one jot that countless photographs have been seen of the great cliffs west of Lulworth, nor that crowds flock to see them too. To be there in person, to look along them and over them and onto them, to feel the breeze on your face, the sound of gulls crying and waves crashing, is

Man-o'-War Bay, part of the larger St Oswald's Bay, is a magnificent piece of coastline.

something momentous and deeply moving. Walking there as part of a week-long journey, is a bonus.

At the northern end of Weymouth's long sandy bay the main road curves away to the left towards Preston while the coastal walker heads over Furzy Cliff near Jordan Hill Roman Temple. Excavated in 1843 the temple foundations, dating from the first to fourth centuries AD, have given up a number of relics including swords, pottery and coins, and at the bottom of a deep shaft the carefully arranged skeletons of many birds, separated by tiles or stones, are thought to have been part of a sacrificial rite.

Seen ahead as you walk over Furzy Cliff is the bleach-white architectural extravaganza of the Hotel Riviera. The Coast Path resumes alongside it towards the brow of Redcliff Point, among gorse and hawthorn bushes and downland grass, with views growing towards Black Head and the projection of White Nothe on the far side of Ringstead Bay. How refreshing it is to be once more away from the loud shrieks and laughter of town, back among wide spaces of cliff and cove. Back on course.

The path climbs and dips again, now on broad grassy ledges, now scrambling and slithering between bushes near the cliff's edge. Then you come to a high fence surrounding Pontin's Holiday Camp—is the fence designed to keep walkers out, or the holiday-makers in?—and just beyond this another landslip has closed the route across Black Head and you have to divert inland as far as Osmington village. Here you catch a view of Britain's only chalk-cut white horse to have a mounted figure; George III, wearing a cocked hat. From it comes the alternative inland route from West Bexington, which you join in the village for the return to the coast at Osmington Mills.

This little cove is a pretty place but the path does not linger here, instead you dodge round the side of The Smugglers' Inn and along a narrow path to pass alongside former Coastguards' cottages, and emerge onto a grassy clifftop. It's a pleasant walk now through a blur of greens and blues as far as the few cottages that comprise the present-day hamlet of Ringstead. Fronting the sea, backs to a gentle farmland bowl, the cottages seem remote from the world, yet on the way to them you pass the site of the original village whose decline and disappearance remain something of a mystery.

A track leads inland a little, skirting the farmlands and ducking through a wood, and climbs on towards Burning Cliff. On joining a narrow metalled lane you pass a creosoted wooden hut-like building that bears a small wooden cross over the door. It's easy to miss it, but this is the church of St Catherine's-by-the-Sea, Holworth. Go inside for a moment's luxury of peace and stillness. Outside, in the precarious clifftop graveyard, orchids grow among the gravestones. But where is the village of Holsworth? There is none, and excavations show that there has been no village here for 500 years, and with the steady decay of Burning Cliff it is hardly likely that the congregation for this tiny place of worship will expand either.

The path climbs on to reach White Nothe, topped by a row of former Coastguard's cottages that are the highest buildings on the Dorset coast. From White Nothe you gain impressive views of the chalk cliffs ahead; Bat's Head, Swyre Head, the top cone of Durdle Door and the unmistakable profile of Lulworth Cove. From here to Lulworth is perhaps the cream of coastal walking, with one enchanting view succeeding another.

The first time I set eyes on the Matterhorn was one of life's unforgettable moments. And when I came over Bat's Head to capture my initial view of Durdle Door, that too was a moment of excitement and pure magic. The whole scene was just as it should be. There was the crown of cropped grass, the savagely steep plunge of chalk cliff, the curious archway of rock with the dazzle of a weltering sea lit by warm sunlight and mounds of cumulus frothing overhead. That the scene was familiar from countless photographs did nothing to diminish its impact. I was hooked.

Below Bat's Head is a smaller 'door' than the more famous Durdle; this is the so-called Bat's Hole, with off-shore rocks known as the Cow and the Calf. The path descends steeply on grass to Scratchy Bottom, then climbs every bit as steeply to Swyre Head. Well-trodden paths come up from Lulworth and Hambury Tout and you'll rarely enjoy Durdle Door in seclusion.

In some respects Man o' War Bay just east of Durdle Door—part of St Oswald's Bay—is the quintessential Dorset cove, and as you wander along the clifftop above it, it is hard to imagine a more lovely coastal scene anywhere. Then up and over Dungy Head and down among the crowds to Lulworth Cove.

The village of West Lulworth, nearly a mile inland, features many of the architectural delights that make Dorset such an attractive county to travel through. Thatched roofs, crooked walled cottages, some white-painted, others of bare stone, arched doorways, gleam-eyed windows. The Coast Path, however, knows nothing of these and heads deliberately round and above the little cove, shaped like an oyster by an inrushing sea that has been actively scouring at the soft Wealden clay, and enters the MoD's firing ranges.

For 7 miles (11km) the path leads through this scarred land, marked every few paces by signs warning of unexploded shells. Campaigners fought for nearly 30 years to gain access to this land, the Ministry of Defence finally submitting in 1974 to open the ranges at specified periods through the year. Some have argued that by their actions the MoD have managed to maintain the original flora and fauna that otherwise might have been destroyed by use of pesticides and intensive farming methods, but walkers passing through the area will be appalled at the tank-scarred landscape and the rusting remains of targets lying in disarray. Of what value are flowers scrunched by tank tracks that you can't see anyway for fear of treading on a shell? The cliff edge certainly displays a rich flora, and there are many butterflies to be seen, but the no-man's land of desert-like barrenness scorches itself upon your conscience as you make for the freedom of Kimmeridge Bay.

Mupe Bay is accessible from the ranges. The Coast Path climbs steeply above it, then descends to Arish Mell where a tired stream leaks into the sea by a concrete landing bay. The map shows Monastery Farm a mile away, the remains of a Trappist community which lasted here for a short period from 1794 until 1817. This too is caught within the Danger Area, while the permitted path takes you across the Iron Age hill fort of Flowers Barrow, through Worbarrow and round Brandy Bay and Hobarrow Bay, then at last with a sense of relief, you leave the ranges near a nodding donkey which pumps oil from the Kimmeridge shales; Britain's most productive inland oil-well.

Above Kimmeridge Bay stands a crumbling folly. This is Clavel's Tower, built by the Reverend John Richards—who later took the name of Clavell—at the beginning of the nineteenth century. With the stucco and plaster falling away it is perhaps just as well that a fence has been erected round it. Having climbed a series of steps to the folly, the Coast Path then edges round the clifftop

Old Harry Rocks are the last stacks on the Dorset Coast Path. At one time they were joined by a long line of chalk cliff to the Needles on the Isle of Wight.

that is cracking and crumbling with even greater potential danger than that of Clavel's Tower. Below the cliffs Kimmeridge Levels project as ledges into the sea, and there are long views ahead to the snout of St Aldhelm's Head. To reach this involves a heart-pounding ascent of more than 160 reinforced steps out of a frustratingly tight cleft, but having attained this there are practically no more really hard climbs to be made.

St Aldhelm's Head is the southern-most point of the walk and from it you can see the cliffs of the Isle of Wight far off in the east. Backwards there is one last look at Portland, an island-like lump that has stubbornly demanded its share of the scene for so long. But now you head north-eastwards, steadily

losing height, to the old limestone quarries at Winspit, and along to Seacombe where there is another abandoned quarry. Farther along the coast, wandering on the margins of sloping meadows, you pass the shelves of rock known as Dancing Ledges jutting over the sea and washed by it at high tide.

Durlston Country Park takes you gently past the squat lighthouse of Anvil Point, and on to Durlston Head with the 40-ton Great Globe carved out of Portland stone, and Durlston Castle—now a café!—above it. Then down among trees and across a grassy sward to Swanage. The walk is nearly over. One feels that this, in some ways, should mark the end as a counter-weight to Lyme Regis. However, this is not to be, and there are yet more cliffs and sandy bays to discover.

Ballard Cliff, at the northern end of Swanage Bay, is a return to open space and the drama of plunging walls of chalk into a sweep of sea. From Ballard Point there are more extensive panoramas to enjoy, but then you continue across the almost level downland table to find the chalk stacks of

first the Pinnacles, then Old Harry Rocks standing out like gigantic stepping stones away from the mainland. Way out to sea rise the Needles on the Isle of Wight announcing that they, too, had once been attached to these cliffs as members of the same family as Old Harry and Old Harry's Wife. That is, until the sea broke through about 8000 or 10,000 years ago, effectively making Wight an island.

The cliffs break off to form the southern limits of Studland Bay, and the path slopes easily down among trees and bushes to Studland village. There then follows a sandy walk round the bay, either on the beach or among the dunes, to Shell Bay looking off to the tower blocks of Bournemouth's busy sprawl. You stumble through the dunes, sea to the right of you, sea ahead. Then there's water to the left, too, and you gaze into Poole Harbour. There's Brownsea Island, Furzey Island and a gay flotilla of sails. And there are queues of cars waiting patiently for the half-hourly ferry across the gap to Bournemouth's suburbs. Suddenly it dawns on you; the walk is over.

WALK 14: *A Dartmoor North-South Walk*

From Belstone Common you gaze north into an agricultural patchwork.

Distance: 32 miles (51km)
Time Required: 2 days.
Type of Walk: Rough and tiring because of the nature of the terrain, but among scenery that is unique in southern England. There are few paths or tracks and as much of the landscape is bare and featureless an understanding of map and compass work is essential.
Start: Belstone.
Finish: Ivybridge.
Maps: O.S. Tourist Map No. 1 'Dartmoor'.
Guidebook: None followed. There are, however, several guides to walks on Dartmoor, including William Crossing's classic *Guide to Dartmoor* (second edition 1912). Of the more recent guides, *Walking on Dartmoor* by John Earle (Cicerone Press) is especially recommended.

By Devious Ways through the National Park

When I began to draw up my short-list of walks for this book, I very much wanted to include one that would cover the wild inner recesses of Dartmoor; the only true wilderness area left in southern England. As a National Park with 7½ million day visitors a year I knew it to be an extremely popular place, especially at such honeypots as Postbridge, Widecombe and Dartmeet. But I knew too that the heart of Dartmoor's 365 square miles (945sq.km) was remote, uninhabited and virtually empty of people. A true wilderness, in fact.

That wilderness, however, is only one view of the moor, a picture best represented by the larger, northern section. The

121

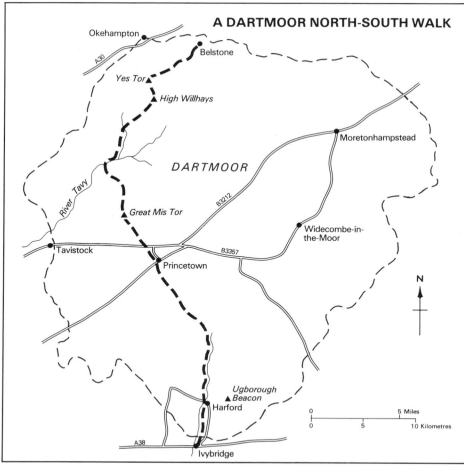

A DARTMOOR NORTH-SOUTH WALK

southern moor is also bare and remote, but less forbidding. It holds three reservoirs and is drained by forceful rivers that have moulded soft, mellow valleys. The eastern moor has a somewhat friendlier face. Contained as it is by a triangle of roads, it offers a much more cultivated landscape dissected by narrow hedge-lined lanes and villages, with woods in the valleys and isolated patches of open moorland standing apart like islands under a broad stretched sky.

Years ago I had scrambled about over some of the outlying tors and wandered a few of the wooded valleys that form a gentle rim round the edge of the National Park. In particular I recalled the splendour of the dawn chorus rippling like liquid gold through one of the woods in early summer. I remembered walking alongside the Teign towards its upper reaches, among ravines and steep woodland slopes, watching the river dash in cascades or lying in deep placid pools where the black shapes of trout came up to catch insects as evening slid from the hills. And from those hills I had gazed off to the mysterious heartland where lonely granite tors stood like sentries, and where mires, fens and 'feather-beds' lay in wait for the unwary. William Crossing, *the* Dartmoor authority, defined these 'feather-beds' (or 'quakers' as they are sometimes known) as deep holes ' . . . not usually more than ten to twelve feet in diameter, filled with ooze, hidden beneath a covering of moss of a beautiful bright green colour.' Mires are to be avoided too. Often called 'Dartmoor Stables' because a number of ponies have found them to be their final resting place, they are another of the moor's hidden dangers.

Researching this book, I fancied, would give me just the excuse I needed to renew my acquaintance with Dartmoor and, hopefully, to learn more about its wild interior.

But what were the classic walks of this wilderness from which to choose something representative of the whole? Just where should I walk? I knew, of course, of the Two Moors Way which crosses both Dartmoor and Exmoor and links with the South-West Peninsula Coast Path after a journey of 103 miles (166km). And I'd heard of the Dartmoor North-South challenge walk.

Belstone is a village tucked away from the world, with Dartmoor sweeping from its very doorsteps.

What else was there?

One of my regular climbing partners of the past twenty-odd years happens to live in Exeter and as he spends a number of weekends, winter as well as summer, wandering about Dartmoor, I wrote to him for advice. He told me then of medieval trackways like the Abbots Way, which leads for about 23 miles (35km) from Buckfast to Tavistock; a route most probably followed by monks as they travelled across the bare open moor between abbeys. He told me too about the Lich Way (or Path of the Dead), a 14 mile (21km) route from Bellever to Lydford Church. This was thought to have been a way used by mourners to reach the Parish Church from various outlying farms. One branch went via Peter Tavy, and another, a drovers' route called Drift Lane, was taken on the occasion of particularly bad weather—one of the regular hazards of travel on Dartmoor. (I learned that the high plateaux of the moor were perfectly capable of, and well-practised in, brewing some of the most appalling weather conditions in all of Britain.) I heard about the Mariners' Way, leading from Ivybridge to Chagford, and the epic Perambulation of 1240, the route taken by a dozen knights who drew up the boundaries of the Forest of Dartmoor in that year. He mentioned the Church Way, and he told me more about the North-South route, an unmarked crossing traditionally begun at Okehampton and heading south for about 25 miles (39km). As a challenge walk this is usually tackled as a day's outing, but as I was to learn, walking on Dartmoor is a strenuous exercise, and 25 miles of tussock grass, bogs, stream crossings, tangles of heather and bilberry, is equal to a much greater distance on, say, the neat-cropped Downs.

'I'll tell you what we'll do,' he said. 'We'll dream up a crossing which links some of the best features of the moor. It won't be an officially recognised route, of course, but you'll get an idea of what Dartmoor's all about, and I can certainly promise you an interesting weekend's walking.'

He did just that.

Day 1: Belstone to Princetown

While Okehampton is the most northerly point of the moor and therefore the obvious place from which to set out on a north-south crossing, it has the drab sprawl of a Ministry of Defence camp on its edge, and military tracks cutting into the wilderness to facilitate army exercises. That the MoD uses some 33,000 acres of this National Park as a firing range and training ground is a matter of some public disquiet, and there can be no doubt that the trackways forced by the army into the wilderness, coupled with low-flying military jets occasionally screaming overhead, do nothing to 'preserve and enhance the natural beauty' of Dartmoor, nor help to 'promote its enjoyment by the public', to conform with principles set out in the National Parks and Access to the Countryside Act of 1949.

Okehampton, then, was passed over in favour of neighbouring Belstone, a quiet, cosy little village on the very fringe of the moor. Here cottages are square-cut, some with thatch on the roof. There's a grey stone-built church typical of the West Country, a set of stocks on the green, a moorside pub and Devonshire cream teas served in a nearby garden. Ponies, cattle and sheep graze side by side, and rabbits chase one another among the heather. Belstone is on the road to nowhere-in-particular. If you've no specific reason for going there, you'll never find it. And that makes it rather special.

A narrow lane heads south out of the village for a short distance alongside dry-stone walls and hedges bright with rhododendrons. There are one or two cottages, then passing through a gate you leave the lane—and civilisation—behind, and emerge onto the open moor. Typical moorland scenery greets the eye; a few scrubby stands of gorse, exposed rocks scattered around, and the bare wind-blown hills rolling into the distance. Ahead to the right rises Belstone Common, and from its rock-cluttered summit a lovely panorama opens to the north as you gaze beyond the National Park to a neat patchwork of agricultural land stretching as far as the eye can see. Belstone Tor rises a little to the south of the Common's brow and is reached by a clear grassy path along an unusually well-defined ridge. Below to one side eases the River Taw, while in the west the indent of the East Okement Valley catches a glimmer of sunlight in a sidling stream.

Heading south-west we descended a ruffled carpet of bilberries and crossed the long low line of dry-stone blocks known as Irishman's Wall. Apparently this was built in the early nineteenth century by a gang of Irish labourers who set about enclosing part of the moor but before they could finish their work, commoners from Belstone and nearby Okehampton drove the Irishmen away and

The village stocks in Belstone, sign of the past when wrong-doers were treated to public scrutiny and abuse.

demolished large sections of their wall.

Whether this story is legend or fact, I do not know, but certainly the Irishman's Wall is there for all to see. Having crossed it and continued down the slope we came to Black-a-Ven Brook, a clear stream rushing with a sense of purpose that outstripped its size.

More Dartmoor ponies were grazing here—a sight familiar to all lovers of the moor. These ponies are often mistakenly believed to be wild, but they are, in fact, all owned by farmers having commoners' rights to graze their livestock on Dartmoor. Twice each year they are rounded up, and well-attended pony fairs are held in the autumn. Some are sold as riding ponies for children, but for the rest it's a particularly ironic fate that lies ahead of them, for these creatures of the wild open moors, much-admired by animal-loving visitors, invariably end up in tins of pet food.

Beyond the brook runs one of the military roads, a tarmac-black intrusion cutting behind a solitary farmhouse. Over this

there's a boggy section fluffed with the tell-tale feathers of cotton grass and with the sizeable lump of Yes Tor rising ahead. Stonechats flitted nervously around us, while skylarks hovered patiently high overhead singing their little hearts out. Buzzards and kestrels are common too.

Yes Tor is a prominent outpost of mangled granite with a clear vision of the unattractive buildings of Okehampton Camp to the north. Elsewhere though an open emptiness beckons; the Dartmoor of imagination becomes the Dartmoor of reality, and as we clambered onto the summit of the tor we were greeted by two men who struck up a conversation with us. They explained how they'd spent the night camping just below the tor, and were then waiting for a group of Venture Scouts to arrive to help them prepare for a disco.

'A disco?' I asked. 'Where?'

'Just here. On Yes Tor!'

I gazed about me. At the huge expanse of moorland to the south and east and west, and out to a northern vista that took in a

wonderland of woods, fields and river valleys. Far away I imagined I could just see Exmoor. (Some claim that you can even see the Bristol Channel from the summit.) And the Scouts were planning to hold a disco here! I remembered it was midsummer. Was this some sort of midsummer madness?

'You've got it. We do something slightly barmy every year. This time we thought we'd have a crack at a disco in the wilds. We've got about a hundred people coming.'

Alan and I fled into the wilderness, determined to be far away from flashing lights, deafening music and people. There are times when you can have just too much of civilisation.

A broad vegetated crest spreads away to the south of Yes Tor and along it you come to High Willhays, a graceful bluff of granite whose summit is the highest point in southern England, at 2039ft above sea level (621m). (Yes Tor is only a few feet lower, and there's nothing higher in all of England until you travel north as far as Ingleborough, in Yorkshire.) A few paces from it

Left: **Black-a-Ven Brook drains the northern moor.**

Above: **Alan Payne makes a silhouette on the top of High Willhays, not only the highest point on Dartmoor, but a height that is not exceeded in England south of Yorkshire.**

stands a lesser tor bearing a cairn and whilst we sat there absorbing the expanse of rolling hill and distant nub of granite, so out of the landscape emerged a brace of walkers bent in search of something they'd apparently lost. 'Letterbox hunters,' explained Alan. 'There are hundreds of them hidden about the moor. Letterboxes, that is.'

'Hundreds?' I questioned.

'One book I've read mentions 450, but another authority says there are occasions when there'll be something like a thousand scattered about the moor. Many of these are just temporary boxes, though.'

One thousand containers secreted in hollows, under tors, hidden among the clutter of rocks. And in them rubber stamps bearing highly individual imprints for the finder to collect.

This curiosity was begun more than a hundred years ago by James Perrott, the 'Dartmoor Guide' who used to take his clients to a place on the northern moor known as Cranmere Pool. (The actual pool was drained by a local shepherd in the 1840s.) Perrott built a cairn there and in it he placed a pickle jar for his clients' visiting cards. A visitors' book followed, and then as postcards became readily available, walkers started leaving stamped, self-addressed cards that would be collected by the next visitors and posted at a conventional postbox—with an additional 'postmark' having been stamped at the moorland 'letterbox'. There is now, inevitably, a club for those who have found more than a hundred such boxes. The '100 Club' meets twice a year for members to share a communal enthusiasm for this unique and somewhat eccentric hobby.

Pricking the distance due south of High Willhays you can see on a clear day the slender television mast on North Hessary Tor above Princetown, about 10 miles (16km) away. Nearer to hand the great bald plateau folds into the valley of the West Okement River, and Alan and I dropped down to it, picking a way over boulders and

125

a familiarity that soon disappeared in a landscape broken by few vertical lines.

Great Links Tor was the largest and most dramatic of the tors so far. These massive granite blocks that are the very bones of Dartmoor, have been eroded into fantastic shapes, weathered into stacks of horizontal pillows and sculpted with imagination by the wind. From them we looked out beyond the moor's western limits, sloping down as though from an escarpment, to rich farmlands that fold away beyond the Tamar and into Cornwall, while south and east the mysterious moor jealously guarded its secrets in undetected grooves and minor ravines. Rattlebrook Hill swelled like an abscess immediately to the south, but we looked beyond that to Sharp Tor and the hazy hint of Hare Tor.

Between Great Links Tor and Rattlebrook Hill, dipped among grass tussocks and yet more tangles of bilberry, were the tell-tale signs of one of the many tin mines that once wrought industrial wealth from the inhospitable moorland. (Seven hundred years ago Dartmoor was the richest producer of tin in all of Europe.)

Sharp Tor has the appearance of the ruined battlements of a one-time Norman castle. Passing by the going became easier, with gentle springy turf underfoot and even the faintest of trails leading up to Hare Tor which supports a flagpole. (There's a military firing range nearby, so presumably warning flags are flown during danger periods.) From the top of Hare Tor clear views showed the lovely River Tavy flowing out to woods and farmland; an enticing scene and a marked contrast to the bleak expanse of the inner plateau.

Cutting across to the head of Tavy Cleave, where the young stream gains independence from the upper moors, we plunged into the green groove of a vale, crossed the river and followed the Tavy downstream. And what a glorious scoop of a narrow valley this was, with the river full of character as it washed over broad plates of smoothed granite, danced in a series of minor cascades and swirled through miniature defiles. Foxgloves and dwarf rowan marked the course of the river and there were tempting wild camp sites everywhere. The Tavy has all the personality of a mountain stream and its company was a constant joy as we wandered beside it for a mile or so.

Then we broke away to climb steeply round the edge of wall-enclosed pasture

Above: **Great Links Tor—a marvel of wind-sculpted rock.**

Below: **The Erme is a cheerful companion on the way out of the southern moor.**

rough heather and bilberry slopes, then steeply up the western side to Kitty Tor. Wretched tussocks and patches of bog made the compass march to Great Links Tor a tortuous affair, but when it eventually came into sight, it gave a fair impression of that much-loved Welsh mountain, Tryfan. It was towards the south-east, then round an attractive circular wood whose outer rim of beeches were growing on top of the lichen- and moss-disguised wall that surrounds it, and headed into the bleak featureless territory of the inner moor. Boggy patches again wore cotton grass as a warning to be noted as we trudged over a steady slope of windswept hillside with a small, but surprisingly prominent, cairn at its crown. South of this cairn rose Great Mis Tor, a black cluster of crags atop a huge bosom of a hill, with the young River Walkham snaking below, having brought itself to life from the high peat bog of Walkham Head and then surging off to join the Tavy outside the National Park at Double Waters, south of Tavistock.

We went down to the stream and crossed by way of greasy boulders. Then followed an energetic struggle up steep slopes of grass to Great Mis Tor. This came as something of a surprise, for the full majesty of this tor is only apparent from the south side where you can properly study the wind-and frost-riven blocks that tower around. There are two small huts standing among the granite shapes on the hilltop and below them a great clutter of rocks and boulders spread unevenly across our path.

Down then to Rundlestone guided by the slender television mast on North Hessary Tor; down to a pattern of dry-stone walls making rectangular enclosures in the valley. Down to a handful of cottages, a stand of pine trees, and the B3357 road. Rundlestone.

A short uphill stroll took us onward to North Hessary Tor, then down again easily to Princetown; a grey town infamous for its prison.

Princetown is indeed a monochrome town in a monochrome landscape, but it makes a natural halfway stage on a north-south crossing. There's a small camp site and bunkhouse offering basic facilities for walkers at the rear of The Plume of Feathers—named, as is the town itself, in honour of the Prince of Wales who, as Duke of Cornwall, owns a large part of Dartmoor. Walkers are made very welcome and there's even a letter box behind the bar!

Day 2: Princetown to Ivybridge

The southern moor is rich in prehistoric remains. From the Bronze Age onward men have tended their flocks on the more hospitable slopes of Dartmoor, and scattered across it—but particularly in the southern half—there are the remains of almost 2000

Bronze Age hut circles to be found. Stone rows are commonplace and on this half of the walk we saw the longest of them all.

The way onto the southern moor is made easy by a wide track leading from the rear of The Plume of Feathers. Well-worn, it soon becomes muddy in bad weather, but continues towards the small but attractive South Hessary Tor, the first landmark to be reached. The track continues to an ancient stone cross just west of Nun's Cross Farm, an isolated place on the edge of wild country, restored by the Duchy of Cornwall and given a new lease of life by pupils from St Peter's School, Exeter, who use it as an outdoor pursuits centre.

Nearby is the head of two valley systems. To the east is the Swincombe Valley, reprieved from plans drawn up a few years ago which would have resulted in its being flooded for a reservoir. Between Nun's Cross and the Swincombe Valley streams drain north to Foxtor Mires, reputed to be the largest bog on Dartmoor; a grim forbidding place where Conan Doyle's Hound of the Baskervilles met its end. But to the west grass slopes spattered with historic remnants lead off to the large Burrator Reservoir, a most attractive man-made lake of a thousand million gallons, which holds Plymouth's main water supply. The valley was flooded a century ago and now 119 acres lie beneath the waters, producing a mature and largely natural appearance with great banks of conifers rising from it.

South of Nun's Cross the going is rather rough and in misty weather navigation problems can easily occur. Our route made for Great Gnat's Head, crossing the route of the Abbots Way on a broad and empty plateau, then veering south-eastward across a vast empty wasteland where hills slide into a misnamed basin of tussock and heather called Erme Plains, at the head of the River Erme. The river, in fact, comes down from Ducks' Pool, a marshy area caught between Great Gnat's Head and Green Hill to the east. Green Hill sees the start of a 2 mile (3km) Stone Row.

Coming down into Erme Plains the lower reaches of the Stone Row are found; an amazing line of upright stones which stretches across the moor, hundreds of them, few more than knee-height and set about a pace apart. At the southern end of the row there's a circle consisting of two dozen or more standing stones, the largest of which is about 5ft (1.5m) high. What do they represent? Why were they set here?

Historians have long puzzled over the significance of Dartmoor's stone rows and circles, but the general consensus of opinion seems to favour the idea that they formed an important role in Bronze Age burial ceremonies, perhaps with an astronomical significance. On the left bank of the Erme, and upstream of the stone circle, there is an enclosed hut group called Erme Pound. This marks a Bronze Age settlement where these early moorsmen built rough shelters, then enclosed them with a sturdy wall, either as a stockade for their animals or as a defence against warring tribes.

There is a choice of route to be taken from Erme Plain. One, the valley route, will take you beside the river to the hamlet of Harford, while the other, upper route, heads along the trackbed of the Red Lake Tramway above the left bank of the river. This goes over Hartford Moor, round the slopes of Three Barrows and Sharp Tor and on to Piles Hill—with yet another stone row for company. This tramway, the rails of which were dismantled in 1932, ran for 7½ miles (12km) from Bittaford, east of Ivybridge, to the china clay workings at Red Lake. The trackway route is the easier under foot and offers a safe escape route from the moor in bad weather, and on clear days it has splendid wide views south to the sea after Piles Hill when you cut across to the south-west towards Harford; but the valley route is also well worth following.

There is a track leading from a weir on the river but you can leave this when it veers away to the west by a lovely beech wood below Sharp Tor to continue through bracken and foxgloves in the valley bed. The river is as vibrant, clear and cheerful as the Tavy, but towards Harford you are forced uphill away from it for a while to cross through a wall-enclosed region and past the final tor of the walk, Tristis Rock, then back to the river bank and down to Harford bridge. A further 2 miles (3km), among trees and flowers, takes you out of the moor and down to Ivybridge where the world is suddenly a very different place.

By the time I reached the village I'd been roasted by the sun and soaked to the skin by horizontal rain. I'd been almost dehydrated on one day, and half-frozen by a cold wind on the next. But I'd seen a fair section of Dartmoor, learnt some of its mysteries and fallen under its spell. I could now understand the passion so many feel for its wild raw beauty, and promised to be back.

Dartmoor had another convert.

WALK 15: *The South-West Peninsula Coast Path*

Distance: 540 miles (869km).
Time Required: About 6 weeks.
Type of Walk: An extremely long and, in places, strenuous walk. There are many days when you must gain and lose a lot of height over cliffs and into deep coombes. Visually spectacular. Because of the necessity of taking ferries over a number of estuaries and wide rivers, the walk should be tackled in the summer season—although sections are practicable at all times of the year.
Start: Minehead, Somerset.
Finish: Shell Bay, Poole Harbour, Dorset.
Maps: O.S. Landranger series 180, 181, 190, 192, 193, 194, 195, 200, 201, 202, 203, 204.

Guidebooks: *South-West Way: Book 1 Minehead to Penzance. Book 2 Penzance to Poole* by Martin Collins (Cicerone Press). *The South-West Peninsula Coast Path* (3 volumes) by Ken Ward and John Mason (Letts). *The Somerset & North Devon Coast Path* by Clive Gunnell; *Cornwall Coast Path* by Edward C Pyatt; *South Devon Coast Path* by Brian Le Messurier—(all HMSO). *A Guide to the South Devon & Dorset Coast Paths* by Roland Gant (Constable).
Information: The South-West Way Association, 1 Orchard Drive, Kingkerswell, Newton Abbot, Devon TQ12 5DG.

Above: **On the North Cornwall Coast Cambeak stands out between Bude and Boscastle.**

Right: **Wandering inland a little the walker catches a blend of farmland and sea, a chequerboard of fields and meadows to contrast the stark cliff scenery elsewhere.**

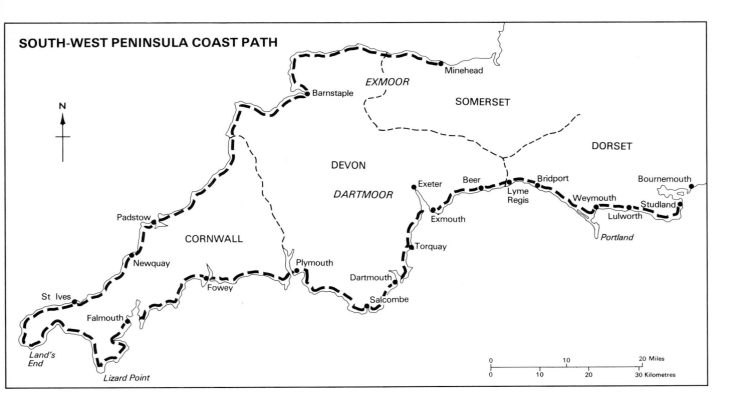

SOUTH-WEST PENINSULA COAST PATH

Rugged Cliffs and Sandy Bays on Britain's Longest Footpath

Coastal walking has an attraction all of its own. Perhaps some of that appeal lies in old childhood pleasures that are stirred again with the smell of salt-laden air, the swish, suck and draw of a gentle sea on a gentle beach, or the thunderous crash of storm-whipped waves against a harbour wall.

Some of that appeal lies in the cry of gulls. Some may be found in the mosaic of wild flowers on lonely clifftops far from habitation. Some of the attraction will surely belong to the wide sweep of an empty bay—seductive in its emptiness—or in the laughter-crowded streets of steep whitewashed villages. Surprisingly perhaps, there is no monotony in day after day of wandering up and down a switchback of green cliff with the sea stretching away forever and ever to the wide dome of an horizon where blue of sea matches blue of sky. For the sky, too, is an important ingredient in the daily vision of the coast path walker, for invariably there will be huge schooner clouds sailing in from the ocean, massing in preparation for some of the finest sunsets England knows.

There is no scenic monotony on the South-West Peninsula Coast Path. Not only are there wild undulating cliffs but there are also low sandy bays, shingle beaches, lunar-like mining landscapes, remote coves, fishing harbours, teeming resorts and industrious ports where ships dock to unload their cargoes. There are neat inlets, lagoons and broad-mouthed estuaries. There are sand dunes and granite blocks and chalk stacks like gigantic stepping stones rising from the surf. At more than 500 miles (800km) it is not only the longest footpath in Britain by far, but it is certainly one of the most varied—and that despite the constant sea. The mood of the constant sea, of course, is always changing too.

Until 1856 Coastguards daily patrolled every part of the South-West Peninsula coast on the lookout for smugglers, and after them officers of the Admiralty until 1913, using the very same footpaths adopted on this walk. Their cottages, often built several miles from the nearest village or town, remain to this day at intervals along the route as a reminder of the path's origins.

In truth the South-West Peninsula Coast Path (or South-West Way, as some prefer to call it) is not one single route, but a combination of four separate Ways: the Somerset and North Devon Coast Path; the Cornwall Coast Path; the South Devon Coast Path and the Dorset Coast Path. That's 540 miles (869km) of delightful and challenging footpath. Some authorities claim the route to be 515 miles long, some 520, some even 560 miles! But whatever the final total may be, it is around twice the length of the Pennine Way and five times the distance of the South Downs Way. To walk in one outing it will take at least six weeks or so to complete, which is more time than most could afford to devote to one single holiday, so those who become addicted to long-distance coast walking often decide to tackle this route piece by piece; one section this year, another next and so on. No long path lends itself to this approach better than the South-West Way.

Days 1–7: Somerset and North Devon Coast Path (104 miles/167km)

The little Somerset town of Minehead, noted for its family amusements and perched on the edge of so much good walking country, marks the beginning of this route. To the east roll the lovely Quantocks; to the south the Brendon hills and to the west, the National Park of Exmoor. You climb out of the harbour on a zig-zag path, gaining height quickly as if eager to escape the town in order to find the solitude of clifftop and seascape, and from a gorse-bright moorland overlook the Bristol Channel. Out there rise the lonely little islands of Steep Holme and Flat Holme; both bird reserves.

Inland by half a mile or so the path descends into Bossington whose roofs are neat with short-back-and-sides thatch. Porlock Bay makes a southerly scoop between Selworthy Beacon and Culbone Hill and you come to it near Porlock Weir, a tiny harbour with an old inn and woods high overhead. Porlock itself stands back from the sea; a village with a sharp hill that has earned a notoriety with over-heating cars climbing onto Exmoor to the west.

In two hours of wandering through woods and fields beyond Porlock Weir, on the first afternoon of this epic walk, you leave Somerset and enter the county of Devon where a fine view looks into the depths of the East Lyn Valley. That river finds its way to the sea through a wooded gorge, joining Farley Water at picturesque Watersmeet and then, linking with the West Lyn at Lynmouth, flows out to the sea. The Coast Path also comes down to Lynmouth, but only after first rounding Foreland Point, 723ft (220m) above the waves with views northward to Wales.

Lynmouth may never forget the tragedy of August 1952 when, in the wake of

The Old Post Office in Tintagel is owned by the National Trust, and is one of the more interesting buildings in the village.

torrential rainstorms, the East and West Lyn rivers brought down 100,000 tons of Exmoor rock and mud, wrecking the village. Thirty-four people were drowned and the resort devastated. But of course Lynmouth was rebuilt and the rivers controlled by wider beds and strengthened banks, and every year the summer crowds return to enjoy the bright combination of sea, moor and river, and to recall the horrors of nearly four decades ago—lest anyone should forget that nature always has the last word.

Lynton dominates the hill above Lynmouth on a site that was occupied in prehistoric times, for in the much-loved Valley of Rocks are traces of Iron Age hut circles and, at Castle Rock, that of a prehistoric pound. Yet again on this route, as on practically every other long walk in this book, we are reminded of the many-thousand-year history of these British Isles and know that others walked these clifftops, moorlands, Downs and valleys long, long before there were such things as acorn waymarks and signposts to guide them!

On then, striding across the western heights of Exmoor, whose edge is blessed by Heritage Coast status, and around Woody Bay along the clifftop towards Heddon's Mouth. But Heddon's Mouth Cleave gets in the way of direct progress and you break away inland to skirt it, coming back to the edge of the sea once more where Exmoor ends; down to delightful Combe Martin Bay. Between the bay and Ilfracombe is an uninspiring stretch, for you share the sea air with fumes from passing traffic as you walk beside the A339 most of the way, but once you escape this busy resort the path remains close to the coast and you wander among gorse and bracken with birds singing in relief to be once more in the freedom of wide open spaces.

Morte Point is a projection marking the northern end of Morte Bay, and from here to the Taw Estuary the coastline is a mixture of flat sandy beaches hidden by sunbathers in summer, and bald slate-grey headlands. At Saunton Sands you cut inland away from the extensive yellow dunes of Braunton Burrows on a lengthy diversion demanded by the intruding estuaries of the Taw and Torridge, and follow then a disused railway track from Barnstaple to Bideford. Here the River Torridge widens as it senses the drawing power of the sea, and on the left bank you take to a riverside path heading seaward to Northam Burrows.

From Westward Ho!, the resort developed

Through Cornwall you pass a number of drystone walls created in a herring-bone pattern. This is known as crazyway walling.

by the Earl of Portsmouth in the mid-nineteenth century and named after the novel by Charles Kingsley, you wander along the curve of Bideford Bay with views ahead to Clovelly—which is far more attractive than Westward Ho! ever was, exclamation mark or not. This little one-time herring-fishing village is surely one of the finest in all of England; a steep cobbled street lined with flower-bright cottages dropping to the quay. Both Kingsley and Charles Dickens worked Clovelly into novels, and its fame has since spread far and wide—as witness the crowds who stumble down (and up) the cobbles on every day of every summer.

Inland from the village, and a short stroll from the Coast Path, a series of earthworks known as Clovelly Dykes have been described through aerial surveys as Bronze Age animal pounds that were later adopted by Iron Age settlers as a hill fort.

Hartland Point is an important headland above a lighthouse where the coast suddenly breaks away to the south. From here to Bude, in Cornwall, the scenery makes a dramatic change. No longer is the coastline wooded but instead the cliffs are bare; near-vertical and gale-hammered, their flat-topped escarpment covered with short grass and masses of flowers, with waterfalls showering into the sea. This is the so-called Iron Coast. Severe and rugged, it is, and gazing west there is nothing but the wide swell of ocean between these gaunt cliffs and the coast of North America.

Days 8–30: Cornwall Coast Path (270 miles/435km)

As you pass from Devon into Cornwall at Marshland Mouth there's nothing to show for it except a broken line on the map. The cliffs continue, split here and there with valley grooves clogged with low-growing trees, and you wander south past Morwenstow church and the large white dish aerials at Cleave Camp, with wildly impressive cliff formations at Lower Sharpnose Point and the rocky projection of Cambeak making a spur ahead at the southern end of Bude Bay. Coombe Valley overlooks the little cove of Duckpool where fine sandy beaches sweep down to the holiday resort of Bude itself.

South of Bude the path is sandwiched between cliff-edge and road until, at Long Cliff above Dizzard Point, the road curves away leaving you to wander alone with the gulls, jackdaws and buzzards, the wild flowers and gorse and the steep plunging cliffs. Above Thorn's Beach, on Castle Point near the hamlet of St Gennys, there's the site of an Iron Age promontory fort; then passing through Crackington Haven you go up to Cambeak's dizzy viewpoint where a superb line of jutting cliffs lead in a mist

beyond the hidden harbour of Boscastle and on towards Tintagel.

Among gorse and heather, rock samphire, bracken and tangles of honeysuckle the path leads above a fine beach broken with rocks imaginatively known as The Strangles. There's a broad doorway arch—Northern Door—cut by the tides, and the contortions of exposed strata clearly showing the ancient folds of this part of the coast. The cliffs here have slipped in several places, undermined by the tides, and running across the beaches and into the sea dislocated cones and ledges make this a dangerous stretch of coast for shipping. (It is said that there is a recorded wreck for every furlong [eighth of a mile] of the Cornish coast.)

Half a mile inland from The Strangles squats Trevigue Farm, its shoulders hunched against Atlantic winds—there are thorn hedges growing at wave-like angles along the field boundaries. It's an old farm, 400 years old and now in the ownership of the National Trust, where the long-distance walker may be tempted to stray to indulge in a typically Cornish cream tea.

Over High Cliff and Rusey Cliff you then

Left: **Port Isaac is a tight squeeze of alleyways and sturdy cottage walls.**

Below: **Port Looe bears its strangely coloured rocks at low tide.**

Right above: **Polperro is one of the classic Cornish fishing villages—with or without the tide.**

Below: **Port Isaac harbour.**

come down to Boscastle's famous sheltered harbour, now also protected by the National Trust—as is so much of this marvellous coastline. Being the only practicable harbour along 40 miles (64km) of coast, Boscastle fared well throughout the last century with ketches and schooners plying a regular trade from the port. But when the railway came to Camelford in 1893, the commercial business of the harbour fell into decline. Tourism today is Boscastle's saviour, as well as its constant threat.

Around Boscastle there is a link with Thomas Hardy. As a young architect he came to the church of St Juliot to oversee restoration work and it was there he met Emma Gifford. Together they visited many of the beaches and cliffs nearby, and he wove some of these landscapes into his third novel, *A Pair of Blue Eyes,* which was to be published in 1873. The following year he and Emma were married.

Tintagel comes next; a summer-busy village straggling at right-angles to the coast. The best part of the village is the Old Post Office, with its thick stone walls and extraordinary undulating roof. Overlooking the village and acting as a landmark is a castle-like building that is, in fact, a nineteenth-century hotel. The real Tintagel Castle, with its fanciful and inappropriate allusions to King Arthur, spreads itself in crumbling lines of grey ruin, exposed to Atlantic storm above a narrow coombe leading from the village. Near the top of this coombe is a fine example of Cornish herring-bone wall known locally as 'curzyway'.

Then follows a deserted stretch of uninhabited coast, up and down through more coombes, and you arrive at the tiny inlet of Port Gaverne where coasters used to ship out slate from the quarries at Delabole. You pass along the foreshore, wander up the hill and there below lies Port Isaac, a bright cottage-crowded village. This is a splendid near-vertical place; grey roofs butting one against another; tiny alleyways, narrow streets with white crooked-walled houses gazing seaward. Port Isaac's lifeboat used to be housed at the top of the hill in what is today the village Post Office and when it was lowered through the streets for launch in the harbour, the ropes cut grooves in the corner walls of buildings.

The tiny harbour makes an attractive scene with the cliffs beyond and the village on three sides. The Coast Path goes past the harbour and up the western side to Lobber

Point and on to Port Quin, which John Seymour described as 'a ghost of a little fishing village'. Pentire Point guards the mouth of the Camel estuary and Padstow Bay, and gives one of the most extensive views of the North Cornwall coast. Great sandy bays swing along the edge of the estuary, and south of Polzeath, surrounded by tamarisk hedges and threatened by the encroaching dunes, sits the church of St Enodoc, much-loved by John Betjeman who now lies in the graveyard here. A short stroll brings you to Rock, where a ferry will take you across the River Camel to Padstow—a crossing for which there has been a ferry for 500 years and more.

From Padstow to Newquay is a day's walk along a coast that is a little gentler than before, with sandy beaches below the cliffs washed with long lines of surf as Atlantic rollers break in a crash and a roar. Newquay is the surfers' capital, a boisterous place of surf-boards and laughter, but continuing down towards St Ives and Land's End, you soon enter the industrial landscape of tin and copper mining country. There are heaps of spoil, the cliffs stained red or green. There are chimneys and the remains of engine houses; a ghostly land when mists are boiling off the sea and dark profiles like cardboard cutouts pock the way ahead.

St Ives is almost a caricature of itself. This is the artists' town, a place of paint and potters' clay, of unfinished canvasses and long hair and ragged jeans, of chintzy corners and fishermen's lofts, of one-time cottages-turned-gallery, of cobbled side-streets where holiday-makers scuff their toes on wet days in fifty pence plastic macs. When the tide is out there are wide sandy beaches, and a neat quay whose curving arm protects a gay flotilla of fishing smacks. From here to Land's End is some of the best of all the Cornish walk; a stretch of coast as popular with rock climbers as it is with long-distance walkers, with huge granite walls rising from the spray—Bosigran's headland and Great Zawn's challenge. The flower-strewn tops have their Iron Age earthworks—promontory forts, ramparts and ditches.

The Granite Coast takes you down to Land's End by way of Cape Cornwall, Whitesand Bay and Sennen Cove, then continues round through Nanjizal Bay—a once-sandy cove now mostly washed bare by the tides—and the headlands of Carn Les Boel and Carn Barra. Out beyond the broken rocks of Land's End itself winks the

Longships light, and farther off in the south-west swell the lighthouse on Wolf Rock sends out its lonely beam.

So you think the back of the walk is broken with the turning of Land's End? Not so, for you've still more than half-way yet to go. Some 300 miles (480km) and more of cliff and cove to draw you on.

Porthcurno's beach is a brush of tide-smoothed sand composed of crushed shells backed by craggy walls from which steps have been carved to create an amphitheatre of delight. Cut by Dorothy Cade, her gardener and a handful of helpers in 1932 England's loveliest open-air theatre is perched above a backdrop of sea. From Minack Theatre the path leads on to round the slow curve of Land's End Peninsula with views east to the Lizard, through Mousehole (pronounced Maozel) and Newlyn to Penzance. And so the landscape changes once more.

Wandering the eastern beaches of Penzance your attention is captivated by the little island of St Michael's Mount, all towers and balustrades rising from a stump of land; a romantic vision in the morning light. But the way is easy now and you can make good time striding down to Lizard Point among wild flowers and round one-time smugglers' coves. There are banks of shingle at Loe Bar, caves and cafés at Mullion Cove and serpentine-glazed rocks at Kynance Cove where crowds gather and solitude is but a dream.

The Lizard is England's farthest south, a notable landmark for the Coast Path walker and as psychologically important as the turning of Land's End, but it's not until you've crossed the Helford River that you can say with confidence that the half-way mark has been passed. You're on the homeward straight. Two hundred-odd miles (320km) of it.

This southern coastline is fretted by river valleys, and all along the remainder of Cornwall's path, and through Devon too, there will be interruptions where you are forced to take a ferry across the water. Not all of these ferries operate throughout the year, so out-of-season walkers may well find themselves forced into making long detours inland.

The ferry across the Helford River puts you in touch with a good stretch of path that leads round by Mawnan, whose circular churchyard has such a fine view, turning Rosemullion Head and on to Falmouth where well-preserved Tudor castles stand on either side of the Carrick Roads, guarding the port entrance; Pendennis on the west bank, St Mawes across the water on the east. More ferries here bridge the Roads and set you on course for Portscatho where you gaze across the curve of Grerrans Bay to breezy Nare Head, which remains unspoilt and protected by the National Trust.

Dodman Point is the next major headland, and on its summit cliff stands a most conspicuous granite cross. There's a Youth Hostel conveniently situated in the little hamlet of Boswinger to the north-west, and another a day's walk away outside Fowey. From Dodman Point to Fowey the Coast Path takes you to the fishing village of Mevagissey. This busy little place, with its quays jammed with laden fishing boats, is also a popular tourist resort, but no less attractive or worth dawdling in for that. But soon after leaving Mevagissey you have a stretch of road walking and face the ugliness of china clay workings around Charlestown and St Austell.

Across St Austell Bay Gribben Head makes a splendid vantage point, then round it you head north-east on a short stroll to Fowey, one of my favourite Cornwall harbours. It cannot match many another for quaintness, but its setting is magnificent, and there's a fair blend of everyday normality and alert tourism about its streets and the long woody creeks cutting back towards Lostwithiel. It is here that the Saints Way ends its 26 mile (42km) journey across the county from Padstow (it has taken almost 190 miles (300km) by Coast Path!). A regular ferry plies back and forth across the estuary to Polruan, and about two hours later you come down from the gaunt cliffs into that wonderful little village of Polperro where the tiny harbour is sucked dry at low tide and the streets are side-on to it. This is the quintessential Cornish fishing village. Trapped below towering crags, the houses butt one against another with the Rafiel stream flowing through the very heart of the place. It is, of course, crammed with tourists in the height of the season but, thankfully, there are few vehicles to fight against since only those on delivery are allowed down towards the harbour.

A few more miles of clifftop walking, then it's down to Looe, where shark fishing and tourism are rivals in the town's bid for prosperity. Looe Bay runs into Whitesand Bay and at the southern end of the latter you turn Rame Head and Penlee Point to overlook the Tamar Estuary and Plymouth

One of the many places on the Coast Path where it is necessary to take a ferry across an inlet. This is South Sands at Salcombe, Devon.

Sound. Across this most famous waterway, with memories of Drake's frisking of the Spanish fleet 400 years ago, and of the Pilgrim Fathers setting sail for a new world in 1620, you leave Cornwall at last and re-enter Devon once more.

Days 31–36: South Devon Coast Path (94 miles/151km)

You shrug off the eye-smarting, ear-thrumming influence of the city and head south towards Wembury Bay where you look out to the rocky islet of the Great Mew Stone spinning the tides. Another ferry takes you across the River Yealm, and on either side of a creek that flows into it sit Newton Ferrers and Nos Mayo, and as you wander along the coast with the sea to your right and a rich agricultural land to the left, so you look out over the blue spread of Bigbury Bay as far as Bolt Tail. Way off inland, high points of the horizon show Dartmoor's rim, and when you wade across the mouth of the River Erme, you splash through waters that were born among the granite tors and peat hags of Devon's great wilderness.

The River Erme marks the western edge of that country known locally as the South Hams, a land of patchwork fields, farms and

tiny villages and hamlets. The coast is lush with a steamy vegetation; the rocks are metamorphic and thrown into ridges that run sharp-edged to the sea, and in all this long walk there is nowhere else quite like it.

From Bolt Tail above Hope Cove to Bolt Head and round towards Salcombe is a very popular section. It's a delight of steep grey cliffs, buckled and shelving into brief coves, the path squeezing through slopes of bracken, gorse and heather, wild flowers everywhere—on the rocks and in the grass. Above Starehole Bay you can look down into the water and pick out the dark outline of the four-masted barque *Herzogin Cecilie* that ran aground in Soar Mill Cove in 1936. Unable to be towed into Salcombe Harbour she sank here, in Starehole Bay amid much publicity, her photograph making most of the national newspapers of the day.

Rounding Bolt Head superb views peer into Salcombe's estuary, a valley flooded at the end of the last Ice Age. On the eastern side sea-cut hills lead off to the headland of Prawle Point and dropping steeply down to South Sands you take yet another ferry which gives access to the continuing path that leads to the headland 4 miles (6km) away. From it you turn north-eastwards, easily now making for Start Point which signals the southern end of Start Bay. On a map showing the whole of the south-west peninsula it is clear that Start Point marks, not only the beginning of Start Bay, but is also the western headland of the great Lyme Bay, whose eastern point is Portland Bill at the end of Chesil Beach. It will be many more days of walking before you turn that point and look to Weymouth Bay.

Shortly after wandering by the lighthouse on Start Point you pass the sad remains of the drowned village of Hallsands, which was beaten by the sea on the night of January 26th 1917 when a combination of gale force winds and a very high tide tore the place apart. Beesands is next, and beyond that the curious freshwater lake of Slapton Ley which is a great place for watching migratory birds in spring. The Ley is 2 miles long and barely a stone's throw from the sea, and you've a dozen miles (19km) to go before coming to Dartmouth and, by crossing the Dart, leaving the South Hams behind.

The ferry takes you across the Dart to Kingswear from which point a fine view looks back to the long line of neat buildings that make up Dartmouth Naval College on a green slope above the town. It's a morning's walk to Brixham's lovely harbour but round Berry Head the hustle of Torbay, with its endless complex of Goodrington, Paignton and Torquay, comes as a crude interruption to the days of long vistas and empty coves. But this is after all the holiday coast, and there's no disputing it. From here to the River Exe, where the last ferry is taken, is one of the less interesting days, but as Lyme Bay begins its eastward curve beyond Exmouth, so the coast improves, and for two days you wander through some fine landscapes; red cliffs studded with thrift, gorse and bell heather, turning to chalk after Sidmouth where the vegetation changes and

you come upon orchids in favoured sites.

All along this curve there is so much to delight in, whether it's the coast itself, or the tidy spread of farmland. Only the bland caravan sites and holiday bungalows intrude. Ladram Bay has a group of six sandstone stacks; High Peak and Peak Hill give splendid views—from the latter you can sometimes see Haytor Rocks on Dartmoor; there's an extremely steep climb to Dunscombe Cliff, and beyond Branscombe Mouth a noted landslip with chalk stacks and pinnacles and a path that winds through the tangly scrub.

Beer and Seaton virtually rub shoulders. Beer is better; Seaton's brash. There's a Youth Hostel in Beer, and setting out from there after breakfast you can be in Lyme Regis for lunch. Devon will be behind you. So will Cornwall, and there's only Dorset's 70 odd miles to go. But what a stage this will be!

Days 37-42: The Dorset Coast Path (72 miles/116km)

If I were to be limited to just one section of the South-West Peninsula Coast Path, this is the one I'd choose. It is the shortest, but in many ways it is also the finest. That is why I have chosen to devote a separate chapter to it. There is never a dull day's walking; barely is there a let-up in interest or scenic grandeur. On the very first day, for example, you cross the highest point on the south coast at Golden Cap; on the second you ex-

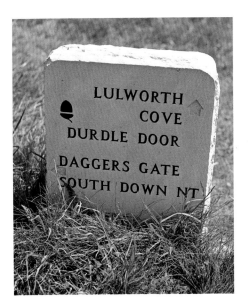

Above: **Lyme Regis, where you pass out of Devon and into Dorset for the final stage of the longest walk in Britain.**

Left: **Coast Path marker stone.**

perience the phenomenon of Chesil beach; then you have the contrasts of Weymouth's holiday fever and the green emptiness of folding hills near Osmington Mills. The day when you approach Lulworth Cove by the fabulous switchback of White Nothe, Bat's Head and Swyre Head, with views to Durdle Door and then the Man o' War Bay, is the very stuff of dreams—no matter how hackneyed those views might be. And there's the long delight of Purbeck—numerous coves and ledges, with breezy headlands and a surprise round every corner. And to complete this epic journey you leave Swanage and go up to Ballard Point, wandering a flat grassy escarpment to look out on the chalk stacks of Old Harry, Old Harry's Wife and the Pinnacles, then descend to the extensive sand dunes of Studland Bay.

Scuffing the soft clean sand under foot, with Poole Harbour opening like a watery mouth ahead, you seem to have come a very long way from Minehead.

But then you have.

MORE TO EXPLORE

Southern England is so richly endowed with worthwhile long-distance walking routes that to treat each one to the depth of description it deserves would be to create a volume much larger than originally intended. The fifteen routes included in the main body of this book are, arguably, among the very best of the bunch but there are plenty of others that ought to be mentioned too. The following brief outline details, being selective rather than comprehensive, and potted descriptions only, are therefore included to draw the attention of all ramblers and prospective ramblers, to various possibilities that abound here.

They are arranged according to geographic span working south and west, from East Anglia to the Cornish peninsula, and are not necessarily in any order of merit, length or degree of seriousness. They cover a diverse range of landscapes and include some of the best walking areas in southern England. Each walk, each area, has its own unique flavour that will help draw out the essence of lowland Britain that only the walker of its footpaths can possibly understand.

WALK 16: *The Peddars Way & North Norfolk Coast Path*

Distance: 93 miles (150km).
Time Required: 6–7 days.
Start: Knettishall, near Thetford, Norfolk.
Finish: Cromer, Norfolk.
Maps: O.S. Landranger series 132, 133, 144.
Guidebooks: *The Peddars Way & North Norfolk Coast Path* by Bruce Robinson (HMSO). *Walking the Peddars Way & North Norfolk Coast Path* (produced by the Peddars Way Association).

This, the tenth of the Countryside Commission's officially designated national long-distance footpaths, is the only one so approved that is situated in East Anglia. It extends from the northern end of the Icknield Way (which in itself was an extension of the Ridgeway Path) and follows the line of an historic track used in prehistoric times, as well as during the Roman occupation.

The route heads roughly northwards through the county of Norfolk among woods and remote, softly undulating farmland, from the Suffolk border to Holme-next-the-Sea on the coast. It then turns east to follow low cliffs, marshes, mudflats, bird reserves and beaches as far as Cromer. A shorter section of Coast Path leads west from Holme to Hunstanton, whilst an additional extension now continues along the coast beyond Cromer for 39 miles (63km) to Great Yarmouth, passing Mundesley and Winterton-on-Sea along the way.

The Peddars Way is a gentle lowland walk with wide horizons and big skies, and the Norfolk Coast Path, whilst overlooking a coastline admittedly not as dramatic as some of those of the West Country, is nonetheless an ever-interesting one—especially for ornithologists. There are four Youth Hostels and a modern bunkhouse accessible from the route.

Norfolk also boasts the Weavers Way (56 miles/90km), a route which links the Coast Path at Cromer with Great Yarmouth by way of parts of the Norfolk Broads—Britain's latest National Park—and through several interesting villages.

WALK 17: *The Suffolk Coast Path*

Distance: 50 miles (80km).
Time Required: 3 days.
Start: Felixstowe.
Finish: Lowestoft.
Maps: O.S. Landranger series 134, 156, 169.
Guide: *Suffolk Coast Path* (produced by Suffolk County Planning Dept., Suffolk County Council, St Edmund House, Ipswich).

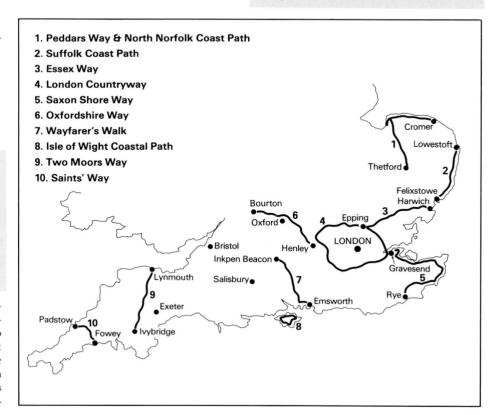

1. Peddars Way & North Norfolk Coast Path
2. Suffolk Coast Path
3. Essex Way
4. London Countryway
5. Saxon Shore Way
6. Oxfordshire Way
7. Wayfarer's Walk
8. Isle of Wight Coastal Path
9. Two Moors Way
10. Saints' Way

and woods. Plant life is rich and varied. There is an abundance of wildlife and the noted bird reserve at Minsmere is justifiably popular among ornithologists.

The Coast Path is not all easy walking; sometimes you're wallowing through soft sand, sometimes on low crumbling cliffs; sometimes dodging mudflats. There are shingle banks and narrow estuaries to negotiate—some by ferry, others by footbridge. There are also raised paths that lead across marshlands with vast reed beds and meres winding through.

Between Aldeburgh and Dunwich a doom-laden shadow is cast by the grim buildings of Sizewell's nuclear power stations but nearby, just before climbing onto the heather mattress of Dunwich Heath, the path leads through the RSPB reserve at Minsmere. Nightingales can often be heard in the woods here (as at Benacre Broad beyond Southwold); bitterns and bearded tits are seen, and in various places along the coast little terns lay their eggs in carefully camouflaged nests on the beach.

Dunwich reflects on the tenuous nature of this coast, for much of the former town that in the Middle Ages had a flourishing port, now lies beneath the waves, and it is said that on nights of low tide a bell can be heard tolling eerily from the depths. Nor is this the only part of the coast being chewed away by the restless North Sea tides and by its very nature the Suffolk Coast Path varies in its precise routing from one year to the next. It is, however, a route worth tackling—either end to end, or in isolated sections. Take a pair of binoculars and a pocket bird identification book and the walk will be memorable not simply because of the path it takes, but because of the variety of wildlife seen on the way.

WALK 18: *The Essex Way*

Distance: 81 miles (130km).
Time Required: 4–5 days.
Start: Epping.
Finish: Harwich. .
Maps: O.S. Landranger series 167, 168, 169.
Guidebook: *The Essex Way* by Fred Matthews & Harry Bitten (privately published—available from F. Matthews, Glen View, London Road, Abridge, Essex).

Essex is an often-maligned county, as far as outdoor enthusiasts are concerned, but its gentle, unspectacular countryside of farmland and woods has a charm all its own,

Walkers on the London Countryway through Kent.

The farmlands of Suffolk have achieved a certain notoriety in recent years for their windblown prairie-like state created by the wholesale destruction of mile upon mile of hedgerow. However, the coast itself has some extremely attractive features: estuaries, crumbling sandy cliffs, marshes and lakes while some of its villages 'out in the sticks' evoke an atmosphere of timelessness with their cob and thatch, their bowed pink walls and crooked windows. The Essex Way explores some of the best of this threatened county.

It was developed by the Council for the Protection of Rural England from a project by pupils of Chelmsford Technical High School; which illustrates the broad range of interest shown in walking and countryside exploration in the south of England. It should be borne in mind, however, that accommodation is a problem on this walk, so it might be better to tackle it in isolated stages, using motorised transport at either end of the day's outing.

The route, which was opened in 1972, begins at Epping station and heads north-eastwards across a gentle, undulating agricultural landscape. It passes the little wooden Saxon church at Greensted, near Ongar, the pleasant off-the-beaten-track village of Willingale, the remains of Pleshey's Norman castle and on to handsome, much-loved Coggeshall, east of Braintree, where the main street is a delight of ageing buildings full of quiet and unassuming history.

Beyond Coggeshall the route begins to bear more towards the east into the Constable countryside of Dedham Vale, and then works its way along the estuary of the Stour to end at Harwich.

Winter walking in Essex can be heavy going underfoot, but there is a raw beauty in its stark outline of tree-clad horizons, while in late summer as you wander through the harvest fields there is often a subtle, dream-like stillness that is almost unique to this corner of England. Elsewhere there are short and pleasant walks to be enjoyed through the glades of Epping Forest; a riverside walk along the Chelmer to Maldon; strolls along the creeks at Heybridge Basin. In fact, once you set out to explore the county by its footpaths, there are many surprise discoveries to be made. Essex, you very soon learn, wears a number of different faces.

WALK 19: *London Countryway*

Distance: 205 miles (330km).
Time Required: 12–14 days.
Start/Finish: By tradition, at the stepping stones below Box Hill, Surrey, but as this is a circular route, it could be started almost anywhere along its course.
Maps: O.S. Landranger series 187, 175, 165, 166, 177, 188, 167.
Guidebook: *A London Countryway* by Keith Chesterton (Constable).

The M25 of walking routes (without the hold-ups), the London Countryway makes a complete circuit of the capital, at the same time maintaining a discreet distance from its suburban sprawl. That distance varies from 13 to 31 miles (21–50km) from London's heart and along it the Countryway explores a surprisingly peaceful range of rural landscapes. Because of its circular nature it crosses half a dozen other long walks, and actually shares the path of two further routes for a short distance.

There are excellent public transport facilities linking with London and elsewhere, which would make this a particularly good walk to tackle on odd weekends over a period of time, rather than in one all-out effort for which, presumably, it was devised by Keith Chesterton and other members of the Long-Distance Walkers' Association. Several Youth Hostels provide accommodation within accessible distance of the path, but there is a notable lack of facilities in the eastern section.

The walk is enriched by superb views over the Weald of Kent. It enjoys attractive hill scenery on the North Downs, Greensand Ridge and Chilterns, follows for a while the Thames towpath, goes through the woods of Epping Forest, and has the opportunity to visit a number of sites of great historic or cultural interest.

Leaving Box Hill the Countryway works a clockwise route heading north-westward across the heaths and woods of Surrey and Berkshire. From Windsor it works along the Thames to Marlow where the Way breaks off to go northward onto the Chilterns. After Great Missenden the countryside becomes more gentle and unassuming, and the easterly course followed then takes the Countryway to the Lea Valley and Epping Forest. To the east of London the Thames is crossed by way of the Tilbury-Gravesend ferry. The route of the Wealdway is briefly touched on the walk towards the North Downs, then veering westward it leads through a part of the Weald and onto the Greensand Ridge. Out of Kent and into Surrey once more, a final day's journey returns to the North Downs for the finish at the stepping stones over the River Mole just outside Dorking.

One of the many good things about the London Countryway is the manner by which it introduces the walker to such varied countryside, and in so doing advertises the accessibility of much of it for future weekend walks. That it is so close to the heart of the capital is one of the surprise factors.

WALK 20: *Saxon Shore Way*

Distance: 135 miles (217km).
Time Required: 7–9 days.
Start: Gravesend, Kent.
Finish: Rye, Sussex.
Maps: O.S. Landranger series 177, 178, 179, 189.
Guidebooks: *The Saxon Shore Way* (a series of route cards produced by the Kent Area of the Ramblers' Association). *The Saxon Shore Way* by Alan Sillitoe and Fay Godwin (Hutchinson).

This is another coastline walk, but with a difference. The coastline of the Saxon Shore Way is the one which the Romans would largely have known, rather than today's boundary between land and sea. In places the sea is several miles from the path, in others the difference is virtually non-existent. But there are sections of the Saxon coast that have now disappeared beneath the waves. In such cases you don't have to trust to a very low tide, but rather hug the coast as it is today, and imagine what it would have been nearly two thousand years ago.

The route curves round the south-eastern heel of England, almost entirely in Kent. In fact it is only the very last 2 or 3 miles (3–5km) of the walk that stray into East Sussex. There are many sites of historic interest along the way, including fortifications from many eras as a constant reminder that this part of Britain has always been at the forefront of invasion. But there is much to enjoy as you follow this walk, especially for the birdwatcher. There is Britain's largest heronry not far from the route. There will be plenty of life in the mudflats and saltings, and along the Swale (the waterway that separates the Isle of Sheppey from the mainland) some 20,000 waders spend the winter. Dunlin, oyster catchers, bar-tailed godwins and clouds of plover can all be seen along here, as well as an occasional sighting of the marsh harrier.

If you could pick a dry week in winter, I'd almost recommend you to walk the Saxon Shore Way then. There's a certain beauty in the bleak, battleship grey coastline in winter, and hour after hour of invigorating exercise through an almost deserted landscape brings its own rewards. But summertime, of course, is when most would set out from Gravesend to stride round to Rye, and then you'll be tempted here and there to break away from the walk for a dip in the sea. And why not!

From Gravesend the Shore Way heads out to the low and lonely lands of the Hoo penisula which borders the Thames Estuary. Cooling Castle surprises with its turrets and solid-looking walls and over one of these you can actually see palm trees growing! When John de Cobham fortified his manor house in 1381 the tides of the estuary washed against the walls. Now they stand high and dry.

The Way continues across Hoo, passing the heronry at High Halstow and on to the Medway's estuary. Upnor Castle is among the best things to be seen here, then across the river and into Rochester with its many memories of Dickens. All along the Swale the route dodges from industrial bustle to empty mudflat and shallow creek. Faversham is a small town with a civic pride that exploits its rich heritage and after leaving this you draw away from the Swale and have much broader sea views.

On reaching the twin Reculver Towers the Saxon Shore Way turns suddenly inland, for where today lie acres of fertile farmland, until the Middle Ages ships used to sail on a major waterway leading to the Channel. This waterway was known as the Wantsum Channel and is what made Thanet an island. It's all silted up and dried out now, and it is not until the walk reaches Sandwich that you gain an impression of what that waterway might once have been like.

The coast is followed from near Deal, through Dover and on to Folkestone, but at Hythe the route again heads inland on low green hills that once were cliffs holding back the sea. Between those cliffs and the sea today stretches Romney Marsh with the long dyke of the Royal Military Canal tracing the Saxon Shore Way round to Rye.

This is an interesting walk with many different facets to it. And to newcomers to this part of the country it will breed plenty of suggestions for further exploration.

Should you wish for just one day's walking along the Saxon Shore Way, I'd opt for the route alongside the Military Canal starting from Appledore. A short but very pleasant circuit could be achieved by heading north-east along one bank to a point just below

Warehorne, then back along the other. Gentle walking, with only birds and sheep for company.

WALK 21: *Oxfordshire Way*

Distance: 65 miles (105km).
Time Required: 4 days.
Start: Bourton-on-the-Water, Gloucestershire.
Finish: Henley-on-Thames, Oxfordshire.
Maps: O.S. Landranger series 163, 164, 165, 175.
Guidebook: *The Oxfordshire Way* by Alison Kemp (Oxfordshire County Council).

From the lovely Cotswold village of Bourton-on-the-Water the Oxfordshire Way explores some extremely pleasant countryside on its meandering route to Henley-on-Thames. There are gentle hills to cross, neat villages, woodlands and open agricultural land. Magnificent Blenheim Palace is on the route and worth a lengthy delay of anyone's time to visit, while other places of interest lie not far from the path.

The Way was inspired by members of the Oxfordshire branch of the Council for the Protection of Rural England, and developed by the County Council. It is signposted but only partially waymarked, and the route is outlined on the O.S. maps.

Initially it heads eastward from Bourton along the Cotswold hills and into the Evenlode Valley, to Shipton-under-Wychwood (what lovely and poetic names there are to conjure with!) and Charlbury where there's a Youth Hostel. Skirting the city of Oxford the path crosses the Oxford Canal, then Otmoor and on to Horton-cum-Studley, then veers south-east via Tetsworth and across country to Pyrton. Over the ancient Icknield Way and onto the Chilterns then, and a final descent among woods to the Thames at Henley.

Oxfordshire is a neat county with a countryside green and welcoming, but it is mellow in places where Cotswold hills flush the lowlands with their golden glow. It's a county with some pleasant walking and the Oxfordshire Way enjoys some of the best available, while the Chilterns (not, of course, restricted to Oxfordshire) are well-known for their footpaths, of which there is a network totalling something like 1500 miles (2400km). The Chilterns Society is both energetic and ever-vigilant in its concern for the region and paths are almost everywhere admirably signposted and kept obstacle-free. For London-based walkers these hills form an obvious attraction.

WALK 22: *The Wayfarer's Walk*

Distance: 70 miles (8133km).
Time Required: 4–5 days.
Start: Emsworth, Hampshire.
Finish: Inkpen Beacon, Berkshire.
Maps: O.S. Landranger series 197, 196, 185, 174.
Guidebook: *The Wayfarer's Walk* by Linda Herbst (Hampshire County Council).

The Wayfarer's Walk, which goes from coastal mudflats to the highest of all southern England's downlands, was the first of its long-distance routes to be developed by Hampshire County Council. Through linking a series of existing footpaths, bridleways, green lanes and quiet country roads, it makes a delightful south-north traverse of the county. It's an easy, well-waymarked route that wanders through calm valleys, tiny villages, woods and fields and onto the Downs of the North Hants Ridgeway. The change from low-lying coast to inland hilltop is a gradual one, with a variety of natural habitats unfolding as you go.

The walk begins at the yacht-busy harbour town of Emsworth on the boundary creek dividing Hampshire from West Sussex to the north of Hayling Island. (The 150 miles [241km] Sussex Border Path also begins here, and the Solent Way finishes its 60 mile [97km] journey from Milford on Sea in Emsworth too.) The Wayfarer's Walk follows the route of the Solent Way westward to the top of Portsdown Hill outside Bedhampton where there are fine views overlooking Portsmouth, its harbour, dockyards and mudflats, and off to the Isle of Wight. The route then turns north through agricultural land that used to be a belt of heath and forest known as the Forest of Bere, and on to Hambledon. Vineyards dress the slopes of nearby Windmill Down; a reminder that southern England's viniculture is rapidly expanding—mostly with German grapes that produce a fruity white wine.

After climbing out of Hambledon the Wayfarer's Walk then descends to the Meon Valley and follows the river upstream to Droxford. In this valley the soil changes from clay to the chalk that is to stay with the route virtually all the way to Inkpen Beacon. After Droxford the path visits the valley of Betty Mundy's Bottom (really!) and onto the wooded South Hants Ridgeway to cross the route of the South Downs Way.

Cheriton, often voted Hampshire's best-kept village, has the glistening River Itchen sidling through. Beyond lies New Alresford and the walk continues over downland, along peaceful green lanes to Drummer, with its splendid twelfth century church lauded by John Betjeman. Once on the crest of the North Hants Ridgeway a track is followed westward across Watership Down and on to the Berkshire border for a finale on the Neolithic barrow of Inkpen Beacon. Here stands Combe Gibbet to mark the spot where, according to legend, in the seventeenth century a man from Combe was hanged with his mistress after being convicted of murdering his wife. (Between Watership Down and the end of the walk, the route is shared by the Inkpen Way; 62 miles (100km) along ancient trackways, paths and roads from the outskirts of Basingstoke to the outskirts of Salisbury.)

The Royal Military Canal, on the route of the Saxon Shore Way.

WALK 23: *Isle of Wight Coastal Path*

Distance: 67 miles (108km).
Time Required: 4–5 days.
Start/Finish: Yarmouth.
Map: O.S. Landranger series 196.
Guidebook; *The Isle of Wight Coastal Path* by Alan Charles (Thornhill Press).

Buckets and spades, crowded beaches, ice cream and candy floss and gaudy amusement arcades may be your picture of the Isle of Wight; but there is another side to it. That is the more appealing vision (to me at least) seen by the wanderer of footpaths. On the coast path there is a variety of scenery to enjoy, some of it surprisingly dramatic. Not that you are ever likely to gain the sense of isolation that is one of the features of wandering across Dartmoor, for example, but even remoteness is relative and out of season there's plenty of peace and solitude to enjoy.

Some of the natural aspects of the island are memorable for their outstanding beauty. There are plunging chalk cliffs, deeply cut chines, estuaries and saltmarshes and wide sandy bays. Green meadows slope inland to streams and neat villages, and if these picture postcard villages are cheek by jowl with visitors during the comparatively short, main summer season, and the narrow roads choked with coaches, then consider walking the Isle of Wight out of high season. Try it in springtime when the flowers are out and blossoms puff the trees, and huge schooners of cloud sail across the sunlit seas. You'll not find it overcrowded then.

The Coastal Path traditionally goes anti-clockwise round the island—at least, that is how the guidebook is written. Starting at Yarmouth (reached by ferry from Lymington across the Solent) the route heads round to Totland Bay and over Headon Warren where burial mounds dating from the Bronze Age are still visible, then to Alum Bay and the fascinating sight of The Needles—those chalk stacks that once were part of a land bridge connecting with the mainland across Poole Bay where Old Harry Rocks stand today. (The stacks of Old Harry are seen clearly from the Dorset Coast Path.)

The path heads east over Tennyson Down above Freshwater Bay, with huge views to enjoy across the island, then curving south-

eastward the cliffs gradually gain height along the 12 miles (19km) of chine-cut coast to Blackgang, just short of St Catherine's Point. These chines are narrow ravines or fissures cut by streams that drain out of the inland fields and meadows and are a major feature of the island, though of course not unique to it.

St Catherine's Point is the southern-most tip of the Isle of Wight. Inevitably it has a lighthouse positioned on the lower cliff, while two more stand on St Catherine's Hill—one redundant, the other unfinished and never used. Below the upper cliff can be seen the Undercliff, with its tangle of vegetation that harbours the rare Granville Fritillary butterfly—the only place in the British Isles, apparently, where it can be found.

Heading through Ventnor, Shanklin and Sandown you run the gauntlet of the holiday crowds, but on Culver Cliff you can gaze back for a last view of the sweep of Sandown Bay, then stroll down to sea-level and the yacht-bright Bembridge Harbour. Ryde is the next major obstacle of town proportions, and beyond that, unfortunately, rather too much road walking to Cowes at the northernmost point of the island, before heading south-west to Yarmouth where the circuit began.

The Isle of Wight has several trails of between 3½ and 15 miles (6–24km) in length that link with the Coastal Path across the inner Downs or over marshland and salting, and, in some cases, link one with another. There is also an Isle of Wight Heritage Trail of about 77 miles (124km) that is waymarked by members of the Cowes Voluntary Activity Centre, and this promises to include some of the best walking on the island. The Isle of Wight Tourist Board at Newport has details.

WALK 24: *The Two Moors Way*

Distance: 103 miles (166km).
Time Required: 7–8 days.
Start: Ivybridge, S.Devon.
Finish: Lynmouth, N.Devon.
Maps: O.S. Landranger series 180, 181, 191, 202.
Guidebook: *Two Moors Way* by H. Rowett (Devon Ramblers' Association).

Tom Stephenson, whose best-known brainchild was the Pennine Way, conceived the idea of a long-distance route across

Devon by way of the National Parks of both Dartmoor and Exmoor, along with members of the Dartmoor Preservation Society and the Exmoor Society, in the early sixties. Despite opposition to a single waymarked route across the moors by the two National Parks Authorities, the Two Moors Way was officially opened in 1976 with the blessing of Devon County Council. Waymarking is mostly confined to the crossing of the midway agricultural belt that separates Dartmoor from Exmoor, but on the early part of the walk there are exposed sections of moorland to tackle where an understanding of map and compass work is all-important.

This is one of the more demanding of lowland walks, with several strenuous sections and exposed tracts of potentially dangerous moorland to cope with. But having said that, it is also a delightfully varied route that experiences deep wooded valleys, chequered farmlands, bleak and somewhat barren heights, clapper bridges, wild tors, picturesque villages, bracken- and heather-clogged slopes and fine views of the North Devon coast. Three Youth Hostels can be used along the way, but this walk would also make a good backpacking trip to save the detours necessary to seek out alternative accommodation.

The Two Moors Way begins on the southern edge of Dartmoor at the village of Ivybridge, which sits beside the A38. It goes north over Dartmoor's wide open southern moor among stone rows that stand witness to the ancient civilisations that were here more than two thousand years ago. Then down to the remote village of Holne, along Holne Chase to Widecombe-in-the-Moor and for a while sharing the Mariners' Way, a route supposedly used by seamen travelling overland between Bideford and Dartmouth.

The River Teign is followed; Castle Drogo (in the care of the National Trust) is passed, and north of Drewsteignton the Way leaves Dartmoor National Park. Now follows a network of field paths and narrow lanes through the undulating mid-Devon countryside—a vibrant landscape in summer—towards Exmoor. Tarr Steps on the River Barle is one of the most popular places on the whole walk. It's also in Somerset; a portion of which is walked as you cross Exmoor National Park on the way to Exe Head where the River Exe rises. Over Cheriton Ridge and down to Cheriton itself (back in Devon once more) the Way soon reaches Lynmouth and the lapping tides of the Bristol Channel.

WALK 25: *The Saints' Way (Forth an Syns)*

Distance: 26 miles (42km).
Time Required: 2 days.
Start: Padstow, N. Cornwall.
Finish: Fowey, S.Cornwall.
Map: O.S. Landranger series 200.
Guidebooks: *The Saints' Way* by Michael Gill (CRS Community Programme).

The walks included in this book have been inspired by many diverse organisations and individuals; from the Countryside Commission to small groups of walkers, and from County Council recreation departments to the Ramblers' Association. This crossing of Cornwall, from Padstow on the Camel Estuary to Fowey on the south coast, was developed by the Co-operative Retail Services Community Programme in 1986.

It traces the course taken by Christian missionaries through central Cornwall, by way of a series of footpaths and tracks that link a number of churches, chapels and holy wells and, for part of its journey, a Bronze Age trading route which is one of the more ancient of all the peninsula's trackways.

Beginning at Padstow on the left bank of the lovely broad estuary of the Camel, the Way skirts the town and climbs Dennis Hill for a splendid view overlooking the estuary, then down to Credis Creek. Woods lead to Little Petherick, once known as Nansventon ('the spring in the valley'). A track leads onto St Breock Downs, spotted with tumuli, and up to St Breock Beacon, the highest part of the whole route, where long views are gained in all directions.

Continuing roughly south-eastwards the Saints' Way goes across country through Withiel and Lanivet, the half-way point, then two hours of walking brings you to Lanlivery to the west of Lostwithiel. (At Helman Tor, between Lanivet and Lanlivery, an alternative route cuts away more to the south and makes a longer journey to Fowey via St Blazey and Tregaminion.) On the main route to St Sampson's church there are views opening ahead into the Fowey Valley. Golant is on the Fowey river; a yachting and fishing village with the only Youth Hostel on the Saint's Way. Fowey, marking the end of the walk, lies just an hour's stroll away to the south; the suck and gurgle of low tide, the slapping of wavelets against timber piles at high tide; the cry of gulls, bobbing of boats; other attractions to dream on.

APPENDIX

Useful Addresses

Countryside Commission
John Dower House
Crescent Place
Cheltenham
Glos GL50 3RA

Long-Distance Walkers' Association
c/o Kevin Uzzell
7 Ford Drive
Yarnfield
Stone
Staffs ST15 0RP

Ramblers' Association
1–2 Wandsworth Road
London SW8 2XX

West Country Tourist Board
Trinity Court
Southerhay East
Exeter
Devon EX1 1QS

English Tourist Board
Thames Tower
Black's Road
Hammersmith
London W6 9EL

National Trust
36 Queen Anne's Gate
London SW1H 9AS

South-East England Tourist Board
1 Warwick Park
Tunbridge Wells
Kent TN2 5BR

YHA National Office
Trevelyan House
St Albans
Herts AL1 2DY

National Parks Authorities:
Dartmoor
Parke
Haytor Road
Bovey Tracey
Newton Abbot
Devon TQ13 9JQ

Exmoor
Exmoor House
Dulverton
Somerset
TA22 9HL

The Broads Authority
Thomas Harvey House
18 Colegate
Norwich
Norfolk NR3 1BQ